Beyond Representational Correctness

*Rethinking Criticism
of Popular Media*

Edward Schiappa

D1065630

State University of New York Press

Cover photo by Venus deMars (www.venusdemars.com).
The self-portrait (cover) photo is entitled "Trashed Open Eyes."

Published by

State University of New York Press, Albany

For information, contact State University of New York Press, Albany, NY
www.sunypress.edu

Production by Diane Ganeles
Marketing by Michael Campochiaro

Library of Congress Cataloging-in-Publication Data

Schiappa, Edward, 1954–
    Beyond representational correctness : rethinking criticism of popular media /
Edward Schiappa.
        p. cm.
    Includes bibliographical references and index.
    ISBN 978-0-7914-7423-5 (hardcover : alk. paper) — ISBN 978-0-7914-7424-2
(pbk. : alk. paper)   1. Stereotypes (Social psychology) in motion pictures.
2. Stereotypes (Social psychology) in mass media.   I. Title.

PN1995.9.S6956S35   2008
791.4—dc22

                                                                                            2007025416

10 9 8 7 6 5 4 3 2 1

Beyond
Representational
Correctness

Dedicated to My Daughters

CONTENTS

ACKNOWLEDGMENTS

Let us start off acknowledging the shortcomings of the subject position of the author: The dominant social categories would place me as white, straight, privileged, and male. In the course of this book I criticize the claims of some popular culture critics who are not white, not straight, and not male. I am aware of the intellectual and political risks associated with speaking for and about social groups that have been discriminated against historically (Alcoff, 1991–1992). My hope is that readers will look past these categorical differences and affirm our similarities: We popular culture critics are engaged in a common struggle against cruelty, oppression, and prejudice. The question before us is how we can best achieve our shared goals of a more tolerant, open, and just society, and, in particular, how media critics can best advance such goals through the practice of media analysis.

I owe many folks a debt of gratitude. Without the support of the Paul W. Frenzel Chair of Liberal Arts, awarded to me by the College of Liberal Arts at the University of Minnesota, this book never would have seen the light of day. Several chapters originally were coauthored journal articles. Chapter 2 was coauthored with Jennifer Stromer-Galley and appeared in *Communication Theory*. Chapter 5 originally was coauthored with Valerie Terry and published in the *Journal of Communication Inquiry*. Patricia Ryden contributed the audience research portion of chapter 5, which our reviewers required us to exclude from the journal version. Peter B. Gregg, Martin Lang, and I conducted the audience research that informs chapter 6, which has not been previously published. Jessica Prody, Emanuelle Wessels, and Pat Schiappa all helped with last-minute research that was crucial to finishing the book.

I am grateful to my colleagues at the University of Minnesota for their feedback on various drafts of the work presented here and to the students in my courses on popular culture, television, and film. Thanks also to audiences at the University of Maryland, Penn State University, the University of Colorado, Boulder, and Loyola University, New Orleans, who provided feedback on public presentations of some of work contained in this book.

I am particularly grateful to those scholars whose work I engage, often quite critically, in the process of developing my arguments. Bonnie Dow is an especially articulate advocate of an approach to criticism with which I disagree, but I want to acknowledge that I have great respect for her and her work. Thanks also to Barry Brummett, Joshua Gunn, Ron Greene, Mary Vavrus, and Beth Bonnstetter for their feedback on various drafts. Our spirited exchanges have made this a better book.

Finally, I want to thank my family. Their contributions go farther than the support and understanding that all writers need. As I write this, my daughter Lauren is an astute 8-year-old media critic; co-watching children's programming with her has been fun and instructive. Daughter Jacqueline is closing in on graduate school, and her insights on popular culture have been enormously helpful. My partner, Liz Murray, is the finest unpaid popular media critic I know, period. This book has been a family project in more ways than one.

Part 1

Provocations

The initial argument of this book is that the most typical modus operandi of popular media criticism concerning representations of race, gender, ethnicity, class, and sexual orientation is problematic. The modus operandi I have in mind performs an analysis of the text of a popular film or television show to argue that the representations conveyed are objectionable because they are stereotypical or otherwise prejudicial toward the group being represented. While I am by no means categorically opposed to such critiques, I wrote this book because I am concerned that (1) the implicit norms of Representational Correctness are impossible to meet, and (2) purely textual analyses may lead critics of popular media to miss the psychological and cultural work such media may perform for specific audiences.

A typical formula for a critical claim is this: Character X is portrayed negatively because X exemplifies the stereotypical behavior or trait Y, therefore the relevant Text perpetuates prejudicial beliefs. To anticipate a later example, let us say a critic notes that Will's lack of baseball ability in an episode of *Will & Grace* perpetuates the stereotype that gay men are feminine ("hits like a girl"), thus reinforcing heterosexism and androcentrism. I contend that such a formula is a legitimate starting place for critics, but we cannot stop there. We need also to examine the range of attributes associated with character X (in this case, Will), particularly given the larger context of multiple episodes in the series and other television programming—the "representational ecology" for a particular social group (in this case, gay men). Otherwise we may very well overestimate the significance of one particular scene or interaction. Furthermore, we need to know whether the way professional critics have decoded *Will & Grace* is adequate to the task of charting the cultural and political

1

work of the show. How do "unpaid" audiences see Will? What sort of judgments do they make about him, and how might that influence their attitudes and beliefs about gay men in general? I suggest that audience research can help provide more thorough answers to such questions than can professional decodings in isolation.

The three chapters that form part 1 of this book, labeled "Provocations," are critiques of certain forms of argument that regularly appear in academic criticism of popular media. In chapter 1 I describe Representational Correctness and lay out an argument for why it should be abandoned. In chapter 2 I argue that if critics wish to make "audience conjectures" about the determinate meaning or effects of popular media texts, then such conjectures would be far more persuasive if bolstered with qualitative or quantitative audience research. In chapter 3, through a discussion of a series of studies about the show *Will & Grace*, I offer a critique of the political economy of textual analysis by arguing that the need to exercise "professional vision" leads some critics to decode popular texts not only in a way different from mainstream viewers but in a way that risks missing how mainstream audiences understand such texts. Indeed, I suggest we may be better off thinking about *all* popular media criticism as based on audience reception analysis—the only question is *which* audience.

In part 2, I attempt to practice what I preach by offering three interventions—one theoretical, one critical, and one pedagogical. The theoretical intervention is offered as one (and certainly not the only) way to conceptualize how consumers of popular media may be influenced by its representational content. I describe what my colleagues and I call the "parasocial contact hypothesis," which suggests that prejudice toward minority groups by majority members can be decreased through learning about the minority group through entertainment media. The question then becomes not whether a representation of a group category as having such-and-such attributes is prejudicial in principle or in the opinion of the critic but whether learning about such group attributes complicates a viewer's understanding of the group category. In chapter 4 I describe a series of studies that suggests that learning about groups "parasocially" can, under certain circumstances, decrease prejudice.

Chapter 5 attempts to illustrate how social group attributes can be represented rhetorically in a text to reinforce or discourage specific social norms. Such analysis must be performed with sensitivity to historical and social context; indeed, context is precisely why we argue that Michael Crichton's *Disclosure* is antifeminist rather than postfeminist. And, practicing what is preached in part 1, such analysis should be bolstered with audience research that illustrates that the critic's decoding is not unintentionally idiosyncratic. Chapter 6 describes classroom efforts to teach students to decode film more critically and to ascertain to what extent media criticism classes can influence student attitudes about gender and sexuality.

It is my hope that these efforts illustrate some of the ways that we can perform academic criticism that moves beyond Representational Correctness. Before proceeding, however, I want to make it clear that I am not claiming that audience research reveals The Real while textual analysis does not. Consistent with contemporary pragmatism or what might be called "sophisticated modernism" (Schiappa, 2002), I see all scholarly writing as rhetorical and argumentative through and through (Gross, 2006). Persuaded by the kind of pragmatism found in Richard Rorty's essay, "Texts and Lumps" (1999, pp. 78–92), I see no reason to rank order methodologies within a grand epistemological or ontological scheme. "Texts," "audiences," and "audience effects" are all socially constructed categories we use to pursue various interests (Hartley, 2006). The questions are pragmatic and strategic: What ought those interests be? Given the *claims* we may wish to advance, what sorts of evidence do we find most compelling?

CHAPTER 1

The Impossible Dream of
Representational Correctness

What academic scholars have in common, regardless of their disciplinary, theoretical, or methodological pieties, is that they advance argumentative claims and propositions. This book is motivated by a conviction that in the practice of popular media criticism certain kinds of claims, assumptions, and patterns of inference have an unwarranted level of acceptance.

The idea that criticism functions as a form of argument is not new. In 1974, communication scholar Wayne Brockriede urged his discipline to view criticism as argument. While not all criticism must be thought of in such terms, Brockriede contends that criticism advancing *analysis* and *evaluation* of communicative phenomena ought to "function as an argument" (1974, p. 165). To the extent critics wish to encourage their readers to view phenomena in a particular way, critics' discourse functions argumentatively if it involves "an inferential leap from existing beliefs to the adoption of a new belief" and "a perceived rationale to justify that leap" (p. 166). Michael C. McGee echoed Brockriede's point some years later when he noted, "Professional criticism functions to persuade readers to make the same judgments of salience, attitude, belief, and action the critic made" (1990, p. 283). The sorts of judgments McGee identifies— salience, attitudes, belief, and action—will all be addressed in this book in the context of the criticism of popular media.

For both ethical and epistemological reasons, criticism as argument entails "a willingness to risk a confrontation of that claim with one's peers" (Brockriede, 1974, p. 166). Ethically, "confrontation" means that critics share their rationale so that criticism remains in the realm of persuasion or invitation rather than coercion; it also means that critics remain open to the possibility that their claims will be modified or even abandoned by readers. Epistemologically, "confrontation" means that critics offer evidence and explain their rationale so the "reader-confronter" has the opportunity to evaluate the soundness of an arguer's claim: "By inviting confrontation, the critic-arguer tries to establish some degree of intersubjective reliability in his [or her] judgment and in his [or her] reasons for the judgment" (p. 167).

Accordingly, this book offers a scholarly confrontation with particular kinds of claims, assumptions, and patterns of inference employed in the criticism of popular culture. My initial argument in this book is that we need to recognize the fallacy of "Representational Correctness" and move beyond it in our analysis. I explain in some detail what I mean by Representational Correctness later, but an example may be helpful at the outset. When the movie version of *The Da Vinci Code* was released in May 2006, it was criticized for its portrayal of Jesus, the Roman Catholic Church, and the *Opus Dei* organization. More of interest for this book is the fact that the National Organization for Albinism and Hypopigmentation (NOAH) "expressed unhappiness" with the fact that the film's assassin is an albino: They claim that *The Da Vinci Code* is the 68th movie since 1960 to feature an evil albino. According to Mike McGowan, NOAH president, "Over the years the stereotyping and misinformation foisted on the albinism community by filmmakers who don't take the time to learn the facts about albinism does real harm to real people" (NOAH, 2005). Concerns such as those voiced by McGowan are not entirely misplaced. Negative portrayals of a group of people in film and television, especially a group unfamiliar to many, certainly can influence how that group is perceived by the population as a whole, and such perceptions can lead to prejudicial attitudes. The core of NOAH's critique is twofold: The representation of albinos in film is *incorrect* (most albinos are not evil assassins) and *harmful* to the extent that such representations encourage prejudice.

The example of the criticism of the albino assassin in *The Da Vinci Code* highlights two key themes that are explored in this book. First, as sensible as the criticism may appear, it implies that there is such a thing as a "correct" representation of albinos to which filmmakers ought to aspire. The dream of a perfectly Correct Representation is unreachable. Now, admittedly, few critics use the specific words "correct," "perfect," or even "accurate" to describe a representation. Yet, as we shall see, such notions are implicit and logically entailed in *many* critiques of representation. For example, typically whenever one uses the term *stereotype* to describe a representation, there is an implicit charge that the representation is somehow an incorrect and inaccurate way to portray a category of people.

Second, the question of whether such representations are, in fact, influential and harmful is an empirical one. One cannot rely solely on a critic's interpretation of what a film, song, or television show may "mean" to its various audiences. I honestly do not know if filmic representations of albinos actually influence audience members' perceptions about albinos or not. I have known only one albino in my life, and he was a funny, kind, high school band teacher. If I were asked, I would certainly espouse no prejudicial attitudes about albinos, and I would hypothesize that films may feature albinos in certain roles primarily because they are visually striking (*Matrix II* comes to mind). But I honestly have no clue as to whether most moviegoers would feel as I do, or if in fact such filmic representations have shaped the perceptions of, and attitudes toward, albinos in our society.

What I have said so far about representations of albinos can be applied to any other social group that may command the attention of critics of popular media. In this chapter, I describe what I mean by Representational Correctness and make the case that critics who have pursued such a dream have created a double bind that no individual representation could ever hope to overcome.

Unpacking Representational Correctness

Representational Correctness refers to a set of beliefs that often implicitly underlies critiques of "popular media texts."[1] As Barry Brummett notes, for many critics representations "sermonize" about how to make sense of our world and thus warrant critical inspection (1991, p. xvi). The fundamental philosophy of Representational Correctness can be traced back to Plato's belief that if art imitates life, then that imitation can and ought to be done *correctly*. This can be thought of as *orthê mimêsis*, or "correct imitation." Plato's objection to the popular entertainment of his time, poetry, was that it "disguises and distorts reality and at the same time distracts us and plays tricks with us by appealing to the shallowest of our sensibilities" (Havelock, 1963, p. 26). In *The Republic*, poetry is censored and poets exiled because such misrepresentations do not serve to educate the masses properly—especially the young—and can be "injurious" to philosophically untrained minds (Cornford, 1941, p. 324). Obviously the idea that representations proffered in "popular media" are worthy of critical inspection, and possible censure, has a long history.

For those who keep up with contemporary popular media criticism, the spirit of Representational Correctness pops up almost constantly, both from the Right and the Left. Consider the following examples, which range from the silly to the very serious:

1. Peter Jackson's blockbuster remake of *King Kong* is described as presenting "an atrocious and offensive depiction of Islanders as a 'savage' population incapable of hygiene with their eyes rolled back in their heads" (Zephoria, 2006).

2. Keanu Reeves's character in the film *Hardball* is described as a stereotypical "great White savior" who rescues an all-Black inner-city baseball team (GRIID, 2003).

3. The animated television series *Jake Long: American Dragon*, which features a teenage Chinese American who transforms into a dragon, is described as presenting "confusing racial stereotyping" (Herman, 2006).

4. The animated action film *The Incredibles* is interpreted as reinforcing "inflated family stereotypes" (Klawans, 2004).

5. U.S. Secretary of Education Margaret Spellings objects to an episode of PBS's animated children's series *Postcards from Buster* for exposing children to a family headed by two lesbians: "Many parents would not want their young children exposed to the life-styles portrayed in this episode" (de Moraes, 2005).

6. On a fan Web site, one viewer complains that Disney's animated series *Kim Possible* is "sexist" due to the fact that all of the male characters are "nerds or jerks" (Doug135711, 2006).

7. The movie version of Chris Van Allsburg's book *The Polar Express* is criticized by some Christian media critics as turning Christmas into Clausmas, "beckoning us to worship the jolly old elf as the heart and soul of this all-important holiday. And that's something that Christians should be very wary of indeed" (Robertson, 2004).

8. Multiple critics note that representations of Arabs in U.S. film, beginning long before 9/11, constitute "slanderous stereotypes" that distort what Arab men, women, and children "are really like" (Shaheen, 2001, p. 1).

9. Nearly every mainstream film ever made about Native Americans in the United States has been criticized for perpetuating overly simplistic and stereotypical representations (Aleiss, 2005; Hilger, 1986; Kilpatrick, 1999).

10. Nearly all Disney movies are criticized for their stereotypical portrayals of women and minorities (Ayres, 2003; Bell, Haas, & Sells, 1995; Brockus, 2004; Budd & Kirsch, 2005; Giroux, 1999; Lacroix, 2004).

11. An irate reader of *The Minneapolis Star-Tribune* complained that the headline of an article, "Pedestrian killed by SUV that fled people," was prejudicial. "You are making a conscious effort to turn opinions against SUVs and the mostly wealthier, suburban, and, yes, mostly Republicans who would own them" (Gelfand, 2002).

12. Apart from criticism of what representations are found in popular television programs or films, critics also have noted the *lack* of representation of most minority groups in such media. Indeed, the only social groups that are not underrepresented are White and Black men.

If these examples lead one to conclude that many people are unhappy with the way the popular media represents social groups, one is right. A study by Stuart Fischoff and colleagues (1999) found that about half of over 1,200 respondents surveyed were offended by representations of their respective social groups; for example, Asians were offended by humor mocking their English skills, their invisibility in film, and the casting of actors from one Asian culture to portray Asians from another.[2]

The point I wish to make with such examples goes beyond the conventional wisdom that you cannot please everyone, true as that might be. It is a testament to human creativity that we can generate evaluative criteria that no human production could ever meet. What I want to argue here is that there are specific criteria that are less useful than they may appear, and these criteria can be summarized usefully under the umbrella of what I am calling "Representational Correctness." What I have in mind is a mélange of ideas that can be found in media criticism, implicitly or explicitly, ideas that advance norms of representational accuracy, purity, and innocence. *Accuracy* implies that a representation should be authentic and true to the social group depicted to avoid the distortion of stereotype. *Purity* implies that a representation should be pure in its liberatory possibilities and avoid ambivalence or ideological contradiction. *Innocence* implies that a representation is devoid of offense or insult to the group depicted. I shall provide examples of these norms throughout the book; for the moment, I would simply assert that a good portion of popular media analysis is guided by the idea that *if* we can attain the goal of Representational Correctness *then* oppressed groups will be empowered or at least encouraged, and mainstream consumers and users of popular media will be motivated toward a more tolerant, open, and just society.

As I noted earlier, these norms function mostly at an unstated, implicit level. If asked, most critics of popular media would not openly embrace such notions as representational accuracy, purity, and innocence. For example, they might claim that they are concerned with the cultural and political work of the text and, following Stuart Hall (1992, 1997), distance themselves from an explicit commitment to Representational Correctness. Nonetheless, throughout this book I will provide numerous examples of criticism of popular media in which I believe the norms of Representational Correctness are at work. Readers will have to decide for themselves whether my examples are fair interpretations of the critical projects I engage. I admit at the outset that in the process of engaging a large body of scholarship, a certain amount of oversimplification is inevitable. I believe, however, that if one steps back to survey the considerable scholarship committed to the criticism of popular media to identify common themes, the norms of Representational Correctness are quickly apparent.

My analysis focuses primarily on what I describe as paid or professional criticism, that is, criticism by academic scholars and media critics whose labor *as* critics is indirectly or directly rewarded financially. The label "professional" links such criticism to what John Frow usefully calls the "knowledge class" (1995), but I do not wish to imply that unpaid criticism, such as might be found in a letter to the editor, fan group communication, or casual conversation, should be valued less because it is "popular" or "unprofessional." I argue later that the need to provide criticism that is "expert" and therefore has added value over unpaid criticism can motivate particular ways of interpreting and critically analyzing popular culture artifacts that are sometimes brilliant but sometimes so out of touch with unpaid audiences as to miss the important work popular media are accomplishing in our culture.

Three major assumptions that inform Representational Correctness (hereafter RC) are problematic. The first is that RC assumes that popular culture texts have a primary, or at least a preferred or dominant, meaning that a discerning critic can *independently* determine and analyze. The vocabulary of "dominant," "negotiated," or "oppositional" readings comes from Stuart Hall's influential essay, "Encoding/Decoding" (1980). The way Hall's terminology is typically deployed by critics follows the logic that *if* the critic understands the culture's dominant ideology, *then* it is a matter of decoding how that dominant ideology manifests itself in a particular text. By definition, a dominant ideology is that which holds sway over most popular media consumers, so if the critic decodes the text appropriately, then she or he can be reasonably confident of how most audience members understand the meaning of the text. Now Hall was quite clear that his categories "need to be empirically tested and refined" (1980, p. 136), and most accounts of "negotiated" or "oppositional" readings are, indeed, informed by audience research (see chapter 2). Too often, however, critics assume they can ascertain the dominant or preferred reading all on their own. I am quite willing to grant that most (though not all) texts have a "dominant" reading *if* it is stipulated that a dominant reading is understood simply as that which is preferred by a majority of readers at a particular point in time—that is, if we define "dominant" in terms of a dominant audience reception and not by particular qualities that inhere in the text.

Later I argue that "textual analysis" of popular culture media is, in a sense, a misleading label: All analysis is a kind of audience reception analysis—what is called "textual analysis" might be more productively thought of as a very specialized kind of audience reception. Meanwhile, the point here is nothing new: *All* movies, television shows, songs, books, and so on are open to multiple interpretations; indeed, sometimes audiences find meanings in popular culture texts that patently contradict what the creators of those texts intended or anticipated. The "text" is silent and meaningless until experienced. The dominant reading is the interpretation that is empirically dominant for a specified audience at a particular point in time.

The second assumption that typically informs criticism guided by a sense of RC is an overly simplistic model of media effects; namely, that sociopolitically good texts cause good effects, and that sociopolitically bad texts cause bad effects. At times, what informs popular media criticism is a version of the old hypodermic needle or "magic bullet" theory of media effects. As the metaphors imply, the theory suggests a direct, causal influence between the transmission or injection of a mass-mediated message and audience reactions. The theory dates back to the 1920s and 1930s when there were concerns about the influence of the era's new media, radio and film. The Payne Fund Studies consisted of an ambitious set of thirteen projects that sought to examine the effects of film in particular. Though there were some serious methodological limitations, the findings of various effects, primarily on children, created a great deal of public concern about the potential negative effects of popular film (Lowery & DeFleur, 1995). Of course, the most famous example of the direct effect of mass media in this era was the panic caused among some listeners to the 1938 radio broadcast by Orson Welles and the Mercury Theater group of H. G. Wells's *War of the Worlds*—a phenomenon that received enormous media coverage and was subsequently the subject of a 1940 academic book *The Invasion from Mars: A Study in the Psychology of Panic* (Cantril, 1982). These early studies provided scholarly credibility to the commonsense intuition that popular media *matters* and can effect those who watch or listen.

Among most mass communication researchers, the simplistic direct effects model was discredited by Paul Lazarsfeld and his colleagues' influential study of media exposure and voting choices in the 1940 elections (Lazarsfeld, Berelson, & Gaudet, 1944) and subsequent scholarship advocating what has come to be called a "limited effects" model. However, the direct effects model has persisted in the criticism of popular culture, both in and out of academia.

Actually, for as long as human history has been recorded, critics have always worried about the potentially negative effects of popular culture—from Plato's critique of poets to the latest panic over violent video games. It is noteworthy that the forms of arguments made have not changed very much. The history of critical responses to popular comic books offers a nice illustration. There have been critics of the corrupting influences of comic books on young readers since 1940 (Beaty, 2005; Heer & Worcester, 2004; Nyberg, 1998), but three are particularly noteworthy for my purposes.

1. Over 50 years ago, Gershon Legman railed against the prevalence of violence in comic books in terms remarkably similar to later

critiques of television violence. He claims that by the time a child is 10 or 11 years old, she or he would have "absorbed" a minimum of 18,000 beatings, shootings, stranglings, and other acts of violence: "With repetition like that, you can teach a child anything" (1949, p. 31). "The effect," Legman claims, "has been to raise an entire generation" that has felt "all the sensations and emotions of committing murder, except pulling the trigger" (p. 32). In addition to encouraging the acceptance of violence, Legman argues that Superman represents a "Nazi-Nietzschean *Übermensch*" whose method of administering justice is indistinguishable "from that of Hitler and the Ku Klux Klan" (p. 40). Describing Wonder Woman in part as "Blondie with a bull-whip," Legman claims she is clearly a lesbian (p. 48).

2. A more influential book on the dangerous effect of comic books was Fredric Wertham's *Seduction of the Innocent* (1954). Among other claims, Wertham argued that young readers are influenced by the "psychologically unmistakable" homosexual subtext of Wonder Woman and the "homosexual and anti-feminine" atmosphere of Batman and Robin comics (pp. 189–93). Wertham also argued for a causal connection between comic book consumption and juvenile delinquency; his research (primarily anecdotal) helped fuel congressional hearings on the hazards of comic books that led to the creation of the Comics Code Authority (Beaty, 2005; Nyberg, 1998).

3. Ariel Dorfman and Armand Mattelart illustrate a somewhat different critique in their book *How to Read Donald Duck: Imperialist Ideology in the Disney Comic* (1975). While earlier comic book critics tend to draw mostly from Freud, Dorfman and Mattelart draw mostly from Marx to make the case that Disney comics create a politically impoverished, colonizing narrative that contributes to the oppression of U.S. minorities and citizens of economically dependent countries: "Reading Disney is like having one's own exploited condition rammed with honey down one's throat" (p. 98). Dorfman and Mattelart's critique is similar to Legman's and Wertham's in the sense that they all "read" comic books as contributing to attitudes and behaviors the critics find problematic.

The argument of these comic book critics relies on a two-step process that we will see again and again in popular culture analysis: *First that a given text "means" such and such (whether the meaning is obvious or subtle, conscious or unconscious, explicit or subtextual) and second that such meanings influence those who experience them.* Even when a critic maintains that an audience is oblivious to the hegemonic or unconscious meaning(s) of the text, there is typically (though not always) an assumption that there *is* an influence on beliefs, feelings, attitudes, or behaviors. Otherwise, why bother with engaging texts?

Effects models have become more sophisticated, of course, though this fact does not mean that critics of popular media have necessarily kept up. A less direct model, again typically unacknowledged but influential among popular media critics, is a version of George Gerbner's cultivation theory (for a summary, see Gerbner, Gross, Morgan, Signorielli, & Shanahan, 2002). Gerbner argues that television is highly repetitive—the more one watches, the more the messages of television "cultivate" a way of (mis)understanding the world. For example, messages on television about violence over years of exposure will socialize television viewers into beliefs about violence that are not true. Television viewers who watch *a lot* of television (more than 4 hours a day) think the world is more dangerous than it is, statistically speaking. Sometimes this effect is called the "drip, drip" effect, as it is assumed that changes in attitudes are the cumulative result of long-term exposure, while at other times it is argued that viewers can be "drenched" by a sudden flood of mass-mediated messages (Greenberg, 1988; Reep & Dambrot, 1989). Some popular culture critics contend that *one* movie or *one* television show will influence viewers to think about some social group in one way or another. If only it were that easy!

To be sure, there are plenty of examples of where popular media had fairly obvious and direct results. Two of my favorites are the fact that applications for library cards briefly skyrocketed after "the Fonz" on *Happy Days* got one (Sparks, 2006, p. 149), and the fact that sales of wine made with pinot noir grapes soared briefly as an apparent result of the praise the wine received in the movie *Sideways* (Verrinder, 2005). Plenty of negative examples of "copycat behavior" can be found as well, including viewers imitating bomb threats, felony crime techniques, professional wrestling moves, and dangerous stunts seen on television. In some cases these imitations had fatal consequences (Sparks, 2006, pp. 81–83). Indeed, the link between children viewing television violence and subsequent violent behavior is well documented.[3]

While there is little doubt that viewers sometimes imitate *behavior* they see in popular media, proving that such media can alter *attitudes* and *beliefs* has not been easy. The most ambitious research in this area has been carried out by scholars informed by cultivation theory studying the effects of television. James Shanahan and Michael Morgan provide a comprehensive overview of this research in their book *Television and Its Viewers: Cultivation Theory and Research* (1999). Using the statistical techniques of meta-analysis, they summarize nearly 6,000 separate findings from 97 study samples, involving tens of thousands of viewers, all published since 1976. Studying attitudes concerning everything from aging, minority groups, abortion, the legalization of marijuana, interracial marriage, crime rates, and sex roles to romance, they found an average correlation of .10, which means that about 1% of the total variance has been explained by television viewing

(Shanahan & Morgan, 1999, p. 115). To put these findings in more practical terms, we could say that 1% of people's beliefs is the result of television viewing; or, put differently, if a hypothetical score of 100% indicates that the media will *wholly* determine a typical person's attitudes on a given subject, then the research indicates that the average score for all individuals is 1%. This is a conservative estimate, of course, and depending on the subject matter of the effected beliefs, the ability of television to alter 1% is not trivial. Nonetheless, the fact that after 30 years of studies researchers can prove only a small overall effect should caution popular culture critics against making dramatic claims about the effects of particular films and programs. Normally, when it comes to an individual film, song, or television show, critics should operate with a Presumption of Negligible Effects absent evidence to the contrary.

Chapter 2 of this book argues that if critics wish to advance what I call "audience conjectures" about the *meaning* or *effects* of pop culture, then their claims would be far more persuasive if they would provide evidence drawn from audience research. I will not anticipate the critique further, except insofar as it informs the third problematic assumption of RC.

The third assumption is that of *simultaneity*; namely, that when a text is judged by the demands of representational accuracy, purity, and innocence, it must meet these requirements *simultaneously*. All three demands are taken as necessary conditions, and none is independently sufficient, to reach a state of RC.

My argument concerning the assumption of simultaneity is that *it is an impossible standard to meet.* The reason it is impossible to meet has to do with the relationships among the central beliefs that reinforce prejudice. In the next section I describe these beliefs as the "triad of prejudice." I then explain how their interrelationships complicate the possibility of simultaneity.

The Triad of Prejudice

Psychologist Sandra Lipsitz Bem (1993) describes three "gender lenses" embedded in our culture that "provide the foundation for a theory of how biology, culture, and individual psyche all interact in historical context to systematically reproduce male power" (p. viii). These three lenses are the widely recognized concepts known as "gender polarization," "androcentrism," and "biological essentialism." Bem provides a concise summary:

> Throughout the history of Western culture, three beliefs about women and men have prevailed: that they have fundamentally different psychological and sexual natures, that men are inherently the dominant or superior sex, and that both male-female difference and male dominance are natural. (1993, p. 1)

Academic scholars have many ways of describing what Bem is after, but whether we describe the lenses of gender as a "terministic screen" or a dominant set of "schemas," these three ideas also can be described simply as "beliefs" that are widely shared in U.S. culture and that perpetuate sexist attitudes, behaviors, and policies. When children are socialized, "the individual gradually internalizes the cultural lenses and thereby becomes motivated to construct an identity that is consistent with them" (Bem, 1993, p. 3). Bem describes this process in terms that some might describe as interpellation: "The discourses and social institutions in which [these beliefs] are embedded automatically channel females and males into different and unequal life situations" (1993, p. 3).

A classic illustration of gender polarization, androcentrism, and biological essentialism can be found in the popular works of John Gray. As nicely documented in a doctoral dissertation by E. S. Weber (2002), Gray's *Men Are from Mars, Women Are from Venus* theme manages to advance all three key beliefs of sexism. Men and women are so different that it is as if they were from different planets, and their differences are caused by their distinctly different psychobiology. Gray's androcentrism plays itself out in two ways. First, the qualities he associates with masculinity tend to coincide with preferred societal values, such as power, competence, career success, problem solving, and public participation. Second, women are not only defined in opposition to men (and thus exhibit qualities less culturally valuable than men), but they are defined primarily by the support roles they play for men—as mothers for men's children and caretakers of men's homes. If one has any doubt of the androcentrism of Gray's views, then consider his advice that some women need to go on the equivalent of an "orgasmic diet" if their sexual needs are not in sync with those of their men (Potts, 1998, p. 170).

Despite the progress of the women's movement, elements of this triad of prejudice remain pervasive. According to a research brief by Joe Kelly and Stacy L. Smith, *Where the Girls Aren't: Gender Disparity Saturates G-Rated Films*, there is a huge imbalance in the number of male and female characters in movies targeted at children and families (Kelly & Smith, 2006). In the 101 top-grossing G-rated films from 1990 through 2004, 75% of the characters were male, 72% of speaking characters were male, 83% of all narrators were male, and 83% of characters in "crowd scenes" were male. Even using a conservative requirement of a ratio of 3 males for every 2 females, only 7% of all films studied were "balanced" by gender, and 46% had an imbalance of at least a 3 to 1 ratio. Of course, G-rated films are not the only source of mass-mediated messages that kids receive, since most also watch television. Unfortunately, females are seen less frequently than males on television as well (Aubrey & Harrison, 2004).

Does such an imbalance really matter? A meta-analysis of research on television programming and sex stereotyping by Herrett-Skjellum and Allen (1996) synthesized scholarship both on the content of television programming and its effects. What message is being provided? "All content analyses illustrate the consistent finding that men are more often on TV, in higher-status roles as characters, and are represented as having greater power than women" (p. 171). Based on such analysis, "we may conclude that the content of the media incorporates a large number of sexual stereotypes" (p. 173). More recently, Patrice A. Oppliger (2007) conducted a meta-analysis involving 33 studies and over 12,000 participants. Twenty-five of the studies she analyzed involved children. She concluded that "as exposure to gender stereotyping increases, sex-typed behavior and sex-role stereotyped attitudes increase" (p. 210). Herrett-Skjellum and Allen (1996) report that "heavy" television viewers are twice as likely as other viewers to profess sex-specific stereotypical attitudes (p. 178).

In other words, the content of film and television programming consistently sends the message that it is a man's world—androcentrism in a nutshell. The available audience research supports the conclusion that the more children consume of such programming, the more likely they are to believe the message. Moreover, Jacob Orlofsky, Ralph Cohen, and Mark Ramsden (1985) found that people with more traditional (stereotyped) sex role attitudes are more likely to have reported sex-typed interests and behaviors. That is, the more people profess to talk the talk of traditional sex roles, the more likely they are to walk the walk.

To understand how mass media advances sexism via androcentrism, gender polarization, and biological essentialism, we need to specify exactly what we are talking about when we say that "stereotypical" beliefs about women are advanced. There are many definitions of "stereotype," and later I want to question whether the term is still useful for media criticism, but for the moment, we can stipulate that stereotypes are *pejorative overgeneralizations*. When we think about a specific group of people in stereotypical fashion, we tend to categorize *all* members of that group as having the same attributes. By "attribute" I mean any quality or characteristic that can be grammatically predicated about a group (Xs are Y), whether such attributes are behavioral (things people do), ethical (good or bad), personality traits, or physical characteristics. In the albino example mentioned earlier, the concern expressed is that representing albinos as assassins in movies advances a particular set of negative category attributes; namely, that albinos are evil and murderous (Xs are Y_1 and Y_2). If audience members' only beliefs about albinos are those beliefs learned from feature films, then cultivation theory suggests that their understanding of the category of albinos will be limited, distorted, and negative. As psychologists Michael A. Hogg and Dominic Abrams (1988) put it, "Categorization can thus be considered to be the process underlying and responsible for stereotyping" (p. 73).

Stereotypical portrayals of women are those that represent the category of women only or primarily with traditionally "feminine" attributes. What are those attributes? Arguably, what people count as masculine, feminine, or gender-neutral attributes is constantly evolving—a point to which I return later. We can begin, however, by noting some of the following attributes identified in the well-known Bem Sex Role Inventory (Bem, 1974):

Masculine	Feminine
Independent	Sensitive to needs of others
Assertive	Yielding
Forceful	Sympathetic
Leadership abilities	Childlike
Dominant	Gullible
Aggressive	Gentle
Analytical	Affectionate
Competitive	Compassionate
Ambitious	Shy
Individualistic	Tender

Bem's Sex Role Inventory was originally developed in the early 1970s. More recently, James Mahalik and his colleagues (2003, 2005) have created the Conformity to Masculine Norms Inventory and the Conformity to Feminine Norms Inventory to update our understanding of what sorts of attributes are expected and treated as normative for men and women. Their lists are worth noting as well:

Masculine Norms Inventory

Winning	Controls emotions	Risk taker
Accepts violence	Playboy	Dominance
Power over women	Self-reliant	Work is primary
Disdain for homosexuality	Pursues status	

Feminine Norms Inventory

Nice in relationships	Values thinness	Modest
Cares for children	Domestic	Values romance
Values sexual fidelity	Interested in appearance	

Several points are worth noting about the gender attributes identified by Bem and later by Mahalik and his colleagues. First, the attributes are largely polar opposites. Masculine men are seen as assertive, feminine women as yielding. Men are analytical, women are compassionate. Manly men are playboys, women value sexual fidelity. Men pursue status, women are modest. This sort of contrast is exactly what Bem is getting at with her concept of gender polarization. Second, in general, the masculine category attributes are more highly valued in contemporary U.S. society than the feminine category attributes. Whether hiring a corporate executive or electing a president, the attributes associated with masculinity are more often privileged than those associated with femininity. This, of course, is what Bem and others mean by androcentrism—Man is the Measure of desirable attributes. Not entirely, of course. It would be oversimplistic to say that none of the attributes associated with femininity is valued. The point is that many of the most important and powerful economic, political, and social roles in our society are coded masculine; that is, the attributes associated with such roles draw more heavily from traditionally masculine attributes than feminine or gender-neutral attributes (Eagley & Karau, 2002). Lastly, persistent stereotypical representations perpetuate the belief that such attributes are "natural," "normal," or "innate." Essentialism implies that being masculine is in the nature of being a man, and that women are naturally feminine.

In short, mass-media representations are important because they do "category work." That is, they play an important socialization role in teaching us about the categories of men and women, masculinity and femininity. As I shall argue later, such category work also creates an opportunity for popular culture media to promote social change.

The Triad of Prejudice: Not Just about Gender

I suggest that what Bem calls the "lenses of gender" can be thought of usefully as a triad of beliefs that informs the discriminatory attitudes, behaviors, and policies involving other social groups. I shall consider only race and sexual orientation here, but an analogous argument could be made with other social categories as well. Bem's categories can be described as beliefs about identity, norms, and differences:

Type of Prejudice	Identity Beliefs	Normative Beliefs	Difference Beliefs
Sexism	Biological essentialism	Androcentrism	Gender polarization
Racism	Biological essentialism	Whiteness	Racial polarization
Heterosexism	Behavioral essentialism	Heteronormativity	Sexual polarization

Essentialism informs beliefs about identity—that is, the belief that a certain group is what it is because it is in its nature. Sexism is rooted in the belief that women are feminine because it is their biological or genetic nature to *be* so. Because the attributes associated with masculinity have a privileged status, androcentrism becomes the norm by which attributes are measured. And because masculine and feminine attributes are assumed to be rooted in *essential* differences, the genders are treated not only as different but as polar opposites (hence the habit of referring to "the opposite sex"). The same sort of logic can be found at work in prejudicial beliefs about race and sexual orientation.

Most racists believe that race is biologically rooted (Goldberg, 1993), and that distinct races have distinct "natures." As Hall puts it, "Stereotyping reduces people to a few, simple, essential characteristics, which are represented as fixed by Nature" (1997, p. 257). Not all racists in the world are White, of course, but in the United States *Whiteness* functions in a parallel normative fashion to *androcentrism* (hooks, 1992; West, 1993). That is, just as "Man" is the measure of all things "normal," so is Whiteness. "At the level of representation," Richard Dyer notes, "whites are not of a certain race, they're just the human race" (1997, p. 3). Whiteness often functions as an "unmarked category against which difference is constructed," but because it has been so deeply normalized, "whiteness never has to speak its name, never has to acknowledge its role as an organizing principle in social and cultural relations" (Lipsitz, 1998, p. 1).

Racial polarization functions in a manner similar to gender polarization. Just as masculine is typically defined culturally by antithesis as *not* feminine, "Whiteness" is typically defined culturally as *not* of color (Lipsitz, 1998; Winant, 1998). Lest we forget, at various times in U.S. history *any* detectable amount of African heritage could be deemed sufficient to classify someone for the purposes of segregation laws as "non-White."

Heterosexism is a bit different from racism. For heterosexists, homosexuality is an immoral lifestyle choice and/or an unnatural perversion. For some heterosexists, it does not matter if one's sexual preferences are learned or innate. For this reason I have chosen to characterize the essentialism of heterosexism as behavioral rather than biological, for in U.S. culture it is *what one does with whom* in one's sexual behavior that defines whether one is straight or gay.

Heteronormativity functions in the same way Whiteness and androcentrism do; that is, "straight" is normal and natural, everything else is perverse. Theorists have argued that such naturalization and normalization is so powerful that it becomes a tacit component of our common sense, thus the psychological and cultural work that normative notions of identity perform is rendered invisible and unnoticed. As Dyer notes, "Heterosexuality as a social reality seems to be invisible to those who benefit from it. In part, this is because of the remorseless construction of heterosexuality as normal" (2002, p. 119). Robert Westerfelhaus and Celeste Lacroix add that "the invisibility of hetrosexual power and privilege to those who possess and benefit from such is strikingly similar to the invis- ibility of the power and privilege associated with whiteness as experi- enced from a 'white' perspective" (2006, p. 428).

Sexual polarization is closely related to heteronormativity. Though dating the invention of the category of "the homosexual" is a matter of some debate, most historians agree that it is a relatively recent construct, even if homosexual activity is as old as humanity. To the extent that one classifies individuals by linking sexual behavior to personality type, one assumes a dichotomy between being straight and not straight. You can- not be both. Bisexuals and transgender individuals are thus typically cat- egorized as not straight.

It is important to recognize that all categories are informed by the very basic schemas of similarity and difference. Stereotypical categories tend to emphasize *difference*, that is, the qualities we use to define a stereo- typed group are ones that are seen as different and "other" (Hall, 1997, pp. 223–77). If we stereotype women as being especially effective care- givers or as physically weak, then we do so because those qualities are in greater or lesser abundance than we consider "normal." Stereotypes thereby presuppose a falsely universalized norm (such as androcentrism), but as noted earlier, they also reinforce essentialism and polarization. The relationships among stereotypes and the beliefs informing the triad of prejudice will become important later when we think about how to com- bat stereotypes through the vehicle of representation.

The good news is that if one can undercut essentialism, then one can simultaneously undercut polarization. For example, if one shows women engaging in activities that are supposedly not in their "nature" to do, then one can both undercut the idea that biology is destiny *and* the idea that men and women, masculinity and femininity, can be defined only in opposition. Indeed, studies have found that young viewers exposed to counterstereotypical sex role portrayals are more likely to change their beliefs about available career choices than those who are not (Miller & Reeves, 1976). Experiments by David M. Marx and Jasmin S. Roman (2002) and Rusty B. McIntyre and colleagues (2003, 2005) found that women exposed to accounts of several successful role models in mathe- matics immediately scored better on a mathematics exam than women who were not exposed to such counterstereotypical models. Such evi- dence suggests why representations in popular culture of women ath- letes, attorneys, doctors, reporters, writers, politicians, scientists, and explorers are a necessary (though clearly not sufficient) step toward chal- lenging the triad of prejudice. Of course, such representations must be *positive* representations. It would merely reinforce sexist beliefs if the only women we saw in such roles were offensive, evil, or incompetent.

Two final introductory comments about this schematization are appropriate before we put it to work. First, the three "isms" identified here work (all too well) together in U.S. culture. The "man" who is the "measure of all things" is manly, white, and straight.

Second, such a schematization obviously oversimplifies the varieties of discriminatory beliefs, attitudes, and practices that permeate U.S. culture. In the space of one book, I cannot begin to catalog all of the forms of prejudice that are related to gender, race, and sexuality, let alone all of the other forms of prejudice at work in society. But I hope that in what follows the usefulness of the triad will become evident.

The Challenge of Simultaneity

Here is the rub. You might think that if John Gray can advance all three key beliefs of sexism at once, then one ought to be able to critique all three at once as well. To be sure, we can do so in analytical prose, but it is much more difficult to do so through popular media representations. Failure to recognize this difficulty can lead critics to impose unrealistic expectations on popular media when criticizing representations or declaring the presence of stereotypes.

To illustrate the point that RC is impossible, I start with a discussion of Bonnie J. Dow's book *Prime-time Feminism: Television, Media Culture, and the Women's Movement since 1970* (1996). Dow's book examines a series of mainstream television shows featuring positive portrayals of women in leading roles, including *The Mary Tyler Moore Show, One Day at a Time, Designing Women, Murphy Brown,* and *Dr. Quinn, Medicine Woman.* Dow's goal is to understand how these shows negotiated issues of feminism that were contemporary with their initial airing. These shows are examined because, for Dow, they offer a vision of the meanings and implications of feminism in the 1970s, 1980s, and 1990s. They have "done important cultural work in representing feminism for the American public" (1996, p. xv).

Dow's modus operandi is characteristic of a good deal of scholarly popular media criticism; namely, her readings describe the popular reception of the shows, she gives a nod toward the progress the show has made in representing women, and she then argues that the representation is not as liberatory as one might think. Typically the final verdict offered by Dow is that a show ends up reinforcing patriarchy in some way or, at best, it offers viewers a representation that is contained by dominant beliefs about gender and thus "ambivalent" (that is, impure).

The Mary Tyler Moore Show, for example, was contained by dominant norms of gender because Mary's character is too feminized and reinforces the stereotypical assumption that women are caretakers. She does not break free from stereotypes enough to be an ideologically "pure" representation. Mary is "domesticated": "Within her family of coworkers, Mary functions in the recognizable roles of idealized mother, wife, and daughter" (1996, p. 40). How? "Mary alternately nurtures, mediates, facilitates, and submits" (ibid.). In short, she is too "fem," and that reinforces the triad of prejudice, and in particular it reinforces biological essentialism and thus gender polarization.

The problem with *Murphy Brown*, in contrast, is that she is too "butch": Dow quotes critic Pyllis Japp's comment that Murphy is "a male persona in a female body" (1996, p. 140). She describes her manner of dress as severe and contrasts it with Corky's ultrafeminine appearance. Murphy's physical presence defines her character as "aggressive," "strong," and "forceful" (pp. 140–41), and her communication style is aggressive and coded masculine: "She is supremely confident about her own opinions, and she expresses them easily, often with little regard for others' feelings" (p. 141). Dow argues that Murphy does not lose her masculine-professional edge after becoming a mother, since post-baby episodes "retain the earlier comedic dynamic of deriving humor from Murphy's lack of feminine qualities" (p. 155). Dow concludes that *Murphy Brown* "has no genuine feministic politics of its own" (p. 161) and participates in the culture's "postfeminist" turn. Indeed, Dow dismisses those who consider *Murphy Brown* a feminist success as proof of how deeply entrenched postfeminist attitudes and expectations are (p. 161).

One might think that *Murphy Brown* would be considered progressive, since Murphy's personality and behavior can be read as directly undercutting biological essentialism and gender polarization. That is, the attributes identified by Dow are found on the masculine side of the personality ledger, proving that a successful, attractive, heterosexual female is not biologically destined for attributes traditionally considered feminine. Indeed, almost any positive portrayal of women that shows them behaving in nonstereotypical fashion would seem to be a step in the right direction. If I may be permitted to translate Dow, the problem is that when Murphy dresses, acts, and communicates in stereotypically masculine ways, *androcentrism* is reinforced.

Maybe you can see what is coming. *When one tries to address the triad of prejudice via representation, one cannot undercut all three beliefs at once.* If one portrays someone in a manner *consistent* with the dominant stereotype, even in a positive way, then one risks reinforcing essentialism and polarization (identity and difference beliefs). But if one undercuts the dominant stereotypes by portraying the member of a social group in a manner *inconsistent* with stereotypical expectations, then one risks reinforcing normative beliefs such as androcentrism, Whiteness, or heteronormativity.

A single representation *cannot* undercut all three sources of prejudice simultaneously, which is why I call Representational Correctness an Impossible Dream. As I argue later, the impossible burden we sometimes put on single representations is why we need to investigate how a character (not just isolated attributes) is understood in a larger representational ecology and to find out what sort of judgments audiences make about them. Consider the critical receptions of "strong" women, such as Lucy Lawless in *Xena*, Sigourney Weaver in *Aliens*, or Linda Hamilton in *Terminator II*—some praise the roles as feminist, while others see them as reinforcing androcentrist beliefs that equate strength with violence. Both positions, of course, may turn out to be correct. What critics need to ponder is *given* a particular historical context and the representational ecology, what sort of cultural and ideological work is the character doing (or, put another way, what is the audience doing with such representations?), and does such work advance or retard specific social goals, such as reducing sex-based discrimination? What we cannot expect from a representation is that it engages all possible cultural and ideological battles successfully at once. As we will see, a similar dilemma faces critics evaluating representations of race and sexual orientation.

"Hawk," on *Spenser: For Hire*, was a character praised by many critics, including African American pundits, for being a strong, self-assured, and successful Black man who did not always follow the (White man's) rules. Nevertheless, his character's attributes are criticized by Dana L. Cloud as reinforcing racist stereotypes about Black men. "Hawk does not decapitate heroines, but his violence is often extreme. He exhibits none of Spenser's reluctance to kill, nor does he wait to attack until attacked himself. This association with the deep-seated type of the native savage might be compelling evidence confirming the racism of an uncritical viewer" (1992, p. 318).

Cloud argues that the show functions hegemonically; that is, the program perpetuates dominant racist beliefs about Black men. "Hawk's oppositional stance and persona, though subject to contradictory critical evaluations, serve the needs of the dominant culture to depict blacks in stereotypical ways" (1992, p. 311). Despite actor Avery Brooks's popularity and the praise the show's depiction of Hawk received from some Black critics, Cloud believes that her "close analysis" of the show "reveals" how the depictions "participate in a conservative, multistructured, yet hegemonic social totality" (p. 314). Like most professional critics, particularly those informed by critical theories of hegemony and/or psychoanalytic theory, Cloud implies that how the text is interpreted by audiences is largely irrelevant, since it is the expert who is best positioned to decode the text and ascertain its likely influence.

Cloud implies that those who attribute positive meaning to Hawk simply are wrong: "Images and articulations that on the surface *seem* positive and empowering can *actually* tap into deeply embedded racist types and can function in racist ways in the dominant culture" (1992, p. 314, emphasis added). Thus the differences between Hawk and Spenser reinforce essentialism and polarization, even though they arguably undercut the normativity of Whiteness.

What happens if an African American is portrayed in ways that run counter to stereotypical assumptions? The central character in the movie *Boyz N the Hood* is Tre, played by Cuba Gooding Jr. Tre's character is constantly being pulled between his friends and his father, between being sexually and physically aggressive versus being responsible, respectful of women, and in control of his anger. The pivotal moment in the movie is when Tre decides not to accompany his friends on their way to avenge the murder of his best friend. Now this is an interesting comparison with Avery Brooks's Hawk character, who certainly would have sought out and killed the killers of his best friend. But John Singleton's message in *Boyz* is that the cycle of violence must end (the tagline for the movie is "Increase the peace"), and so Tre's decision *not* to kill is key.

Sadly (to me, at least), African American feminist critic bell hooks is less than sympathetic. In an interview with Ice Cube, who played the character Doughboy (who murders his stepbrother's murderers), hooks objects: "But Tre just came off like a wimp, a crybaby. He was just so weak. He came off weak in the movie" (1994, p. 132). Ice Cube objects: "No, to me he came off tryin' to do the right thing. The neighborhood was really frustratin' him out, because he was trying' to do the right thing and everybody else was doin' the wrong thing. And I think Doughboy woulda been just like him if [he] had the right guidance, the right father. It's a thin line between 'em all. Tre was about to be like Doughboy for a minute until he thought about it." And hooks responds, "I feel like if I was a kid lookin' at that move, I wouldn't wanna be him, I'd wanna be you, because your character had the jazz" (1994, p. 132).[4]

The "damned if you do, damned if you don't" logic in Representational Correctness has been noted by other critics as well. Donald Bogle (2001a, 2001b), historian of Black film and television, has been accused by one conservative critic as playing a game called "Can You Find the Stereotype?" (McWhorter, 2003, pp. 104–37). Though he oversimplifies Bogle's work, John McWhorter's argument is that Bogle's interpretive framework leads to the conclusion that virtually all Black representations fail, either because they reinforce stereotypes or because the characters are inaccurate or inauthentic. It is a dilemma that McWhorter charges imposes "an unrealizable requirement upon the medium" (p. 129). Even when a "wholly new" kind of African American character comes along, such as Jaleel White's

Urkel on *Family Matters*, either he is considered inauthentic or inaccurate (Bogle suggests, "in some respects, Urkel was deracialized"), or he is described as an updated version of a stereotype (quoting another critic)—"a modern Stepin Fetchit in the making" (Bogle, 2001a, p. 332).

I will revisit the clash between Bogle and McWhorter in chapter 7. At the moment, the point I want to stress is that media critics can end up creating a double bind for representations. Perpetuate a stereotype and one reinforces essentialism and polarization—even if a positive spin on a stereotype challenges normative beliefs such as androcentrism or White supremacy. Challenge a stereotype and one may undercut essentialism and polarization, but one can end up accused of either reinforcing discriminatory normative beliefs (like androcentrism with Murphy Brown) or failing to provide representational accuracy or purity (as with Tre or Urkel).

Such a double bind also has been applied in critiques of representations of sexual orientation. For example, some critics deride "Jack" on *Will & Grace* for being *too* gay and reinforcing stereotypes, and then they turn around and critique Will for not being gay *enough!* It is the same catch-22. A scholarly essay by Kathleen Battles and Wendy Hilton-Morrow (2002) offers an in-depth analysis of *Will & Grace*. The "threat" that Jack poses to heteronormativity is acknowledged as significant but considered fatally compromised (strategically impure) by the fact that Jack is a "minor" character too campy to be taken seriously. Will is criticized for being too feminine in some scenes (making him stereotypical) and too masculine in others (reinforcing heteronormativity). For these and other reasons the authors claim that *Will & Grace* relies on conventions that reinforce heteronormativity as well as homophobia. They come to the counterintuitive conclusion that the show actually reinforces all three elements of the triad of sexual prejudice. Similarly, Robert Brookey and Robert Westerfelhaus (2001) note that portrayals of gay men in *To Wong Foo* are "positive," but they claim they are *too* positive: "The deification of these characters results in remarginalization" (p. 153). The question, of course, is whether anyone else "reads" these texts in the same way these academic critics have, and I attempt to answer that question in later chapters.

Recall that an emphasis on *difference* can be read as reinforcing essentialism and polarization, while an emphasis on *similarity* can be read as reinforcing the false universalism of androcentrism, Whiteness, and heteronormativity. This is not an easy double bind to escape. Indeed, the civil rights movement splintered in the 1960s over whether the goal of the movement should be integration or Black power; Kathleen Hall Jamieson (1995) points out that the women's movement still wrestles with whether to emphasize similarity or difference between the sexes; and R. A. Slagle (1995) argues that gay and lesbian rights movements emphasize similarities with straight folks, while queer politics rely on strategies of difference.

Stuart Hall has conceded, "We hardly begin to know how to conduct a popular anti-racist struggle or how to bend the twig of racist common sense which currently dominates popular thinking" (1981, p. 52). Such disagreements in the political realm over what the appropriate *ends* should be for these movements parallel the disagreements over what the appropriate *means* of representation should be in the mass media.

What To Do Differently: An Overview of the Rest of This Book

Overall, we paid critics need to raise our expectations so that our work is more sophisticated than it is now. How we should go about such a task is the subject of the remainder of this book, but as a starting point we must recognize that no representation is going to be perfectly accurate, ideologically pure, and innocent of any possible offense. We need to get past the point where we damn representations with the label "ambivalent." All images are ambivalent and ambiguous. All are impure from someone's perspective. To understand the social significance of a particular representation requires a critic to understand the psychological and cultural work it performs for specific audiences. The remainder of this book explores some possible paths to such an understanding.

In chapter 2 I argue that we professional critics need to do more audience research. Recall that there is typically a two-step process in most (though not all) criticism of popular media. First an argument is made that a given text *means* such and such (whether the meaning is obvious or subtle, conscious or unconscious, explicit or subtextual) and second that such meanings *influence* those who experience them. Even if we grant to certain schools of criticism that mass audiences are unaware of the ideological work of various popular texts, there remains an argumentative burden to prove the second step—that such audiences are influenced in the way(s) we think they are. We need to find out what people are doing with representations rather than being limited to making claims about what we think representations are doing to people. By using contrasting approaches to the films *The Firm* and *Jurassic Park*, I suggest that one's audience conjectures are much more persuasive if supported through audience research.

In chapter 3 I suggest that we need to recognize multiple audiences. It has been thoroughly documented that different social groups use media and read texts differently. What is rhetorically salient to one audience may not be so for another, and what an audience member finds important plays a pivotal role in her or his decoding of a text. It simply does not make sense to make claims of the form X is Y or X causes Y without adding *for audience Z*. Through an analysis of a number of studies of the popular television show *Will & Grace*, we can learn a lot about how the critique of popular criticism succeeds or fails by noting how differently professional and unpaid critics create and decode texts; specifically, I critique the political economy of textual analysis by arguing that the need to exercise "professional vision" leads some critics to decode popular texts in a way that risks missing how mainstream audiences understand such texts. One way to reconceptualize academic criticism is to view *all* popular media criticism as based on audience reception analysis—the only question is *which* audience.

In chapter 4 I contend that a key element of audience analysis ought to be understanding the sorts of *judgments* that audience members make about characters—their likability, perceived similarity, trustworthiness, attractiveness, and so on. More important than a critic's ability to spot the similarity between an individual character and a recognizable stereotype is the sort of judgment that audience members are making, not only about the individual character but also about the social group of which the individual is a part. By explicating what my colleagues and I call the "parasocial contact hypothesis," I suggest that the key to understanding how representations can influence attitudes about social groups, such as gay men and male transvestites, is to understand the "category work" that popular media such as *Six Feet Under, Queer Eye for the Straight Guy,* and *Eddie Izzard: Dress to Kill* can perform. What do we *learn* about a category of people with whom we may be relatively unfamiliar? And if we have positive feelings toward and judgments about minority group representatives in a popular culture text, then how might our feelings and judgments transfer to the minority group as a whole?

In chapter 5 I attempt to illustrate how we can make our talk about representations more precise and productive by moving past the "Can You Find the Stereotype?" game. While it is easy enough to spot the stereotypes in Michael Crichton's *Disclosure,* their significance depends on the psychological and cultural work they perform in the early 1990s with U.S. audiences. Such rhetorical work is performed in the way a particular character instantiates a recognizable social type: the attributes the character demonstrates, whether the character's dramatic choices are rewarded or punished, and how the audience is "coached" to judge the character through a process I call "vicarious operant conditioning." By making specific, recognizable character and social types appealing and other recognizable character and social types unappealing, a text can contribute to or retard social progress. Though critics' conjectures about the judgments audiences make about various characters should be subject to verification, textual and audience analysis can work together to chart the rhetorical work of popular texts.

In chapter 6 I describe my efforts in a class on "Masculinity and Film" to teach critical media literacy so that students can become more sophisticated critics of the representational work that film performs. Data gathered from a sample classroom effort suggest that students can learn to be more critical viewers, become more tolerant toward minority groups, but they are unlikely to change the way they believe they "ought" to behave in terms of gender performance.

In chapter 7 I summarize my suggestions for moving beyond Representational Correctness. I suggest that we need to strategize about which parts of the triad of prejudice are most important to undercut for specific social groups and audiences in order to understand how media representations contribute to such a process. Our readings of popular media need to be context-sensitive yet multidimensional and recognize that representations function in multiple ways. For example, a study in Australia suggests that just having gay characters in mainstream media may play an important role in overcoming "the low self-esteem and suicidal tendencies of young gay men" (McKee, 2000). In such a context, I would happily trade off a little essentializing and polarization if it would decrease the potentially fatal consequences of heteronormativity.

Throughout this book, it will be clear that I believe scholars need to integrate social scientific with humanistic theories and methodologies. Rhetorical (text-centered) critical media scholars are very good at analyzing texts and telling a compelling story about what happens in and through public discourse and representations. We have tended to situate our stories into grand narratives that involve the dominance of patriarchy and/or capitalism. We have generally done a far less successful job of integrating our stories with theories of social psychology (on stereotypes and attitude theory, for example) or with theories about how the media influences people (cultivation theory, or social learning theory) and how people use the media (uses and gratification theory) (cf. Livingstone, 1998b). *None* of the textual analyses discussed previously makes any connection to relevant social psychological literature. I suspect that we can do better than that.

CHAPTER 2

The Argumentative Burdens of Audience Conjectures

As noted at the outset of this book, criticism may be viewed as a form of argument. Not surprisingly, different sorts of claims and judgments require different sorts of evidence. The central claim of this chapter is that *criticism of popular media that advances claims positing specific effects of popular texts on audiences or claims describing a determinate meaning of the text for audiences can be enhanced with evidence garnered through audience research.* In such cases, the critic offers claims about what texts do *to* audiences or what audiences do *with* popular culture texts; both sorts of claims can be described as "audience conjectures."

Several key terms should be clarified. In this chapter, "text" refers to whatever fragments or phenomena are constituted and contextualized by the critic as an "object" of critical inquiry apart from the audience, including what is treated as discrete artifacts or practices (Dow, 2001a; McGee, 1990).[1]

"Audience" is a more slippery concept than it may appear, as various constructions of "audience" are at work in popular culture research, each one guided by the particular cluster of theoretical beliefs informing individual critics (Allor, 1988; Brummett, 1991; Dow, 2001a; Seiter, Borchers, Kreutzner, & Warth, 1989). "Audience" as a concept has a long history, and any particular use of it implicates a set of ideological, theoretical, and methodological assumptions. Nor is there any shortage of typologies of audience research. Klaus Jensen and Klaus Rosengren (1990) identified

---

Originally written with Jennifer Stromer-Galley.

29

five traditions of audience research, namely, effects research, uses and gratifications research, literary criticism, cultural studies, and reception analysis. Thomas Lindlof (1991) describes five styles of qualitative audience research; specifically, social-phenomenological, communication-rules, cultural studies, reception studies, and feminist research.

James Anderson (1996) divides the competing conceptualizations of "audience" into two categories: formal and empirical. Audiences understood as created or constituted in and through discourse are described as *formal*, including "encoded" and "analytic" audiences: The discourse itself defines encoded audiences, while scientific or critical claims define analytic audiences. *Empirical* conceptions of audience posit an audience that is "out there," consisting of a set or sets of empirically verifiable members. Anderson identifies seven sorts of empirical audiences, ranging from the transcendent audience (categories of people rather than those specifically situated) to the engaged audience (people identified as an audience by their multiple layers of connection to a message). Sonia Livingstone (1998a), adapting descriptions from Jeffrey Alexander and Bernhard Giesen (1987), suggests that there are five competing conceptions of the audience: the audience as consumer (or market), the active and creative audience, the audience as public (the citizen viewer), the audience as potentially resistant, and the audience as a duped mass.

Importantly, criticisms of popular culture texts do not always stipulate a specific conceptualization of audience, even though, as illustrated later, explicit references to audiences often are made. Such scholarship frequently uses a relatively commonsense, empirical notion of audience as the specific consumers (viewers, listeners, and readers) of the texts analyzed. Another benefit of audience research is that it may encourage scholars to clarify more precisely who "the audience" of the text analyzed is and how that audience is constructed both by the scholar and by the text. It certainly seems reasonable to stipulate that scholars should move to more specific conceptualizations. As Livingstone suggests, "Let us stop asking how audiences are affected by the mass media and start asking how particular audience groups engage in different ways with particular forms and genres of the mass media in different contexts" (1993, p. 10).

In any case, the debate over how to best theorize or define "audience" need not be settled for the purposes of this chapter. No matter how "audience" is understood by any particular critic, *if* audience conjectures are set forth, *then* audience research is beneficial.

This chapter begins with a theoretical, argumentative rationale for audience research. Next I note that audience research is an underutilized resource in criticism that engages popular culture texts. I then provide a case study, originally conducted and written with Jennifer Stromer-Galley, contrasting the audience conjectures in a text-centered rhetorical criticism of the movies and novels *The Firm* and *Jurassic Park*

(Goodnight, 1995) with audience interpretations gathered through a series of focus group interviews. I conclude by noting three theoretical implications of the chapter's argument; namely, that wording in scholarly writing matters, that the lines between social scientific and humanistic research should be blurred, and that audience research enhances the connections between rhetorical and cultural studies.

Theoretical and Argumentative Rationale for Audience Research

I want to be clear that it is not my contention that all scholarly criticism of popular culture texts ought to engage in audience research. The point is that *if* critics make claims concerning the determinate meanings of the text or the effects those texts have on audiences, *then* the critic should turn to the audience to support those claims.

Audience research is not necessary to support audience conjectures if one of two assumptions is true: first, that all mass-mediated messages have universal deterministic effects on audiences; second, that popular media texts have one unequivocal meaning. If it were the case that all mass-mediated messages have an ascertainable, direct causal effect on most or all audiences, then critics merely would have to ascertain what that effect was on them and we would know what sort of effect the message would have on everybody else. Or, if it were the case that everyone experiencing a given popular culture text always agreed on what the text "means," then again audience research would be unnecessary. There would be only one possible reading of any and all texts, and thus critics could be confident that their reading of a text would be shared by all.

Both common experience and empirical research challenge these two assumptions. All one need do is think of a case where two people were affected differently by a movie, song, novel, or television show, and we can safely assume that mass-mediated messages do not always have a universal effect. And if one can imagine even one case of two people disagreeing over what a given movie, song, novel, or television show was "about," or what "lesson" it offered, or what the text "meant" to them, then the notion that all popular culture texts are unequivocal is refuted (Fiske, 1986). Most readers can provide their own anecdotal evidence. Anthony Swofford (2003) notes in *Jarhead* that battle scenes in antiwar movies became ecstatic "pornography" for his fellow marines,[2] while John Fiske (1989b) reports that young urban Aborigines in Australia watch "old Westerns" and cheer on the Indians as they kill the White men (p. 25)—interpretations that are quite the opposite of the films' putative intentions. Indeed, a good deal of scholarly research makes it clear that it is not safe to make audience conjectures without audience data.

David Morley's *The "Nationwide" Audience* (1980) studies how different audiences decode the popular British news program *Nationwide*. His audience research grew out of the close textual analysis that he and Charlotte Brunsdon did in 1978 on *Nationwide*. Morley tested a hypothesized relationship between the socioeconomic status of audience members and their specific interpretation of the television show. Audience members were grouped by occupation, socioeconomic status, race, and gender. Although Morley's methods have been criticized, he found that interpretations did vary by socioeconomic status at least on some topics. Janice Radway's influential *Reading the Romance* (1984) found that female fans of romance novels, far from being passive or uncritical dupes of false consciousness, put their reading efforts to a variety of educational, therapeutic, and leisure purposes that Radway interprets as being partially resistant to, rather than wholly co-opted by, patriarchy. Her results were noteworthy in part because the literary genre involved had been dismissed by previous critics as being reactionary and regressive.

Tamar Liebes and Elihu Katz conducted audience research to test the critical reaction of audiences of different nationalities and cultures to an episode of *Dallas*. They found that Arabs were more likely to criticize *Dallas* because of its associations with the Western colonial administration under which they suffered, but that Japanese and Russian audiences associated *Dallas* with the end of the era of the American rich (1989, 1990). Liebes and Katz also found that Western audiences surpassed the other groups in critical explanations of the television text, and that within the various nationalities those with a higher education made most of the critical statements. Thus national culture and education played a role in the various viewing practices and meaning construction of audiences.

Research on soap operas indicates that women viewers easily alternate between a detached, critical mode of viewing and a more involved, uncritical mode (Liebes & Katz, 1990; Press, 1991). According to Dorothy Hobson (1989, 1990), each mode of viewing facilitates different social tasks, including providing a topic of common discussion and critique (not unlike sports viewing for men) to enabling discussion of personal problems and feelings that might have been too painful to discuss directly (see also Seiter et al., 1989, pp. 223–47). Sonia Livingstone's (1998b) study of British viewers of the soap opera *Coronation Street* found that viewers' interpretation of a plot development (a controversial marriage) depended on how they felt about individual characters; their interpretations were partly explained by age and gender but also by the sort of relationship (such as level of identification) felt between the viewer and key characters. In a study of working-class and middle-class women, Andrea L. Press found that women viewers with varied class backgrounds respond differently to the images that television in general and soap operas in particular present to them (1990, 1991). Press found that the "hegemonic function" of television varied in ways that were more gender-specific for middle-class women and more class-specific for working-class women (1991, p. 176).

Several audience studies have reported that White viewers are uncomfortable or resistant to interpretative disputes involving racial representations. Naomi Rockler (2002b), for example, found that Black students generally were cognizant of the racial politics of the comic strips *The Boondocks* and *Jump Start*, but White students failed to find racial politics relevant to the strips. In a different research project, Rockler (2001b) found that her interview subjects were resistant to seeing any problematic racial overtones in *The Lion King*. Interestingly, an audience study of the reception of *Rush Hour 2*, starring Jackie Chan and Chris Tucker, found that Black and Asian viewers were just as resistant as White viewers to finding race-based humor offensive, though the reasons viewers of color did not find the humor offensive were different than those of White viewers (Park, Gabbadon, & Chernin, 2006).

Analyzing the role of "killer women" in films such as *Thelma & Louise*, *Terminator 2*, *The Quick and the Dead*, and *Tank Girl*, Tiina Vares (2002) argues that "it is not possible to theorize how audiences will respond to representations of violent women from textual analysis or anecdotal accounts alone" (p. 213). In her audience research, she found that female viewers make sense of such roles largely in term of the genre in which the film is identified. Thus those who enjoyed *The Quick and the Dead*, for example, did so in part because it disrupts the genre's traditional representations of women, while those who disliked the film found the genre itself boring. Vares concludes that viewers' sense of "taste" in movies was more often explained by genre preferences than by explicit references to gender politics: "Both genre and generic forms were shown to structure viewer expectations and thus influence the perception, selection, and interpretation of films" (p. 225).

Much of the audience research described here has been motivated by the belief that text-centered analyses cannot go very far in explaining how and why popular culture texts *become* popular. Despite content considered problematic by feminist critics, for example, various texts and genres remain popular even among feminists themselves (Dow, 1996, pp. 21–22; van Zoonen, 1994, p. 106; Winship, 1987). I agree with Dutch scholar Liesbet van Zoonen that "such developments seem impossible to explain by textual analysis only" (1994, p. 106).

Despite the provocative results of audience studies so far, the *theoretical* significance of audience research is a matter of some dispute. Critics of audience research believe that the polysemy of popular culture texts has been exaggerated, and that some audience research underestimates the mass media's ability to maintain and reproduce the beliefs and desires of the "dominant culture" (see, for example, Condit, 1989; Dow, 1996). In Celeste Condit's study (1989) of two viewers' responses to an episode of *Cagney and Lacey*, for example, she found evidence that there was a "dominant reading" that was easily and pleasurably engaged by the viewer who agreed with the show's putative message but required notable effort and ability to resist by the viewer who disagreed. Accordingly, Condit suggests that many texts may be *polyvalent* rather than polysemous; that is, texts have a dominant message that most or all viewers "get," even if they *value* such messages differently.

Condit's study is important because it has reassured some text-centered critics that texts do indeed have a "dominant" or "preferred" reading, thus making audience research less urgent (see, for example, Cloud, 1992, p. 313; Dow, 1996, pp. 12–13). As long as the critic can confidently access the "dominant" or "preferred" reading of a text, the reasoning goes, then that critic can assume that she or he is analyzing the message that "most" audience members receive. Of course Condit would be the first to admit that one cannot generalize from *one* example, particularly when there were only two participants and arguably atypical stimuli.[3] From the standpoint of theory development, Condit's study illustrates the need for *more* audience research, not less: While it may be that many or most mainstream popular culture texts have preferred readings that function to perpetuate the dominant culture, strictly text-centered studies preach mostly to the choir and are unlikely to prove this to be the case to skeptics of hegemony theory. The best way to explore such theories is through audience research, since only through further audience research will the limits of polysemy be confidently and persuasively articulated. As Justin Lewis puts it, "The question that should be put to textual analysis that purports to tell us how a cultural product 'works' in contemporary culture is almost embarrassingly simple: where's the evidence? Without evidence, everything is pure speculation" (1991, p. 49). While I would not go so far as to describe all such textual analysis as "pure speculation," I do believe that audience research would virtually always enhance a critic's argument.

A range of intriguing theoretical questions now faces the critic of popular media texts: Which textual and audience factors influence how polysemous a popular culture text is?[4] Just how influential are popular culture texts in changing or reinforcing beliefs and behaviors? Which methods of data gathering about audience responses are most reliable? Why are some members of subordinated groups more productive or more resistant viewers than others? How do meanings stabilize within a given discourse community—or do they? How influential are critics and opinion leaders in shaping the reception of popular culture texts? How much persuasion happens at an unconscious level? To what extent might a text affect audience members without them knowing it? These are just a few of the important theoretical questions that concern all popular culture critics, and such questions will receive richer and more persuasive answers if critics are assisted by audience research. Of course, audience research should not be pursued to the exclusion of textual analysis—arguably the most interesting and persuasive studies combine both (see, e.g., Rarick, Duncan, Lee, & Porter, 1977; Cohen, 1991; Press, 1991). Indeed, Livingstone argues, "Text and audience can no longer be seen as independent or studied separately" (1993, p. 7). Instead, she proposes that the text, audience, and context should be considered in any research project.

The rationale for audience research need not be based on any particular body of literature critical of the notion of media determinism or on recent theories concerning the polysemic character of popular culture texts. Audience research is needed to support claims about audience responses regardless of one's specific theoretical pieties regarding media effects and meaning formation. Readers need only agree that the initial assumptions identified earlier are dubious in their absolute form to understand that audience research is beneficial if and when audience conjectures are advanced.

Of course this is not the first call for augmenting textual analysis of popular culture texts with audience research. Many scholars—mostly in cultural and media studies—recognize the need to combine textual and audience research to understand how and why audiences react very differently to the "same" text. For some readers, this is old news (Livingstone, 1998b). Furthermore, most researchers would agree with Press's conclusion that audiences cannot be described either as wholly passive or active: "My findings stand in contradiction to those theorists who would argue that viewers use the mass media to resist cultural hegemony all the time, or to hegemony theorists who might argue that the mass media operate as a cultural monolith" (1991, p. 177). Clearly there is a good deal of theoretical and empirical support for the idea that conjectures about the meaning(s) and effects of texts on audiences require specific evidence.

Old news or not, a good deal of scholarly criticism concerned with popular media still does not include audience research *even when* claims are made about how and why audiences respond to a text. My colleagues and I reviewed the 1991–2005 issues of the journals published by the National Communication Association—*Quarterly Journal of Speech, Critical Studies in Media Communication, Communication Monographs, Communication and Critical/Cultural Studies,* and *Text and Performance Quarterly*—to identify articles concerned with popular culture texts that include audience conjectures.[5] Of the dozens of such articles, only a handful provided evidence for such claims based on audience research. Our selection of journals betrays a particular disciplinary bias due to the fact we are most familiar with the scholarship in communication studies. Our forays into the literature produced by film critics, popular culture scholars, and critical media scholars outside of the communication studies discipline (as constituted by the National Communication Association) suggest that the patterns we found are typical. Based on a review of the content of journals, including *Feminist Media Studies, Cultural Studies, Journal of Communication Inquiry, Media, Culture & Society, Television and New Media, Screen, Camera Obscura, Wide Angle, The Velvet Light Trap, Cinema Journal, Popular Communication, Journal of Popular Film & Television,* and *The Journal of Popular Culture,* it seems safe to make the generalization that audience research rarely informs popular media critics' work.[6]

It is not that essays containing audience conjectures without audience-generated data are "wrong" or somehow deeply flawed. Rather, the point is that audience conjectures would be more interesting as arguments, important for theory development, and persuasive as scholarship if they were supported with evidence generated through audience research. To restate the claim: I am not asking critics to compare or confirm their textual analysis with an audience when that analysis does *not* include claims about how audiences "read" texts or the effects texts have on audiences. Critics simply need to be aware of the argumentative burdens of specific types of critical claims. If critics make audience conjectures, then they should support such conjectures with audience research.

Many critics see themselves as "expert" readers of socially significant texts. As professional critics, they assume that they "see" and understand texts in a more sophisticated manner than the general public—that, after all, would be the point of an advanced education and training in theories of communication and culture. They exercise what Charles Goodwin (1994) usefully describes as "professional vision"—a concept I will revisit in chapter 3. It is neither expected nor especially desired that expert readings of popular culture texts be limited by how "lay" audiences interpret or react to them. Nonetheless, along the way to offering expert critical insights about popular culture texts, critics often make assumptions or explicit claims about audiences that deserve further investigation. Among the assumptions that require investigation is whether professional critics are as immune to the ideological workings of popular culture texts as some textual analysis implies. Van Zoonen describes this as the "unsatisfactory politics hidden in the textual politics," namely, the assumption that critics can "recognize the hegemonic thrust of media output and are able to resist its devastating effects, while the audience is still lured by its attractions and temptations" (1994, p. 106). Just how obliged critics ought to be to the practice of supplementing textual analysis with audience research depends on the specific modes of analysis they engage.

A Taxonomy of Audience Conjectures

Though any taxonomy of criticism is bound to fail to capture the complexity of critical projects, the following categories can serve as a starting place to describe the modes of rhetorical analysis of popular culture texts: illustrative, descriptive and explanatory, corrective, audience-interpretive, and creative-mediational. A common mode of analysis is *illustrative*; that is, a particular popular culture text is engaged primarily to illustrate a contribution to rhetorical, media, or cultural theory. If such analysis is purely formal and the claims are text-oriented, such as Bruno Giuliana's postmodern reading of the film *Blade Runner* (1993), then audience research is not necessary. If, on the other hand, the critic makes claims about probable *effects* of certain artistic choices and techniques, then audience research would be beneficial. Criticism that seeks to describe and explain a popular culture text also may or may not require audience research—it depends on the sort of claims advanced. Dick Hebdige's (1979) study of the subculture of punk rock in the late 1970s in Great Britain, for example, is an effort primarily to describe and explain the roots and cultural significance of the punk "style." It is only when Hebdige seeks to advance claims about what punk *meant* or what the social *effects* of punk were to different segments of British society in the 1970s that he advances audience conjectures.

The remaining three modes of analysis are adapted from an essay by G. Thomas Goodnight in which he describes three "modes of argument" commonly advanced in criticism: *corrective, audience-interpretive*, and *creative-mediational*: "Arguments may be adduced to reform audience reception, to identify responses and make audiences more self-aware, or to prepare an audience for alternative responses" (1987, p. 62). The corrective argument "adjusts the work to its public by questioning the appropriateness of audience response," while the interpretive argument "expands understanding of the relationships between a work and its reception. So critics offer reasons why acceptance of a work is suggestive of an audience's predispositions or even definitive of its identity" (1987, p. 61). Note that for both of these modes of argument, audience conjectures inform the critic's position and audience research would be beneficial. A critic cannot "correct" or reform audience reception without knowing what such responses are, and a critic cannot make audiences more self-aware without first identifying their responses and giving them meaning.

The last mode is creative-mediational. Goodnight explains that such analysis mediates between a work and "its possible audiences. Here argument functions as a way of explaining new contexts of meaning. Focused discussion on unexamined or routinely overlooked aspects of a work or its production process may create opportunities for novel appreciation"

(1987, pp. 61–62). In support of such an approach, Dow (2001a) encourages the critic to embrace the model of the creative artist rather than the scientist, pursuing the goal of illumination rather than "truth." In this mode of argument, audience research is largely superfluous as it is the critic's goal to open up new interpretive possibilities rather than to identify and assess how audiences have made texts meaningful or to determine what effects those texts may have had. Annette Kolodny defends feminist criticism in part for its ability to provide new and different meaning from texts and to ask new and different questions to enhance the range of critical possibilities (1985; see also Dow, 1996, pp. 5–6). As Dow puts it, "Criticism in the artistic mode seeks to move us, to interest us, to create works that make us think about our world in new ways" (2001a, p. 347).

For example, in her analysis of *Boys Don't Cry*, Brenda Cooper (2002) argues, "Kimberly Peirce's film can be read as a liberatory narrative that effectively 'queers the center' of heteroideology by centering female masculinity in opposition to what society and its mass media typically depict as 'normal' (p. 49). Admitting that her reading "may not reflect the interpretations of average spectators," Cooper claims her goal borrows from Dow's argument that "criticism should be a process of argumentation whereby the goal is to convince readers that their own insights into a text may be enhanced by reading the text similarly" (p. 49). In arguing that the text challenges heteronormativity, Cooper focuses on four elements: (1) "dismantling the myth of 'America's heartland'"; (2) "problematizing heteromasculinity"; (3) "centering female masculinity"; and, (4) "blurring the boundaries of female masculinity" (p. 49). The dismantling of the myth of Americas heartland, argues Coopers, serves to set the stage for the greater challenges of the film but throws into question the idyllic image of the heartland and the normalcy of social expectations, such as the nuclear family. The greater challenge comes when the female masculinity of the main character, transgendered Brandon Teena, is juxtaposed against the heteromasculinities of the film's other male characters. In this pairing, Teena's masculinity is shown, through the narrative of romance and sexual desire, to be more appealing. The message Cooper finds in the film is further reinforced as the truth of Teena's gender is discovered, as Teena's girlfriend continues to accept Teena as a man, even making love with him after seeing his fully female body. In her conclusion, Cooper again acknowledges the openness of textual analysis. She notes, "While there are multiple ways to interpret *Boys Don't Cry* and other media representations of sexuality, critical readings such as this one, which privilege gender fluidity and liberation from heteronormative straightjackets, also have the potential to contribute to broadening our understanding of gender and sexuality, in both mass media and in society" (p. 58).

In addition to criticism that invites, rather than reports, audience reception of a particular text, scholars of popular culture may intervene in other ways that do not require the sort of audience research described here. Analysis that provides a big picture of the sociocultural significance of new technologies (iPod), genres (reality TV), icons (Madonna), and so on will draw upon audience receptions but will situate them in a larger narrative. For example, Gilbert Rodman's book *Elvis after Elvis* (1996) documents how popular culture practices and artifacts related to Elvis Presley become the terrain in which a number of cultural forces are played out: One cannot talk about the role that Elvis played in the history of rock and roll without engaging issues of race, class, gender, and even religion. Among other topics, Rodman systematically recounts the controversies over Sam Phillips's oft-cited comments about how he could get rich if he could find a White person who could sing like an African American (the terminology varies in the telling) in order to chart the complex relationships among Elvis, early African American rock-and-roll performers, and the music industry. To what extent was Elvis rock and roll's equivalent of a "Great White Hope"? Rodman does not attempt to provide a definitive answer but instead finds significance in the manner in which the question has been approached by a variety of music historians and critics. Indeed, part of Rodman's explanation for the enduring significance of Elvis is that his career serves as a symbolic gold mine that is continually used as evidence for alternative accounts of U.S. popular culture history. Rodman advances his argument through the analysis of a wide variety of texts and artifacts, providing accounts of various receptions of Elvis and relatively detailed descriptions of specific events (such as Elvis's "pivotal" performance on Milton Berle's TV show).

In short, a good deal of popular culture criticism offers analysis in such a creative mode that does not depend on explicit or implicit audience conjectures. While some such criticism may be offered as speculation, creative interpretation, or even entertainment, most theorists agree that all criticism functions persuasively and argumentatively: "The critic says implicitly, 'See as I see, know as I know, value as I value'" (Brock, Scott, & Chesebro, 1990, p. 16). McGee puts the point more forcefully when he declares that scholarly critics "differ from everyday critics in that *they are always trying to make the world conform to their will*" (1990, p. 282, emphasis in original). Thus all critics take on a rhetorical or an argumentative burden in advancing their claims about popular culture texts, whether or not those burdens include support for audience conjectures or not.

The Burdens of Audience Conjectures: Four Examples

A series of examples of essays containing audience conjectures without audience research can further clarify the argument. The first is an example of what has been described as *illustrative* analysis. In Sonja K. Foss and Karen A. Foss's "The Construction of Feminine Spectatorship in Garrison Keillor's Radio Monologues," the authors indicate: "We are interested in discovering how a feminine reader or spectator is constructed rhetorically in a text and how that construction can be used to subvert dominant meanings about women in popular culture" (1994, p. 411). Based on their listening experience of Keillor's popular radio program, Foss and Foss argue that Keillor's monologues illustrate a "feminine spectator stance" through "refusal to privilege sight, dismantling of the male gaze, creation of Lake Wobegon as a feminine setting, and feminine speaking style" (1994, p. 412). Most of their analysis in the essay provides textual evidence to support their claims, but in the conclusion Foss and Foss make specific claims about the effects Keillor's radio monologues have on listeners. They are interested in the social and cultural consequences of Keillor's monologues, thus the question of whether his monologues "constitute an emancipatory rhetoric" is very important. Their claims are not framed as hoped-for effects, nor are they offered solely as self-reports of the authors' own experience of Keillor's monologues. Rather, they are specific conjectures about the possible linear effects of Keillor's construction of "the feminist spectator stance":

> As audience members position themselves in the feminine spectator stance suggested by the texts, they actually experience the concomitant feminist epistemology. They come to know through or from within a feminist perspective—they are able to try it on and to discover how it works and feels in their lives. Moreover, because their experience of the perspective is associated with pleasure, interest, and humor, listeners are likely to view the experience as a positive one; they are less likely to evaluate it as negative or to remain detached from and thus unaffected by it. (1994, p. 424)

As fascinating and important as the claims are about Keillor's monologues, they would be much stronger as arguments if they had been supported through some form of audience research. The specific causal claim made—"*because* their experience of the perspective is associated with pleasure, interest, and humor, listeners *are likely* to view the experience as a positive one" (1994, p. 424, emphasis added)—potentially could be investigated through any one of a variety of audience research methods, including the use of focus groups, personal interviews, surveys, ethnographies, or a host of experimental methodologies.

Martin J. Medhurst's "The Rhetorical Structure of Oliver Stone's *JFK*" *describes* and *explains* how the film *JFK* affects its audiences. Medhurst contends that the mythic structure of *JFK* functions rhetorically so that "the narrative on the screen is an artistic and poetic exemplification of the rhetorical action demanded of the viewer" (1993, p. 129). The actions by the protagonist, Jim Garrison, are "models for action that viewers are invited to emulate" (1993, p. 129). Throughout the essay Medhurst describes how the artistic choices made by Oliver Stone induce the audience to become "instruments of sociopolitical change" (1993, p. 128). Describing the effects of Stone's portrayal of Garrison's investigations of the assassination, Medhurst proposes that, "Like Garrison, the viewer is becoming increasingly skeptical of the official version of events" (1993, p. 132). Medhurst is convinced that audiences are persuaded that John F. Kennedy's assassination was part of a high-level government conspiracy: "It is the conclusion that Garrison and the viewing audience necessarily reach after having 'thought'—through visual imagery and memories—about the possibilities" (1993, p. 135). Medhurst conjectures a fairly direct cause-and-effect relationship between the film's rhetorical structure and audiences' responses. Consider the following claims:

> As Garrison awakens from his slumber, so too does the audience. (p. 133)

> Shot composition, framing, editing, lighting, and sound all conspire to compel the viewer to consider a government-led conspiracy as the answer to Kennedy's killer. (pp. 135–36)

> Slowly but inexorably the viewer is led to the conclusion that no external source can be trusted. (p. 136)

Medhurst admits that not all audience members will be persuaded, but by invoking the very biblical language with which he prefaces his essay, he implies that it is the fault of those who remain unpersuaded rather than the film's: "Stone's film is an artistic wake-up call to those having ears to hear and eyes to see. Clearly not everyone will understand, and even among those who do, not all will believe. But this is the nature of any rhetorical situation" (1993, p. 139).[7]

As was the case with the essay by Foss and Foss, it is not that Medhurst is "wrong" but that he offers claims that can and should be supported by audience research. Though he offers theoretical rationale for why the artistic choices made by Stone should have certain consequences for viewers, he offers no evidence that a majority (or even a significant segment) of *JFK's* viewers was influenced in the manner Medhurst conjectures. For example, he suggests that when the film depicts light reflecting off of Garrison's and Earl Warren's glasses, "The Platonic overtones are unmistakable" (1993, p. 135). Perhaps for Medhurst the allusion is "unmistakable," but a counterassertion that "most audience members do not catch the Platonic overtones" is equally plausible—absent audience research.

Perhaps the most forceful claim of the film's effects concerns its direct political consequences. Medhurst argues that elected "leaders have felt the force of an outraged citizenry," a citizenry provoked in part by *JFK,* and hence "the film has had a discernible effect on the willingness of governmental leaders to declassify documents pertaining to the Kennedy assassination" (1993, p. 140). While the timing of the passage of the Kennedy Assassination Records Collection Act supports the claim that *JFK* had a "discernable effect," just what sort of effect is not as clear. None of the sources cited by Medhurst on this point offers any evidence that public opinion was significantly affected by *JFK;* rather, the bill was passed to dispel "rumors" or "suspicion" of a conspiracy especially among people too young to remember the event themselves (Cope, 1992; Clymer 1992).

Nonetheless, Stone's *JFK* may very well have influenced public opinion. In a poll conducted in October 1988, 66% of those surveyed said they believed "there was a conspiracy to kill President Kennedy," and 61% believed that there was an official cover-up (Shenon, 1988). *JFK* was released in late 1991, and by February 1992 "77 percent said they believed that people besides Lee Harvey Oswald were involved in the killing. And 75 percent said there was an official cover-up in the case" (Carter, 1992). In a Gallup poll taken in December 1993, 75% still professed belief in a conspiracy (Gallup, 1995, p. 193). What factors increased the number of people who doubted that Oswald acted alone? Was it the publicity surrounding the film *JFK* or the government's reaction to the film? Or was it the film itself? And if so, what made the film so effective? We suspect that the most thorough and persuasive answers to such questions can be had only by *combining* audience research with the sort of careful textual analysis that Medhurst performs.

In addition to audience conjectures concerning the *effects* caused by certain texts, rhetorical critics also offer conjectures about the *meaning* that audiences derive from popular culture texts. In Dana Cloud's "The Limits of Interpretation: Ambivalence and the Stereotype in *Spenser: For Hire*" (1992), the argument is set forth that the character "Hawk" is constructed in such a way as to be "ambivalent"; that is, the meanings associated with Hawk are both positive and negative, supportive of the status quo and subversive. According to Cloud, "Hawk is simultaneously allied with white power and culture via Spenser, and resistant to it in his associations with Boston's criminal elements and antagonism toward the police and other institutionalized authorities" (1992, p. 313). Cloud suggests that the text has a dominant meaning for audiences and that meaning is ambivalence, though she admits how that ambivalence is evaluated can vary as a result "of viewer interpretation. Either side of Hawk (the side allied with white power or the side that resists it) can be evaluated in either a positive or negative way" (ibid.). Cloud contends that "it could be argued that the pleasure of watching Hawk is found in between Hawk's role as ally and his role as enemy of white culture, or in the dialectic interplay between these poles, the glimpses of irony and possible critique that the play of opposite positions entails" (1992, p. 316).

Cloud's analysis is *corrective* in the sense that she believes the praise Hawk's portrayal has received is misguided because the net effect of Hawk's portrayal is to perpetuate stereotypical racist images of the "native savage" (1992, p. 318). Furthermore, because the television show focuses on individual action rather than institutional critique, the naïve ideological stance of the show props up modern racism: "When issues of difference, power, and politics are reduced in discourse to matters of individual morality, as they are in *Spenser: For Hire*, the result is not only the silencing of a vision of collective action but also the legitimation of social and institutional discipline of groups whose political crises become reinterpreted as moral crises, the failure of individuals to meet their individual responsibilities" (p. 321). As noted in the previous chapter, Cloud contends that there are limits to interpretations of popular culture texts so that the program perpetuates dominant racist beliefs about Black men.

While Cloud's reading of *Spenser: For Hire* is provocative and important, it would be far more compelling if aided by audience research, because her central thesis rests on unproven assumptions about the meanings typical television viewers attribute to the show. Most evidence offered concerning audience reactions in her essay—reviews and fan reactions—indicates that audiences did not read Hawk in a racist manner. Indeed, after *Spenser: For Hire* was cancelled, there was such enthusiasm for Hawk's character that a short-lived series was launched that focused on him—*A Man Called Hawk*. Cloud conjectures that *Spenser: For Hire*'s "overt positive messages about race issues and articulation of empowered difference *cannot outweigh* the [negative] associations with which that difference is continually articulated in the text"; she concludes that "the dominant or preferred reading of this program is one that allows the racial stereotype to work" (1992, p. 317, emphasis added). But how can we know what the dominant or preferred reading is without checking our conjectures with audiences other than ourselves? Especially with a text acknowledged to be "ambivalent," how can we know what meanings outweigh others without asking audiences how they interpret the text? Cloud does an excellent job of providing evidence, both textual and intertextual, that certain aspects of Hawk's characterization *could* be read in a racist manner. The key question, of course, is how did different audiences read or interpretively "use" Hawk? *Spenser: For Hire* would seem an ideal vehicle for audience research to investigate how class, race, and gender factors correlate with various interpretations. Even if we do not trust audience interpretive reports, a host of qualitative and quantitative methods exists for investigating whether viewers' beliefs, attitudes, or behaviors were influenced by the show.

Similarities are evident between Cloud's analysis of *Spenser: For Hire* and audience conjectures made about *The Cosby Show* (Jhally & Lewis, 1992, pp. 3–8). Some critics praised the show's depiction of successful African Americans and claimed that the show provided a positive role model for minorities and promoted tolerance among White people. Other critics claimed that the main characters' economic success could foster the belief that racism was no longer a significant problem in America by perpetuating the myth that social mobility is determined solely by personal ambition and effort. Critics on each side of the issue offered arguments informed by their own readings of the show, but there was little hope of resolving the interpretive stalemate without turning to audience research. In an audience-centered research project published in 1992, Jhally and Lewis were motivated by the interpretive disagreements "to go beyond conjecture and seek the answer from the show's viewers, about whom both arguments make assumptions" (1992, p. 8). They found a much more complex reading of the show by audience members than previous critics had suggested. In a sense, both sides were proven right. The show did provide positive images that not only influenced *The Cosby Show's* immediate audiences but also were credited for a dramatic improvement and increase in television programming featuring African Americans (Gray, 1995). On the other hand, some (though by no means all) viewers did find in the show a reaffirmation of the myth of the American Dream so that the problems of racism were minimized.[8] Obviously Jhally and Lewis need not have the final word on the subject, but their audience research advances and refines the debate on *The Cosby Show* in a way that critics wanting to make audience conjectures without audience research could not. The debate has been taken to a new level of sophistication and persuasiveness through their effort to determine how audiences interpreted and comprehended the television show and why the show resonated with such a large viewing public. Similarly, how the character Hawk is used by different audiences could be explored empirically rather than assuming that audiences will attribute meaning in a stereotypical fashion. As Jodi R. Cohen's (1991) research on competing readings by audiences of Harvey Fierstein's *Tidy Endings* suggests, we cannot safely assume that the meaning audiences construe from a text will always neatly fit into the dichotomous categories of "dominant" and "resistant."

Though not a perfect fit, Nick Trujillo's "Hegemonic Masculinity on the Mound: Media Representations of Nolan Ryan and American Sports Culture" can be described as an example of the *audience-interpretive* mode of analysis. As Goodnight notes, critics can argue that "acceptance of a work is suggestive of an audience's predispositions or even definitive of its identity" (1987, p. 61). Trujillo contends that "hegemonic masculinity" is definitive of dominant American culture, and that media representations of the famed baseball pitcher Nolan Ryan reflect and reproduce masculinist predispositions. Specifically, Ryan has been represented in a sufficiently consistent and dominant manner in popular culture that "the media have functioned hegemonically by personifying Ryan as an archetypal male athletic hero" (1991, p. 290). Reviewing print and television representations of Ryan, Trujillo provides an artful combination of metaphor analysis, critical theory, gender theory, semiotics, and psychoanalysis. Trujillo implies that the media have portrayed Ryan in a sufficiently monolithic manner that what Ryan "means" to the American public as a symbol is stable and predictable: "In the final analysis, Nolan Ryan represents a white, middle-aged, upper-class, banker-athlete, with working-class cowboy values, who was raised by a middle-class family in a small rural town, and who is a strong father and devoted heterosexual husband" (1991, p. 303). Such representations function hegemonically by resisting the challenges posed to "the dominant image of masculinity" by women's sports, increased visibility of homosexual athletes, charges of racism, and an increasingly heterogeneous sports-viewing public. Furthermore, hegemonic masculinity in sports coverage "has negative consequences for men" such as encouraging excessive competition, sexist attitudes, and lack of trust and feeling (ibid.).

Trujillo may very well be correct, but two key conjectures he offers would gain significant support with the assistance of audience research. First, it would be relatively simple to investigate whether Trujillo's reading of sports coverage of Nolan Ryan is consistent with that of the general public. How consistently and monolithically has Ryan been represented? To what extent have various audiences accepted and adopted those representations? Such questions would be answered fairly easily with audience research. Indeed, in his subsequent book on Nolan Ryan, Trujillo (1994) includes a chapter that details his ethnographic research of fans and ballpark workers to determine what Ryan means to them. Although he does not survey a general audience, he does examine an important audience—fans and ballpark workers. Second, though sometimes the conclusions of media "effects" research are controversial because of the difficulty of isolating causal influences, theories and methods are available that would allow a critic to seek confirmation of the conjectured relationship between the types and amounts of sports coverage and various attitudes and emotional characteristics. In fact, research by Thomas C. Johnson (2006) suggests that watching major league baseball does *not* correlate with Mahalik's and his colleagues' (2003) masculine norms, with the exception of the (questionably) gendered norm of "winning." In contrast, Johnson found that viewing frequency of sports such as "Ultimate Fighting Championship" matches or professional boxing correlates with a number of masculine norms, including winning, emotional control, violence, power over women, being a playboy, and prejudice toward gay men.

So far a case has been advanced for the benefits of audience research if and when critics wish to make audience conjectures. In the parlance of debaters, it would be "comparatively advantageous" for scholars to support audience conjectures with audience research. The following case study further illustrates the thesis.

The Benefits of Audience Research: A Case Study

Goodnight's essay, "The Firm, the Park, and the University: Fear and Trembling on the Postmodern Trail" (1995), makes a series of claims about the meanings of two popular culture texts, *The Firm* and *Jurassic Park*, and it offers inferences concerning the effects that these popular culture texts have had on audiences. Because Goodnight's essay is lengthy, complex, and difficult to categorize, a few words are in order about how to interpret his criticism. Obviously a rhetorical criticism, like any text, is open to multiple readings. I fully recognize that the interpretation of the essay advanced here may have nothing to do with Goodnight's intentions.[9] Consistent with a commitment to audience research, the summary of Goodnight's essay was formulated after discussions with over 20 graduate students and faculty at three universities who were asked what they felt the "basic point" of Goodnight's article was. The reading represents the most common responses, and none of the participants offered an interpretation significantly at odds with it. Even if it is the case that Goodnight's project has been seriously misunderstood, the following "misreading" has heuristic value for the discussion of the benefits of audience research.

Accordingly, I focus on Goodnight's claim that the mass media are preying on the fears and already-present skepticism of post-baby boomers, specifically Goodnight's exploration of the "play of mass-mediated, postmodern performances in which skeptical audiences are induced to entertain the collapse of the social worlds" (1995, p. 269). Two best-selling novels turned into movies, *Jurassic Park* and *The Firm*, exemplify such "fused and fueled" postmodern themes at work (p. 281).

Goodnight is concerned that postmodernism, a "skepticism sweeping into and out of the academy for well over two decades" (p. 269), influences the so-called "Generation X." He contends that postmodernism has taken up the cultural space in much the same way that Greek skepticism took up the Hellenic cultural space, creating relativism, anti-essentialism, and undecidability, and in general calling into question notions of what constitutes "knowledge." For Goodnight, Generation X is silenced by institutions such as the media that absorb and then further compound and elaborate a code of cultural skepticism. He explains that Generation X has been celebrated and reviled as a label fixed by "boomer" marketing strategists trying to target a crucial market of new consumers elusive to "traditional" marketing strategies. Gen Xers are typically described as post-baby boomers who are skeptical, angry, and unhappy about the state of the world and of American society (Coupland, 1991). Goodnight describes them as sharing one key characteristic: "This generation without a consensual identity seems to display the shattering cohesion of postmodernity itself" (1995, p. 272).

Goodnight charges the authors and directors of *Jurassic Park* and *The Firm* with "exploiting" the fears of Generation X because the texts absorb and reinforce "chaotic" postmodern themes and aesthetics (1995, pp. 273, 281). He identifies *The Firm's* political messages in both novel and film as encouraging a "disdain for all institutions," offering a "cynical vision of the human condition" while tossing out the political messages of an "earlier generation" (1995, p. 273, cf. Wall, 1993, p. 731). Both novel and movie, he claims, invert the American Dream "with a profusion of postmodern themes that appear to well up from a Baudrillian fun house" (Goodnight, 1995, p. 273). As evidence for this claim he identifies the corrupt and "faux reality" of the firm, even though it appears respectful and proper, and the law firm affirms a "traditional code of propriety" of wife and children—designed not to ensure a healthy community but instead to create a liability for a partner who needs to be controlled (p. 274). Mitch McDeere has intermittent contacts with government agents, who, like the partners of the law firm, play the young attorney and his wife as pawns in clandestine games of institutional power. As a result, "skepticism [of institutions] is fed continually in novel and film alike" (ibid.).

In *Jurassic Park*, Goodnight also finds a variety of postmodern themes and aesthetics in both novel and film, however, the postmodern skepticism at work is downplayed in the movie because of Spielberg's inability to represent visually the terrors of institutional power. Nonetheless, Goodnight identifies "gestures of institutional disrespect" that "pepper the film" through characterizations that serve as symbolic representations of the ills of institutions. The "technocrats" who create this great dinosaur amusement park range from Nedry, the computer genius, who is "whiny, corrupt, and slovenly," to the lawyer, who is overly eager in his rush to get the cash flowing "but who, in a Freudian spinout, runs to a portable toilet for sanctuary only to get munched on the commode by a tyrannosaur— a subtle sign perhaps that in the face of raw nature rationalists retreat to the primal and perish," to Hammond, the "capitalist ogre" and mastermind of Jurassic Park, who is too greedy and egotistical to see the dangers in his theme park (1995, pp. 278–79).

As well as making claims about the supposed meaning or reception of *Jurassic Park* and *The Firm*, Goodnight makes claims about the effects that these texts have on audiences. He posits a causal relationship between text and specific audience attitudes and behaviors: "Audiences are induced neither to investigate the limits of current situations nor to evaluate common choices, but only to enjoy tastes of 'terror' and 'panic' that linger on the mind less than the popcorn on the palate" (1995, p. 270). The impact that the plot of *The Firm* has on audiences is clearly stated: *The Firm* "exploits suspicion of the law and animosity toward lawyers" (p. 273). Even the differences in the endings of the novels and movies "exploit aesthetic spaces of postmodernity so as to converge epistemic differences among media" (p. 269). For viewers and readers, *Jurassic Park* and *The Firm* "exploit generational anxieties, celebrate public absence, suppress a space for reflection, and promote some dreadful institutional dependencies" (p. 273). In sum, Goodnight believes that *Jurassic Park* and *The Firm* reinforce an attitude of institutional skepticism that is deplorable because it leads to inactivity in the public sphere: "The net result is the playful reductions of public life for an emergent generation" (p. 269).

Goodnight's description of *The Firm* and *Jurassic Park* yields the following audience conjectures, the first of which concerns the *meaning* or reception of the texts, while the second is a conjecture about the *effects* the texts have had on audiences. While other conjectures could also be teased out of Goodnight's essays, these are the two most central to his interpretation.

Conjecture 1: For members of Generation X, the plots portray "postmodern" heroes grappling with the corrupt and failing institutions of law and science. The movies offer cynical views of "the human condition" that suggest that the only "outs" are to escape or to "play" the game better than one's opponents.

Conjecture 2: Audience members, especially Gen Xers, are encouraged by *Jurassic Park* and *The Firm* to be skeptical toward institutions in general (especially the law and science). By discouraging faith in such institutions, interest in seeking societal improvement through participating in the public sphere is diminished.

In order to demonstrate the usefulness and importance of audience research, not long after the publication of Goodnight's essay Jennifer Stromer-Galley and I conducted research in an effort to determine how a set of audience members "read" the movies and novels of *Jurassic Park* and *The Firm* in order to test Goodnight's conjectures. Following Richard A. Krueger's work on focus group methodology (1994), we conducted four focus groups with a total of 23 volunteer college students ranging from ages 18 to 22. Participants in this age range were solicited specifically because they fit Goodnight's description of Generation X—the empirical audience conjectured to be the most defined or influenced by these texts. Furthermore, in the beginning of the essay, Goodnight notes that *The Firm* and *Jurassic Park* were very popular on college campuses, an observation that becomes particularly meaningful to his reading as he notes ominously in his conclusion that "the next spectacle, after *Firm* and *Park*, will be undoubtedly THE UNIVERSITY" (1995, p. 286). Focus group participants were volunteers from eight different communication classes and were required to have seen either *Jurassic Park*, *The Firm*, or both, and it was helpful but not necessary if they had read the books. Twenty-two of the 23 participants had seen both *Jurassic Park* and *The Firm* (one respondent had only seen *Jurassic Park*). Of 23 participants, only two had read the novel *Jurassic Park*, and four had read *The Firm*. A funnel sequence was used, beginning with open-ended questions about plot and moving to more specific questions involving interpretation of the texts' meaning. The interview schedule was followed closely, and additional questions concerning the positive and negative messages of the movies were asked of two focus groups to flesh out their interpretations. Each group was tape-recorded by the focus group moderator (Gen X) to allow for accurate recording of participants' answers, notes were made during the focus group interview by the assistant moderator (baby boomer), and partial transcripts were made of each focus group. Because this is a small sample, no claims are made as to the generalizability of the findings; instead, the purpose is to supplement and compare Goodnight's audience conjectures and text-centered analysis of *Jurassic Park* and *The Firm* to audience research.

Discussion of Audience Conjecture 1

When asked to describe the plot and meaning of the texts, it is fair to say that the focus groups did not experience the same films Goodnight describes. When focus group participants explained the plots of *The Firm* and *Jurassic Park*, traditional tales of good versus evil emerged, even if the tales were set in innovative settings. None of the 23 participants understood the stories as being primarily "about" the institutions of science and law, and only one saw evidence of institutional critique. The most consistent descriptions focused on characters or plot details having no apparent political or epistemological dimension. Regarding *The Firm,* one respondent explained the movie in this way:

> A hotshot lawyer graduates from Harvard, then he gets all these different proposals and he picks one from down South and he goes there and they give him an offer he can't refuse, and he goes there and finds out it is like a mafia-based law firm. People are trying to get out of there and when they leave the firm they get killed. And he finds out about all of this. And he's got the FBI against him, and the mafia is against him. . . . Then he finds out a way to get the firm in trouble with the IRS and then black-mail the mob so they can't do anything about him either. (R1)

Concerning *Jurassic Park,* another participant echoed similar plot and character-driven themes:

> An inventor created a way to bring back the dinosaur, on an is-land where he thinks it can be contained, then trouble arises when he starts bringing in people, he brings in his family mem-bers, and the whole park kinda goes into chaos; people are dying, and there is lots of trouble. (R2)

Often participants painted the stories in very traditional "good versus evil" terms that are hard to distinguish from very common modernist fare:

> The whole idea of the movie is that good overcomes evil. The evil law firm actually lost out in the end. And the good lawyer, Tom Cruise, won out because he knew how to use his legal skills to get himself out of the bind he was in. His whole reason for doing what he did was to keep practicing law so he would not lose his honor. (R3)

> I think like in the middle of the movie when they bring in the two kids and the two scientists or whatever, like at first they're like "this is really great" and then all of a sudden they're like "but you guys need to think about this" and then at the end, after like everything happens and everything's so bad, like, like, the good overcomes the evil, and like, like "hey, this is wrong: you need to destroy this." (R4)

When participants offered plot descriptions that included a political or an ethical dimension, those descriptions most often involved individual greed threatening the lives of innocent and well-meaning people. The implicit notions of autonomous individuals having sufficient agency to make ethical choices are hardly postmodern, and indeed they represent the most traditional modernist assumptions. Unless one associates a critique of capitalist greed with postmodernism—a link hard to reconcile with the history of Marxism—such interpretations are most easily read as reflective of modernism. Another respondent described the individual instances of greed as follows:

> [*The Firm* is] about how when lawyers come out of law school they are desperate to find a job, that they'll get sucked into whatever, you know, seems good to them, and about how much they have to work right at the beginning, like the movie shows that if they got paid off well enough, then they would do it, regardless of what they were asked to do. . . . [It is about] how your ethics get compromised when money is involved. (R5)

> [Concerning *Jurassic Park*] once again the ethical question coming into play with all the competition and what gets compromised. (R2)

> Creating dinosaurs sounds like a really good idea, but look what happens when greed and other human emotions get involved; it like, all goes haywire. (R5)

The closest statements that support Goodnight's interpretation came from one of the only two participants who were openly skeptical about the institutions of law or science: "I think the institution corrupted the lawyers. Especially the part that Gene Hackman played. You get the feeling that he was kind of a good guy, but he was just corrupted by the system. And he couldn't really escape from it, just like any of the other guys couldn't" (R6). The same respondent commented on *Jurassic Park*: "I identified with [Ian Malcolm] too. Because he was more cynical and disbelieving than any of those people in that park at first. And the archeologists were all gung ho to build it, even with reservations." But even this statement, in context, tended to be more about the evils of greed and capitalism than of postmodern skepticism about institutional reason.

Discussion of Audience Conjecture 2

Before discussing Goodnight's second conjecture, an additional issue should be addressed. Concepts such as "postmodernism" and "skepticism" are used in Goodnight's essay at such a sufficiently high level of abstraction that their translation across scholars and respondents is not secure. As a result of these complications, one cannot make a claim *definitively* proving or refuting Goodnight's second conjecture. It could be that these texts affected audiences in ways in which they are unaware. No questions were asked regarding participants' beliefs about how *Jurassic Park* and *The Firm* affected them directly. We did, however, elicit participants' general feelings about the institutions of science and law with such questions as "What would you say is your attitude towards the institution of science?" and "What would you say your attitude is towards legal institutions?" Answers to such questions provide one form of test of Goodnight's assumptions about preexisting audience attitudes that he believes are reinforced by the texts. They also provide some insight into the different ways that audience members "use" the texts.

All but two participants were generally positive rather than skeptical about the institutions of law and science—a finding that appears to challenge Goodnight's assumptions about the skepticism of Generation X. Further, when pressed about the meaning of the texts, the participants' discussion suggests that they did not "get" the skeptical message that Goodnight conjectures dominates *The Firm* and *Jurassic Park*. A typical response about the institution of law highlighted the corruption of individuals but the sanctity of the institution:

> I've always had the impression that we live in the best nation on earth. And I've always had a respect for the law and I always will. And, yeah, there is a lot of corruption out there, but I think if you look at the overall picture there is a lot of good people. (R7)

One participant mentioned being arrested "a couple of times" and having to go to court: "I was treated pretty fairly, so I guess I would say that I don't really think it [the legal institution] is bad" (R3). Other participants' comments were generally supportive of legal institutions:

> About the law itself, I feel that it is good. I have more [of a] problem with some of the people in law . . . I feel that they give the society a feeling that they are corrupt—more so than in the law itself. (R8)

> Overall I think the legal institution is good, I mean, I don't know, I have no experience with it, or whatever, but I think it is scary too because everything you hear about is, you hear the bad cases, usually, you know, and like, O. J. was so widely publicized. . . . But I think, on the whole, it can't be infallible and everything has its faults, and I think it's the best system, um, I think it's working, it's doing it's job, but I don't know. (R2)

> There are two sides to it . . . I think there is a lot of corruption involved . . . but at the same time I think that the legal profession is good, because our legal system is probably the best in the world. (R5)

Comments regarding science as an institution also were positive, even when participants noted the corruption of individuals. One participant's answer specifically debunks the portrayal of science in *Jurassic Park*:

> I think the science institution is great. I think that it's, the way it's portrayed in *Jurassic Park*, is pretty false. I don't think that that would ever happen in real life. I think it's totally fake, and I don't think that is how the science profession is. I see the science profession as the two doctors and how their life's work was with dinosaurs and they weren't out to make a buck, and I think that most scientists aren't out to make a buck. I think that they're in it for the advancement of science and not to make money. (R3)

Participants who expressed mixed feelings about science typically believed that the good outweighs the bad:

> I think it [science] can go both ways; obviously there is a lot of bad, but I think that there is more good to offset it with all the cures and medicine that they've come up with and other things. I'd say that it's more positive than negative but there's a lot on both sides. (R9)

Even those who expressed concerns about the institutions did so very much within a modernist framework. That is, they described the relevant institution as value-neutral, even if what certain individuals do with it represents good or bad values (cf. Bronowski, 1956).

> As far as Jurassic Park is concerned, it is not the science that made it bad, it was the publicity—making it into a park that made it bad. . . . It is not the science that blew up the project, it was the making it into a park. (R8)

R6's statement about *The Firm*, quoted earlier, was the only interpretation offered that resonated with Goodnight's own description of the plot. Her description was shaped by a similar interpretative frame that Goodnight brought to the same movie. That is, for those audience members already cynical about the legal institution, *The Firm* provides grist for the mill: "I think I tend to be really cynical, and I would believe something more easily like *The Firm* than I would believe something that was promoting the good things about our 'wonderful' judicial system. . . . There is no room for individuality, and there is a status quo that has to be maintained. And you know no one can break away from that because the consequences would be too bad for it." Similarly, R10 stated, "I don't trust the legal system," and described it as a "game" with "no rules." Such sentiments strike us as very much in line with Goodnight's reading of *The Firm*. Given that these participants were the only 2 of the 23 participants who proffered such a reading, the question is, how typical are such readings?

There is reason to doubt just how rampant postmodern skepticism is among Generation Xers. Public opinion researchers criticized the media hype in the early 1990s that described Generation X as being unusually disillusioned (Ladd, 1993). A Gallup poll in 1992, which sought to assess public sentiments of dissatisfaction, found that "The youngest generation of voting-age Americans (18–31 years) have the most optimistic view of the country," showing the highest level of satisfaction of all age groups overall and on such issues as "the way the political process is working," "the honesty and ethical standards of people in this country," "the state of the American family," and "the sense of community in this country today" (Hugick & McAneny, 1992, pp. 2–4), as well as "the way things are going in your own personal life" (Hugick, 1992). When asked about trusting institutions, including the government, news media, and corporations, the same group was at least as trustful as baby boomers, silent generation members, and the GI generation—and sometimes more so (Hugick & McAneny, 1992, p. 7).

Even the two "skeptics" in the focus groups can be described as more modernist than postmodern, because their interpretations identified the cause of problems within science and the law as personal greed and free-market capitalism. In R6's case, her skepticism extended to the institution of science: "I think progress and advancement is an inherent part of our nature, but we don't think about the consequences, and that is what I thought about the whole time when I saw that movie [*Jurassic Park*]." In some respects, such a sentiment is consistent with those participants who saw science as basically good, even though some scientists go wrong through haste or lack of caution. However, R6 seems less than optimistic about the future: "That is what I think is the difference between real scientists, like Einstein, who want to know just for the knowledge, and a whole different branch of scientists *now* who want to find out something to exploit it, to make money off of it. Every scientist's invention is just another profit-making thing." Though skeptical about the law, R10 expressed confidence in the institution of science. The problems in the movie *Jurassic Park* resulted from the pursuit of profit, leading to "moving so fast." Her solution is thoroughly modernist: Claiming that science is a "benefit to society," she believed that the moral of *Jurassic Park* is "the more you know, the better."

We concluded the focus groups by summarizing the main themes and messages the participants identified about the texts and asking group members if we had understood their comments correctly. During the debriefing process, we asked the participants directly if they felt the texts were about the institutions of law and science and whether they felt the texts encouraged skepticism toward such institutions. None of the 23 participants agreed with such a characterization. The following comment by R11 was met with a round of nods from other focus group participants: "I think [the movies were] more about the people, the way the people use the institutions, not exactly a portrayal of the institutions themselves." Another respondent summed up her interpretation of both movies this way:

> They showed that it's individuals who are manipulating things and not the institutions acting on them, they are acting within the institutions. So it's not like their course is predetermined by what the institution says. I think they show that their own motives get in the way and influence what they do. (R5)

Of course, the comments produced by our participants are open to more than one interpretation. One could argue that their comments prove that they have been successfully "duped" by the texts in question. By extension, it could be argued that audience research is unnecessary for media criticism informed and guided by certain critical neo-Marxist or psychoanalytic theories, because such theories assume that audiences are influenced on levels of which they are not consciously aware. But to make such arguments would require a specific theory of reading that explains how the critic is immune to the texts' hegemonic effects and yet can still know what is "really" happening to "average" audience members. Goodnight, at least, offers no such theory of reading.

Furthermore, if an argument is made that a given text "means" such and such—even when that meaning is argued to be subtle or operating at an unconscious or a subtextual level—then an audience conjecture is still being forwarded if it is proposed that such meanings *influence* audiences. Thus even if we dismiss all of the comments that flatly contradict Goodnight's interpretation, we are left with absolutely no evidence that young viewers were influenced in the manner conjectured. Enough audience research has been guided by psychoanalytic or critical theory to demonstrate that audience research is compatible with such theories (see, e.g., Radway, 1984; Hall, 1978; Walkerdine, 1986). If one wishes to make audience conjectures, then there does not appear to be a good reason not to engage in audience research.

In this study, it is fair to say that focus group participants generally did not comprehend or interpret the meanings of *Jurassic Park* and *The Firm* in the manner that Goodnight conjectures. It may be the case that the sort of negative aesthetics that combines postmodern style with a cynical attitude toward institutions can be found far more readily in such movies as *Blade Runner, Brazil,* or *Natural Born Killers* rather than in those discussed by Goodnight. Although Goodnight's claims about the effects these texts may have had on audiences cannot be proved right or wrong at this stage, his assumptions about the pervasiveness of postmodern skepticism are questionable. At this point, Goodnight's second conjecture about the persuasive effects of the texts must be viewed as an unsupported assertion absent audience research procedures informed by a specific theory of persuasion.

Conclusion: Wording Matters, Methodological Pluralism, and Cultural Studies

If the contention that "essays containing audience conjectures can be enhanced through the use of audience research" is accepted, then popular culture critics have two choices: avoid audience conjectures or consider incorporating some sort of audience research. Either way, scholarship will be enhanced. I conclude this chapter by identifying three theoretical implications, two of which are in response to some of the feedback received on earlier versions.[10]

The first implication is that word choices *matter*. A common reaction to the argument has been that "critics need only change the wording of their claims" either to avoid audience conjectures, frame their interpretations as artistic and creative interventions (Dow, 2001a), or frame audience conjectures as speculative. I agree completely. However, such wording changes are far from trivial. As Condit puts it, changing one's phraseology to admit the "partiality" of one's interpretations has "weighty consequences" (1990, p. 336). There is considerable difference between the act of offering a speculative, creative, or admittedly idiosyncratic reading of a popular culture text and the act of making definitive claims about the text's meaning or positing a causal claim about what that text is doing to audiences. Condit critiques Michael Leff's "close reading" of Abraham Lincoln's Second Inaugural on the basis that it was "accurate only for those socialized to the dominant culture (which was northern and white)" (1990, p. 336). To the extent that we see ourselves in academia as advancing knowledge claims, the clarity and specificity of those claims are important so that we avoid turning a particularized reading into an "implied universal" reading (ibid.).

For example, Goodnight's reading of *The Firm* and *Jurassic Park* could be categorized as a speculative or mediational argument proffered as a creative interpretation and not at all about audience reactions. After all, Goodnight admits that the two examples are not enough to prove a general case about the "trajectory of the code of cultural skepticism" in public discourse (1995, p. 285). However, Goodnight's other two categories seem to be better fits: Goodnight is out to *correct* an overly positive public reception, or to *interpret* these texts as definitive of our current social identity and to make us aware of that identity. In either case, his essay rests on assumptions about the meanings audiences took from the texts and how they may have been influenced by them. Specifically, there is sufficient causal language in the essay to invite the inference by readers that *Jurassic Park* and *The Firm* contribute to the demise of public discourse that Goodnight laments in a well-known series of essays (1982). Indeed, editor Robert L. Ivie's introduction to the issue in which Goodnight's essay appears is titled "What's at stake for public discourse?" Ivie suggests that Goodnight's essay is important, because "the negative aesthetics of a postmodern condition" presumably enacted by *The Firm* and *Jurassic Park* "undermines the recovery of an authentic public sphere" (1995, p. 266). Proving such a hypothesis would be no easy matter. Even if Goodnight can *interpret* the books and movies as he has, there is no evidence offered either that audiences *comprehended* the specific messages that Goodnight decoded from the texts or were influenced in the way he and Ivie imply that they are (Bordwell, 1989, pp. 1–18).

Alternatively, if the contrary position were admitted (namely, that *The Firm* and *Jurassic Park* do *not* contribute to the demise of public discourse), then what would be the point of Goodnight's essay? Certainly there is room for popular culture criticism that is creative, provocative, and highly speculative. But let us be clear about the different sorts of claims made (and thus the evidence required) in criticism that aims to edify and entertain fellow scholars compared to criticism that attempts to explain or evaluate socially significant popular culture texts. While many critics may not intend to make empirical statements about effects, they sometimes write as if they do. The result is conceptual and argumentative fuzziness. Claims about individual texts, and the cause of rhetorical and media criticism generally, could be advanced if we were clearer about what we were doing.[11] Audience research is irrelevant to criticism aimed at illustrating interpretive possibilities but potentially very valuable to criticism aimed at assessing the social and political significance of popular culture texts.

The second theoretical implication to which interlocutors have drawn attention is that this discussion blurs the line between humanistic and social scientific research (cf. Edwards, 1996, p. 262). Again, I agree completely and think that such a blurring is all for the good. After all, it has been over 35 years since the Committee on Rhetorical Criticism of the National Developmental Project's report on "the prospect of rhetoric" noted that "it is both possible and desirable to join the roles of the 'critic-scientist' and 'critic-artist'" (Sloan, 1971, p. 224). Efforts by philosophers to draw a sharp distinction between science and non-science—including the humanities—on epistemological or ontological grounds have been unsuccessful (Rorty, 1991, pp. 21–110). As much of the rhetoric-of-inquiry scholarship has noted, what humanists and social scientists have in common is that they advance *arguments* (Brockriede, 1971, pp. 131–32). Arguments concerning popular culture texts can be enhanced by the critic who draws from multiple research traditions without regard to the labels of humanities or social science: "Just as a debater makes a convincing case by using varied evidence, so the research scholar can argue a theoretical position more convincingly by blending the powerful evidence of experimental research with the vivid evidence of criticism" (pp. 137–38). Such a position does not return us to John Waite Bowers's notion of rhetorical criticism as "pre-scientific" (1968) but instead to a view of *all* scholarly writing as thoroughly rhetorical and argumentative—discourse drawing from the available means of persuasion to influence specific communities of readers (Gross, 2006; Prelli, 1989).

The third and final point is that audience research in support of audience conjectures enhances the interconnections between rhetorical and cultural studies. Particularly when engaging popular culture texts, rhetorical critics often align themselves with the aims of the cultural studies movement (Rosteck, 1995). The common denominator among the essays engaged in this chapter is that popular culture texts *matter* to the critics. As we read them, Foss and Foss forward Keillor as exemplary in part because they oppose the patriarchal biases of contemporary society and hope to see it change. Medhurst believes that Oliver Stone's *JFK* matters not only because of the historical importance of its subject matter but also because considering the impact of competing historical narratives reminds us that we are "symbol created" as well as symbol creators, and with such insight, "we can begin to know ourselves" (1993, p. 141). Cloud explicitly opposes the racism she believes is advanced in *Spenser: For Hire*, just as Trujillo implies that the stereotypical notion of masculinity he believes is dominant ought to be replaced. And Goodnight's impressive body of work for nearly 30 years makes clear his desire for a reinvigorated public sphere of discourse. Cumulatively these works contribute to what Steven Mailloux describes as *rhetorical cultural studies*, which "attempts to describe and explain past and present configurations of rhetorical practices as they affect each other and as they extend and manipulate the social practices, political structures, and material circumstances in which they are embedded at particular historical moments" (1991, p. 234; see also 1994, pp. 82–88).

I share a commitment to the belief that rhetorical scholars ought to engage socially significant texts, and that the end or *telos* of our engagement ought to be social change itself. As McGee puts it, the discourse of professional critics "is on its face that sort of action which intervenes in the world" (1990, p. 282). As Justin Lewis declares, "If we are concerned with the meaning and significance of popular culture in contemporary society, with how cultural forms work ideologically or politically, then we need to understand cultural products (or 'texts') as they are understood by audiences" (1991, p. 47). Thus part of the motivation to write this chapter is the conviction that the stronger and more thorough our scholarly arguments are, the better the chance to influence a broader audience—in my own discipline of communication studies, in other disciplines, and even outside of academia.[12]

CHAPTER 3

The Phenomenal Text of *Will & Grace*
Revisiting the Text/Audience Divide

The previous chapter argues for the usefulness of audience research for critics interested in making what were called "audience conjectures." In this chapter, I pursue this point further but with a somewhat different agenda. The initial theoretical points I want to make are far from novel: Texts in themselves do not exist, thus when a critic offers a reading she or he simultaneously constitutes a text. Furthermore, professional critics engage texts in ways that are different from unpaid critics or the hypothetical "uncritical viewer." The more provocative point I wish to make, however, follows from the first two points; namely, I wish to suggest that what are often called "textual analyses" might be thought of as a specialized form of audience reception research.

In his 1787 *Critique of Pure Reason*, Immanuel Kant called "things-in-themselves" (*Dinge an sich*) noumena and argued that they are unknowable in principle; all we can know are *phenomena*—things as we perceive and experience them (1965). Similarly, texts are silent until experienced. We do not have access to the Pure Text, or to its single correct interpretation. All we have is the *phenomenal* text—the text as its various readers perceive and experience it. Each textual encounter is *partial* in the sense that it represents one of many possible ways to encounter any given text, and in the sense that our individual histories, abilities, values, and interests influence the "meaning" that we glean from a text.

So far I have not said anything that has not already been said by a wide variety of philosophers, theorists, and media critics. What I wish to add to our understanding of the phenomenal text is a discussion of how our histories, abilities, values, and interests—what Martin Heidegger (1962, ¶32)

61

would call our "fore-structure" or Hans-Georg Gadamer (1989, p. 270) calls "prejudice"—guide what we find *rhetorically salient* in the act of critical analysis. Consider the following thought experiment: If someone were to ask you to think about the past two hours of your life and to provide an account, you would have to go through a two-step process. First, you would gather your thoughts about what you have been doing, and I assume it is uncontroversial to note that our perceptions and memories are selective. They *have* to be selective in order to make sense of the potentially infinite number of stimuli to which we could attend in the flux of everyday experience (Schiappa, 2003, pp. 13–17). Second, we would have to decide *what* to talk about and *how* to talk about it: We might create a list or tell a narrative, for example. In either case, again there is a process of selection involved, not only in deciding what is *worth telling* but also *how to tell it.* Deciding what is relevant or salient to tell about is a function, at least in part, of our rhetorical goals—What do we want to accomplish in our narrative? How do we want our audience to react? Furthermore, even beyond our conscious intentions, whatever language we choose can be described as persuasive and rhetorical because there is no neutral way to describe events or experiences—*all* descriptions enact a particular point of view and implicitly or explicitly invite a particular response (Schiappa, 2003, pp. 151–60).

Instead of describing the past two hours of your life, instead consider what happens if one is asked to describe a two-hour movie, a book, a television series, or some other popular culture text. The same processes of selective *perception* and *description* are necessarily at work. What we notice and deem worthwhile to talk about, and how we talk about it, cannot help but be selective, guided by our foreknowledge, and influenced by our persuasive goals (Livingstone, 1998b). Because in the process of crafting our account we "re-create" the text, some media critics describe the process as "constituting" a text, in part to recognize the fact that their phenomenal text is not necessarily the same as anyone else's, and in part to recognize that in the process of re-creation the critic brings to life a text that would not have existed without them (Dow, 2001a, pp. 340–43; Brummett, 1991).

As noted earlier, some media criticism is paid criticism. Professional critics may be compensated directly through the sale of book or essay manuscripts to publishers, or indirectly through the academic credit earned through scholarly publication (which can have direct, material benefits in the form of merit raises, tenure, awards, etc.). Such criticism is assumed to be worthy of compensation because its authors use a set of skills not shared by all popular culture consumers. Paid critics can be described as members of the "knowledge class": "The formation of the knowledge class characteristically takes place around the professional claim to, and the professional mystique of, autonomy of judgment; this forms the basis both for the struggle over the organization of work and for individual self-respect (that is, for a particular mode of subjectivity) grounded in this relation to work" (Frow, 1995, p. 125). A central part of how academic criticism is culturally valued is linked to professional critics deploying skills that demonstrate "professional vision."

In his essay "Professional Vision," anthropologist Charles Goodwin (1994) states: "Central to the social and cognitive organization of a profession is its ability to shape events in the domain of its scrutiny into the phenomenal objects around which the discourse of the professional is organized" (p. 626). Goodwin contends that the process of engaging phenomena and producing knowledge claims about them involves three practices: "(1) *coding*, which transforms phenomena observed in a specific setting into the objects of knowledge that animate the discourse of a profession; (2) *highlighting*, which makes specific phenomena in a complex perceptual field salient by marking them in some fashion; and (3) *producing and articulating material representations*" (p. 606). Goodwin illustrates these practices with respect to an archaeological dig and the use of the infamous Rodney King video in the criminal and civil trials resulting from his violent beating by police officers.

Coding can be thought of in a simple or sophisticated way. It is simple enough to refer to the book or film version of *The Firm*, for example, just as it is simple to refer to "dirt" and "a videotape." These are social categories widely shared and understood by just about any English-speaking person. If someone wants to describe such phenomena in something more than a mundane manner, however, greater sophistication is required. In the process of producing an account of a popular culture text (Goodwin's third set of practices), professional critics deploy a specialized vocabulary that draws our attention to what the critic believes are salient features of the phenomenal text that make it meaningful. As Goodwin notes, the practices of coding and highlighting are closely related: "A quite general class of cognitive practices consists of methods for highlighting [the] perceptual field so that relevant phenomena are made salient. This process simultaneously helps classify those phenomena, for example, as an archaeological feature rather than an irrelevant patch of color in the dirt, or as an aggressive movement" (1994, p. 628). Notice that the meaning being constructed is both denotative and connotative; that is, coding/highlighting tells us what something is and how it ought to fit into our larger understanding of the world—whether it is good or bad, valuable or not, and so on.

The only limit on the number of accounts or descriptions of a text is that of human imagination. Though I do not want to underestimate the sophistication of unpaid criticism, generally speaking we can assume that professional critics will produce accounts that are more "valuable" than those by most unpaid critics. Discussing film criticism in particular, Clive James notes, "Critics must either be able to express opinions like ours better than we can, or else they must be in charge of a big idea, preferably one that can be dignified as being called a theory" (2006, p. 36). Academic critics must be theoretically and methodologically sophisticated and draw from the specialized vocabularies and discursive practices in which they have been trained. This may lead critics to analyze a text's linkages to historical and contemporary counterparts, the political economy of the text, its genre, or medium, the techniques of aesthetic production, the strategies of representation at work, or any of a number of other issues made salient by the cultural, psychological, ideological, psychoanalytical, and/or rhetorical theories favored by the critic. As Richard Rorty puts it, there are as many possible descriptions "as there are purposes to be served," and all descriptions have to be "evaluated according to their efficacy as instruments for purposes" (1999, p. 134).

The descriptions produced by different disciplines, or theories within a discipline, function in a manner that is analogous to the way different maps work (Dorling, 1997). The "same" phenomenon can be mapped in a variety of ways—metereological, demographic, economic, biological, topographical, transportation, geological, hydrological, bathymetric, historical, political, and so on. It is pointless to ask about a "pecking order" of maps, or to ask which depicts reality as it "really is." Maps are necessarily selective, "partial," and constructed to serve specific interests and purposes (Wood, 1992). They can be judged for their usefulness only with respect to such interests and purposes. Even such notions as "accuracy" only make sense relative to the specific function of a map (Monmonier, 1991).

The question then becomes, what are the *purposes* served by professional, and especially academic, criticism of popular culture texts? Of course, there are many purposes served through professional criticism, ranging from personal recognition to the desire to contribute to a better world. One might view one's criticism as a pedagogical exercise to promote critical media literacy, a contribution to theory, a political intervention, as an artistic creation in its own right, and so forth. The range of critical purposes also is illustrated by the variety of types of claims described in the previous chapter. To that list we can add *historical* claims ("*Gremlins* is symptomatic of emerging technophobia") *ethical* claims ("it is wrong to portray Native Americans as savage"), and *artistic* claims ("*Bladerunner* creates a stunning postmodern aesthetic").

I think almost all professional critics would agree that one purpose is to interpret or describe the relevant text or texts in a manner that is *different* from the sort of descriptions that might be produced by the "typical" or "average" viewer. That is, after all, what would make a professional critic's work worthy of compensation. The political economy of professional criticism encourages the logic that the more radically different a critic's description of a text is from the dominant reading from mainstream culture the better, because the more unusual and distinctive the description the more clear it is what the "added value" a particular critic's contribution is. The problem is that the need to produce unusual and distinctive descriptions can lead to a "trained incapacity" that leads the critic to miss the cultural and political work a text may perform among the general population.[1]

For example, some critics decode the dialogue and behavior of the character "Scar" in *The Lion King* as gay (Harris, 1994; Newberger, 1994), even though a more plausible case can be made that Jeremy Irons was cast to convey the sort of upper-class snobbishness evinced by George Sanders's performance as Shere Khan in *The Jungle Book*. It is arguably less of a stretch to read an effete lion or tiger in *class* terms (especially when voiced with an upper-class British accent) than in terms of sexual orientation. As evidence for a gay reading of Scar, some critics quote the line he utters in response to Simba's comment, "Uncle Scar, you're weird." Scar replies, "You have no idea." As critic Chris Hewitt (1997) notes, however, this line is an in-joke borrowed from Jeremy Irons's performance as Claus von Bülow in *Reversal of Fortune*: When his attorney, Alan Dershowitz, says, "You are a very strange man," Irons as von Bülow replied, "You have no idea."

Similarly, "King Louie" in *The Jungle Book* is deemed an example of negative racial stereotyping due to the orangutan's love of jazz and his famous song "I Wanna Be Like You." Critics Susan Miller and Greg Rode (1995, p. 92) describe the tune as performed in a "familiar black-coded voice," which, when sung to Mowgli (a South Asian Indian apparently coded white for the purpose of their critique), represents "a humiliating revelation" of the desire of African Americans to be accepted as human. Such claims probably would have surprised the original viewers of the film in 1967, since King Louie was performed by the then-famous Italian American jazz icon Louis Prima. Indeed, the song's performance in the movie even recreates the sort of jazz parade for which Prima and his band were well known.

Such examples could be multiplied many times over. Psychologist Carolyn Newberger (1994) and critic John E. Harris (1994) both decode the hyenas of *The Lion King* as "urban blacks," despite being voiced by a multiracial grouping of Cheech Marin (Mexican American), Whoopi Goldberg (African American), and Jim Cummings (Anglo-American). Certainly the hyenas *could* be read in such a way in an allegorical interpretation of *The Lion King* as a polemic on class and social order; but if we do, then how does one adjudicate between *that* decoding and Annalee R. Ward's (1996) decoding of the story as a Christian allegory? Or between *those* readings and a decoding that sees *The Lion King* as driven by an intense fear of illegal immigration (Elahi, 2001; Martin-Rodriguez, 2000)? Or those who see *The Lion King* in Shakespearean terms as a retelling of *Hamlet* (Buhler, 2003; Gavin, 1996; Stenberg, 1996)? Or even those who contend that the movie is an allegory between the relationship between the dead "father" Walt Disney himself and his successor, Michael Eisner (Hoberman, 1994; Krämer, 2000)? Of course, some of these interpretations are deliberately fanciful and are best understood as creative-mediational. But most are *corrective* inasmuch as they advance audience conjectures. The question is, how should we evaluate competing conjectures? How do we arbitrate between those who decode Disney's representations of women as oppressive (see, e.g., Bell, 1995) and a decoding that positions them as Disney's coded homage to goddess worship and the sacred feminine (Brown, 2003, pp. 261–62)?

One could spend an entire career just analyzing the various interpretations of Disney films and programs by professional critics. I strongly suspect that at the end of that career one would come to four conclusions. First, professional critics have found Disney products complicit with just about every imaginable evil in the United States.[2] Second, such professional critics rarely engage in audience research. Third, the decodings of professional critics often are radically at odds with those of unpaid viewers and critics. And fourth, when faced with unpaid viewers' conflicting interpretations, professional critics typically dismiss them as evidence of Disney's hegemonic power and/or the poor state of critical media literacy in the United States (Rockler, 1999a; Sun & Scharrer, 2004).

I hasten to add that I am *not* advocating that critics must be limited to the popular receptions of any particular text. And I am not trying to claim that all critiques based on the critic's sense of what is important about the text are wrong. Rather, I am trying to construct a cautionary tale that encourages colleagues to be wary of how the pressure to produce the unusual can lead us to produce accounts that may, in the end, undercut the larger purposes of our criticism.

When engaging a popular culture text, critics must, in Goodwin's terms, code and highlight the perceptual field so that relevant phenomena are made salient. Because our theories, methods, values, and interests vary, what I find salient in a text to my life and judgment as a critic may be very different than another critic; and obviously what an academic finds significant in a text may be quite different than an unpaid critic. Critics are guided by what I describe as "rhetorical salience" to attend to those features of the text that are most interesting or important for their purposes. Such features may be as simple as decoding an animated character's accent to make inferences about the character's coded identity or as complex as reading the story line of a movie in allegorical terms. We should not expect professional critics to decode popular media in precisely the same ways that mainstream audiences do, but when the exercise of professional vision is linked to audience conjectures, the question of what different viewers find salient becomes directly relevant to the assessment of such conjectures.

For most critics, what is most immediately salient about *Will & Grace* is that it is the first successful mainstream TV show ever to portray two gay men as leading characters, so how those men are represented is important. As noted earlier, critics often have a notion of Representational Correctness that informs their work. When the norms of RC are reinforced by the need to produce unusual or distinctive accounts and descriptions, odd things can happen.

Competing Textualizations and Receptions of *Will & Grace*

When the National Broadcasting Company (NBC) first began to air *Will & Grace* in 1998, gay rights advocates and media critics applauded the program for its positive portrayal of two gay men with very different personalities (Battles & Hilton-Morrow, 2002, pp. 87–89). The show features four main characters living in Manhattan. The title characters are Will Truman, a gay attorney, and his best friend Grace Adler, a heterosexual interior decorator. They often are joined by Jack McFarland, a "flamboyantly gay, continually unemployed, self-described actor/dancer/choreographer," and Karen Walker, a wealthy, married "socialite and alcoholic" who works for Grace (p. 88). The show has been very successful and has won critical praise and numerous awards. By the spring of 2001, *Will & Grace* was being watched by an average of 17.3 million viewers each week (Cagle, 2002); in 2002, the series entered syndication and now can be viewed daily in most media markets, despite the official end of the series in May 2006.

Will & Grace is an unusual popular culture phenomenon. In the United States homosexuals are still targets of prejudice, which is manifested "in a wide range of behaviors ranging from verbal expressions of dislike to violent attacks" (Herek, 1988, p. 451). Negative attitudes toward homosexuals have been documented as being pervasive among adolescents (Morrison, Parriag, & Morrison, 1999), college students (D'Augelli & Rose, 1990; Kurdek, 1988), and the general adult population in the United States (Herek & Glunt, 1993). We still live in a culture in which if someone even *thinks* you are gay, you could be harassed, assaulted, or killed (Wilchins, 2002). Attitudes toward homosexuals are slowly changing, however (Altemeyer, 2001; Yang, 1997), and it seems reasonable to explore what role television could have in influencing sexual prejudice (Gross, 1984, 2001; Shanahan & Morgan, 1999).

In the first decades of television, homosexuals were mostly absent or were portrayed negatively as deviants in mainstream shows such as *Marcus*

Welby, M.D. or *Hawaii Five-0* (Gould, 1973; Gross, 1991; Simms, 1981). Lesbian representations have fared better than gay men (Moritz, 1989), and both have fared better in film than on television (Nelson, 1985). Content analysis by Alfred Kielwasser and Michelle Wolf (1992) and Fred Fejes and Kevin Petrich (1993) suggests that at least through the early 1990s positive representations of gay men and lesbians on mainstream television were few and far between. Billy Crystal's portrayal of a gay character, Jodie Dallas, on *Soap* is noteworthy as television history but did not appear to lead to more gay characters in mainstream television. By 1995, homosexual characters accounted for 0.6% of the TV population, significantly less than estimated rates of homosexuality in the U.S. population (Shanahan & Morgan, 1999, p. 94). In the 1990s, the number of gay characters on television increased significantly, though the beneficence of increased visibility is a matter of some dispute (Hart, 2000; Walters, 2001).

While many pundits considered *Ellen* an important cultural breakthrough in the United States, I am not aware of any research done investigating attitudes associated with viewing the show; furthermore, one cannot assume that positive attitudes toward lesbian characters result in positive attitudes about gay men (Herek, 1988, p. 470; Kite & Whitley, 1998, p. 56). While positive portrayals of homosexual characters are scattered across various television shows, no previous broadcast network show that features two gay male characters in leading roles has reached the sort of enduring popularity and critical acclaim that *Will & Grace* has. It is impossible, of course, to predict the future direction of television content. The popularity of cable network shows with more diverse portrayals of gay men, such as *Queer as Folk*, *Six Feet Under*, and *Queer Eye for the Straight Guy*, may lead to a greater range of representations on broadcast network shows. In any case, the distinctive place *Will & Grace* has in broadcast television history warrants the attention of television and popular culture scholars.

Study 1: The Textualists

Battles and Hilton-Morrow (2002) contend that because *Will & Grace* conforms to the genre demands of situation comedy and conventional patterns of representing gay men, the show fails to "represent a challenge to the dominant norms of U.S. culture" (p. 102). Indeed, they argue that the individualistic focus of the sitcom genre, combined with representations that feminize the gay characters and infantilize the program's most subversive characters, results in a program that ends up "reinforcing heterosexism" (p. 89).[3]

To understand how the concept of rhetorical salience manifests itself in Battles and Hilton-Morrow's critique, it is necessary to examine how their specific arguments are constructed. Obviously, their essay is, itself, a text, and I am guided by my own sense of rhetorical salience in choosing which specific points to address.

First, Battles and Hilton-Morrow (2002) contend that the individualistic focus of the situation comedy genre diminishes the ability of *Will & Grace* to challenge dominant social norms. All issues concerned with prejudice about homosexuality are presented as *personal* issues rather than as larger political issues. Furthermore, "The emphasis on interpersonal relationships prevents a consideration of gay politics and leads to a failure to acknowledge the social consequences of gay and lesbian persons living in our heterosexist culture" (p. 99). They rely here on syllogistic reasoning that is widely shared in critiques of situation comedies from ideological critics, which I call the "flawed genre argument":

1. Situation comedies have an individualistic focus that prevents such shows from engaging in serious political critique.
2. *Will & Grace* is a situation comedy. Therefore,
3. *Will & Grace's* individualistic focus prevents it from engaging in serious political critique.

In one sense, Battles and Hilton-Morrow are clearly correct. The situation comedy genre succeeds, as do most television genres, by developing characters that we enjoy watching. Comedy functions by exaggeration, so much of the humor of this genre results from putting flawed but funny characters in different situations in which their flaws repeatedly emerge (Altman, 1999; King, 2002). Even situation comedies that attempt to engage larger social issues, such as *All in the Family* or the early seasons of *Good Times*, succeed or fail depending on whether viewers enjoy watching the characters and find the experience of watching the show pleasurable.

The examples of *All in the Family* and *Good Times* are not randomly selected—each provides an important lesson in what happens with commercially successful situation comedies. *All in the Family* is one of the most successful situation comedies of all time, and it tackled prejudice and politics explicitly, but it also falls victim to the same critique as *Will & Grace*. The show certainly never provided a sustained case for institutional change. Furthermore, how some viewers responded to leading characters, particularly the bigoted Archie Bunker, ended up at odds with producer Norman Lear's noble intentions. Audience research found that viewers with higher levels of prejudice laughed *with* Archie Bunker rather than *at* him and were twice as likely as viewers with lower levels of prejudice to say that Archie usually "wins" the conflict by the end of the show (Vidmar & Rokeach, 1974). Indeed, despite the "obvious" satirical bent of the show, Vidmar and Rokeach found that the show appealed "more to the racially and ethically prejudiced members of society than to the less prejudiced members" (1974, p. 45)

Good Times was another Norman Lear production that initially won praise for being "edgy, pushy, and in-your-face about its issues" (Bogle, 2001a, p. 199). Episodes dealt with issues such as teen alcoholism, child abuse, gang warfare, unemployment, and racism. Once again, however, the show could not sustain a robust political agenda as it became increasingly trivialized with the departure of John Amos, who played the father of the family, and as the clownish character of "J. J.," whose trademark phrase was "*dyn-o-mite*," became increasingly popular.

In short, situation comedies illustrate perfectly Neil Postman's (1985) claim that the epistemology of television is entertainment, and that the "best" (i.e., most watched) fictive television consists of programming that encourages "amusement" and "enjoyment" at the expense of thoughtful, considered, rational reflection about the political and social issues of the day. Postman's argument is that a particular medium can only sustain a particular level of ideas, and that television is a medium ill suited to promoting intellectual involvement. Even if one feels that Postman overgeneralizes about the medium of television (cf. Brummett, 1991, pp. 18–30), his critique seems especially apt for the genre of situation comedies. Postman probably would agree with Battles and Hilton-Morrow (2002) about the limitations of televised situation comedies to engage important political and social issues, even if he would trace the cause to the need for commercial television to provide unchallenging entertainment rather than characteristics of the genre.

Indeed, if the flawed genre argument is correct, then it is virtually impossible to imagine a successful situation comedy that *could* engage in institutional critique and encourage viewers to engage in serious political thought. One cannot visually depict a social-political institution such as capitalism or patriarchy. One can only portray characters that *talk* about such institutions, or *personify* such institutions. But then we are back where we started—with an individualistic, character-driven focus. Even a television program such as M*A*S*H, which managed to be comedic, entertaining, and, at times, quite serious, cannot be said to deliver more than a generic political message that "war is hell," and the program never engaged in a serious discussion of the rationale for and against the Korean War.

Do the aforementioned limitations mean that situation comedies can never contribute to social or political change? Not at all. But such limitations *do* imply that we need to change the questions we ask of situation comedies. It just does not make sense to criticize a comedy for not being serious enough, or to criticize an entertainment medium for not promoting intellectual engagement, or to criticize character-driven genres for forsaking the political for the personal. If a situation comedy is going to gain an audience, then it must be funny, entertaining, and driven by the interplay between characters and the situations they encounter. These parameters imply a different set of research questions that we ought to consider when evaluating the cultural work of situation comedies. We need to have a better understanding of what situation comedies *can* do that builds on our understanding of the limitations of the genre: Can sitcoms encourage empathy and understanding for the characters that translate into an understanding of the social groups that such characters represent? Can sitcoms educate viewers about material circumstances that might, in turn, influence attitudes about larger social and political issues? In short, we need to ask ourselves how the vices of the genre might function as virtues. I will explore such ideas further in the next chapter, but for the moment I return to Battles and Hilton-Morrow's critique of *Will & Grace*.

The second point that Battles and Hilton-Morrow find problematic is that *Will & Grace* fails to be an accurate representation of a sufficiently broad spectrum of the gay community. Citing an online review by Rahul Gairola (2001), Battles and Hilton-Morrow note that Will's character "has been criticized for confining the portrayal of gay men to those who are white and upper-middle class, making his character more acceptable to a mainstream heterosexual audience at the expense of alienating a large portion of the gay community" (2002, p. 90). This argumentative move is probably familiar to many popular culture critics because it invokes the notion of "innocence" that I described in chapter 1. If *Will & Grace* offends *some* gay men or a subset of gay men, then it fails the requirements of Representative Correctness. I call this move the *Omnia Perfectissima* requirement—everything completely perfect. I exaggerate, of course, but the point I want to make of this criticism is that it is clearly a slippery slope. *No* text can ever be expected to address the complexities of all potentially relevant social groups or subgroups. Given that *Will & Grace* is the first-ever prime-time television show to feature two main characters who are gay men, it strikes me as unreasonable to impose the burden of representing *all* gay men (an obvious impossibility) or anything approaching a truly representative sample.

The third point that Battles and Hilton-Morrow find problematic is that *Will & Grace* "feminizes" the gay male characters of Will and Jack. Their argument relies on very careful readings of specific scenes and interactions; for example, Jack is feminized *compared to Will*: "Will provides the norm of masculinity against which Jack's gayness is defined" (2002, p. 91). But *Will* is feminized "whenever *Will & Grace* specifically deals with Will's sexuality" (p. 90). Such depictions "reinforce a definition of gayness as that which is not masculine," which reinforces the "heteronormative understanding of desire—as existing between a masculine person and a feminine person" (p. 91).

Even if one grants that Battles and Hilton-Morrow's account is coherent and internally consistent, the manner in which they decode or map the gendered attributes of Jack and Will prompts several questions. First, precisely because their reading is so careful and nuanced, it remains an open question of whether mainstream viewers would perceive the characters as Battles and Hilton-Morrow do. The specific contexts that they feel *define* Will and Jack may not be the ones that most viewers would identify. Only audience research could tell us that. Second, what *counts* as masculine and feminine is no longer as obvious as it once might have been. As noted in chapter 1, research on gender norms suggests that they change over time. This means that certain behaviors (concern for one's appearance, fashion sensibility, lack of athletic ability) that are mapped as "feminine" by Battles and Hilton-Morrow may not be decoded in the same way by viewers. For example, in a scene recounted by Battles and Hilton-Morrow in which Grace provides batting lessons to Will, her ability to hit the ball and parody "macho-style ball playing" is not enough to recode Grace as "masculinized," so why should we assume that Will's initial lack of baseball ability is enough to feminize him? Third, it is not entirely clear why it is bad to be feminized. Arguably, if likable male characters do display "feminine" attributes, regardless of their sexual orientation, then it could contribute to the weakening of androcentric norms. Again, one could ascertain this sort of effect only with audience research. I suspect that Battles and Hilton-Morrow would agree that there is nothing wrong with feminine qualities, but that in context the enactment of feminine attributes by gay men reinforces heterosexism. But that too is an empirical audience conjecture.

The fourth point that Battles and Hilton-Morrow find problematic is that *Will & Grace* "infantalizes" the subversive characters of Jack and Karen. Most critics agree that Jack and Karen are the funniest and most outrageous characters, and ideological critics agree that they are the most subversive: "Both characters continually call into question the assumptions and beliefs of a heterosexist culture through their dialogue and actions" (Battles & Hilton-Morrow, 2002, p. 96). However, in Battles and Hilton-Morrow's opinion, their subversive potential is "contained," because they are presented as childish buffoons not to be taken seriously (pp. 96–99). Once again, it seems an open question whether most viewers would agree with such an interpretation. Categorizing Karen and Jack as children or buffoons is an act of decoding or mapping that is informed by Battles and Hilton-Morrow's particular theoretical understanding of "the sitcom narrative structure" (p. 96). They may be absolutely correct, but again their conjectures would be strengthened with even a modest amount of audience research.

The bottom line for Battles and Hilton-Morrow is that *Will & Grace* reinforces heterosexism and heteronormativity. Such a conclusion would be more persuasive if there had been a more explicit definition or theoretical explication of what the authors mean by these two terms; too often, critics will deploy highly charged words such as sexist, racist, or heterosexist without identifying precisely what attitudes, beliefs, or behaviors are being reinforced. As psychologist Gregory Herek notes, "A single definition of heteronormativity is not forthcoming in the writings of queer theorists" (2004, p. 16). A wealth of scholarship has been devoted to unpacking distinctions among the concepts of homophobia, heterosexism, and sexual prejudice, as well as the development of various survey instruments designed to identify and measure such attitudes. One also can distinguish heterosexism as a "cultural ideology" from what can be described as psychological heterosexism or simply "sexual prejudice" (ibid.). Thus whether *Will & Grace* reinforces heterosexism and heteronormativity hinges, in part, on how one defines such terms. As argued later, it is possible that *Will & Grace* does not mount a systematic challenge to the cultural ideology of heterosexism but nonetheless contributes to a reduction of sexual prejudice.

Study 2: Textualism, Take Two

Danielle M. Mitchell's critiques (2005, 2006) are similar to Battles and Hilton-Morrow's to the extent that she argues that *Will & Grace* "*appears* socially progressive" while "*actually* functioning to contain transformative change" (2006, pp. 275–76, emphasis added; see also 2005, p. 1064). While acknowledging that the show is a "far cry from a hateful homophobic harangue," Mitchell contends that the program should be understood "as a contradictory site, rather than an exemplar of progressive politics" (2006, pp. 275–76). She suggests that the show attempts to take an "apolitical stance" as a comedy so that neither the inclusion of gay characters nor the use of "homophobic" humor should be taken seriously by viewers; *Will & Grace* is offered as "mere entertainment" (2006, p. 277). Nonetheless, Mitchell believes that the humor *does* function politically and argues that "the comedic structure of gay bashing is central to its rhetorical appeals" as she quotes approvingly an early critic's description of the show as doing "little more than call each other 'homo' and 'queer' while mincing about" (2006, p. 277). Mitchell also faults the show for perpetuating the "myth" of "gay affluence" and for failing to include meaningful non-White or lesbian characters; thus "*Will & Grace* reproduces sexist and racist inequities that have plagued the LGBT community for years" (2006, p. 278). She claims that *Will & Grace* represents the New Homophobia on television that "works to enforce hegemonic social relations of inequity" (2005, p. 1052). Her final assessment of *Will & Grace's* "rhetoric of incorporation" is very similar to that of Battles and Hilton-Morrow: *Will & Grace* "persuades us to consent to the perpetuation of oppressive ideologies and to the containment of transformative social change" (2006, p. 279; see also 2005, p. 1064).

The charge of verbal gay bashing within the show is a serious one that is taken up in more detail in the next study I discuss, so I will set it aside momentarily. Beyond that, Mitchell's analysis follows the criteria of Representational Correctness as described in chapter 1. *Will & Grace* fails the "purity" test, because it is "contained" and "impure" and offends some gay viewers and leaves others unrepresented (the *Omnia Perfectissima* requirement). Again we find the genre of commercially viable situation comedies as failing to challenge the dominant political structures sufficiently. Lastly, her stance is another good example of the exercise of professional vision: The show *appears* socially progressive, but when decoded by an ideological critic is revealed as *actually* reproducing oppression.

Again, though internally coherent, it is an open question whether Mitchell's phenomenal text is the same as those understood by mainstream audiences. Like the analysis by Battles and Hilton-Morrow, the text constituted as *Will & Grace* is based on selective perception, coding, and highlighting. Since all texts must be constituted in such a fashion, there is a sense in which these critics are engaging in "audience reception research" of a very special kind—an elite, professional audience of theoretically and methodologically sophisticated critics sharing certain ideological commitments. Whether *Will & Grace*, or any other text, for that matter, functions in society the way anticipated by such critics is a conjecture worthy of further investigation.

Study 3: Textualist and Audience Analysis, Take One

Sociologist Thomas Linneman combines textual and audience analysis in his study of *Will & Grace*, sponsored in part by GLAAD (Gay and Lesbian Alliance against Defamation); his study was originally published on GLAAD's Web site in 2001, described by the author in an online magazine (2004), and updated and published in the academic journal *Men and Masculinities* (2007). The primary textual issue that Linneman examines is what he calls the use of a "feminine appellation" to describe one of the two gay men in the show. Based on content analysis of all 162 episodes from the first seven seasons of *Will & Grace*, Linneman and his research assistants "located every instance" where a man was referred to in the feminine: as a woman, as a girl, as a she, as a wife, as a queen, as Dorothy, as Cher, as Madame Butterfly, and so on (2007). In a nutshell, they found a lot of such references—there were 605 references to gay men with feminine appellations over the first seven seasons.

This is, of course, "rhetorical salience" at work. As noted previously, selective perception, coding, and highlighting are unavoidable. For Linneman, *the* most important and relevant textual feature of the show is the use of feminine appellations, a practice known in the gay community as "shebonics." Linneman acknowledges that *Will & Grace* is an important, breakthrough television program, but he is concerned that the consistent use of feminine appellations perpetuates the stereotype of the feminized homosexual. Will Truman's character strikes Linneman as "a poster boy for hegemonic masculinity" (a reading quite different from that by Battles and Hilton-Morrow), but he is concerned that the show "eases tension for hegemonic masculinity by pushing its gay characters again and again into the realm of femininity" (2006, p. 6). Linneman's argument differs from Battles and Hilton-Morrow's in that he argues that the major vehicle for feminizing Will is through the use of feminine appellations. As feminized gay men, neither Will nor Jack represents a serious challenge or threat to hegemonic masculinity or heteronormativity.

Linneman takes the need to understand audience interpretations seriously, so he and his colleagues conducted focus group discussions involving 39 participants organized into groups according to age and sexual orientation: (1) eight gay and lesbian youth group members (ranging from 16 to 21 years of age), (2) five heterosexual high school students, (3) seven gay and lesbian college students, (4) seven heterosexual college students, (5) five gay and lesbian adults, and (6) five heterosexual adults (2002, 2007). In addition to asking a series of open-ended questions about the show and its characters, Linneman presented each group with a 13-minute tape with 25 clips from the show, each having a feminine reference within it. Participants were told *prior* to watching the clips that they would all have something in common, and that they would be asked to identify that commonality.

In compiling adjectives from the participants to describe Will and Jack, Linneman concedes that, "Themes regarding gender representations did not arise as frequently as I had expected" (2002, p. 33). In particular, Will was not described in the sort of feminized language that Linneman had anticipated. Unless one wishes to map "dressy" or "fashionable" as feminine, *none* of the adjectives provided by participants was feminine, and four participants specifically described him as "masculine, male, or butch" (ibid.). The most common adjectives used to describe Will included good friend, loyal, loving, attractive, good looking, cute, reserved, serious, introverted, successful, professional, and lawyer. Interestingly, even Jack was described as "effeminate, feminine, or queen" by less than 25% of the participants. *All* participants described Jack as "flamboyant, flaming, or outrageous" (ibid.). But given that more than 75% of the participants did *not* describe him as "effeminate, feminine, or queen," critics need to be cautious about assuming that viewers automatically associate gayness with femininity.

The creation of a 13-minute tape with 25 examples of feminine appellations is a literal example of how critics must constitute a text. There is no way to engage a text without first "entitling" something first *as* a text, and we are guided by our values and interests in that act of constitution. As Kenneth Burke says, "A constitution is a substance—and as such, it is a set of motives" (1945, p. 342). I understand Burke as saying that implicit in any constitutive act is a set of implicit motives and interests. This cannot be escaped. But at the same time, we need to recognize that how professional critics constitute texts and how unpaid critics constitute texts will vary in proportion to their interests, values, and training. In Linneman's study, his key belief is that the speech-act of using feminine appellations is very important in understanding the cultural work of *Will & Grace*. Interestingly enough, despite his stacking the deck with 25 examples, his participants largely disagreed.

Half of the gay and lesbian viewers "completely got it," compared to less than a third of the heterosexual participants (Linneman, 2007, p. 13). Linneman confesses that he was surprised by this result and characterizes those who answered not with the expected or "desired" response as "oblivious" (ibid.), but a more fair reaction would be that his audience conjecture concerning the "meaning" of these scenes was simply disproven. That is, what the selected scenes meant to Linneman was not the same as what they meant to most of his participants. To describe those who agreed with his interpretation as having "got it" or "on the right track" (p. 13) implies that the text has only one meaning, which of course Linneman would concede is false.

Linneman reports that "some" (he does not say how many) of his participants "were angry or at least concerned that these references could reinforce stereotypes," but he notes that the more common response was "acceptance" (2007, pp. 15–17). Participants noted that such speech-acts constitute "in jokes" that are acceptable among the gay community and argued that some gay men do, in fact, talk in such ways with each other. Indeed, some of Linneman's gay participants praised such moments as evidence that the show was "reaching out" to the gay community (p. 16). An ethnographic study by Matti Bunzl (2000), published in *Discourse & Society*, argues that feminine appellations are an important linguistic tool for the gay community to provide a disruptive critique of traditional, heterosexist gender norms and to resist their discursive naturalization. If Bunzl is correct, in the long run the use of feminine appellations toward male characters (including the gay Will Truman, mapped by some viewers in masculine terms) may have the opposite effect as that originally hypothesized by Linneman.

It is relevant to note that Linneman (2007) records that more than half of the instances of feminine appellations are either self-references or are spoken from one gay man to another. Such a finding supports the contention that shebonics is an accepted part of the linguistic practices of the gay community. A good deal of what Linneman identifies can be described as in-group *teasing*. Research on teasing suggests that such banter can be an important verbal behavior for building group identification, particularly among disaffected social groups—including gay men and lesbians (Bruhn & Murray, 1985; Heisterkamp & Alberts, 2000; Pratt, 1996). Whether teasing is considered humorous or hurtful depends on the relationship context (Charpentier, 2006); given how close the four central characters are portrayed on *Will & Grace*, it is hard to read such banter as serious interpersonal attacks.

In a passage in the 2002 version of his study but not included in the shorter version, published in 2007, Linneman concedes that "the results from the focus group discussions serve to comfort a mind troubled by these feminizing references" (p. 46). While it is clear that when a football coach or drill sergeant calls a man "a girl," it is meant to be insulting and derogatory, it is not so clear that such is the case when shebonics is employed among friends. The fact that most of Linneman's participants either did not find such speech-acts salient enough even to notice them, or accepted them when they did notice them, suggests that *Will & Grace* may not be performing the sort of cultural work he originally surmised. Linneman's study is not only valuable for what it found but also for what it did not.

Study 4: Textualist and Audience Analysis, Take Two

Sociologist Evan Cooper (2003) also provides an analysis of *Will & Grace* informed by his own reading of the text and by audience research. Interestingly, Cooper interprets the use of gay labels ("queer," "fruit") and feminine appellations by the cast of *Will & Grace* in a manner consistent with some of Linneman's participants. Rather than viewing such practices as negative, Cooper sees them as evidence "of the show's intimacy with gay culture" (p. 518).

As a result of his reading of the show, Cooper hypothesized that audiences would describe Jack as their favorite, funniest character. Similar to Battles and Hilton-Morrow, he also hypothesized that Jack would be seen as "a fatuous fool and the most frequent butt of humor" by most respondents; that is, he would be seen as silly or stupid rather than as genuinely transgressive (p. 521). To test his audience conjectures, Cooper surveyed 136 college students who watched the show and asked a combination of open-ended and closed-ended questions. To his surprise, most of his hypotheses were not confirmed.

Not quite half (49%) of his respondents said that they thought Jack was the funniest character, with 30% declaring Karen the funniest and 11% describing both Jack and Karen the funniest (p. 524). However, Jack, Karen, and Grace were in a virtual tie for the "favorite character" category (p. 523). If we assume that there is a potential relationship between which characters give us the most pleasure and the possible cultural "work" that such representations perform, it is noteworthy that 90% of the respondents agreed that the most transgressive characters, Jack and Karen, were found to be the funniest.

Even more significant is Cooper's finding that Jack was *not* dismissed by his respondents in the way he (or Battles and Hilton-Morrow) conjectured. Less than half (44%) of the respondents said that they thought Jack was most often the butt of jokes. Far from being seen as a fool or buffoon, Cooper found that Jack was seen more as a "trickster" character combining positive and negative attributes (p. 529). Indeed, the vast majority of adjectives used to describe Jack were positive, and only 9 of the 136 respondents described him as silly, ditzy, or worse (pp. 526–28). Positive terms included fun, entertaining, and funny but also enthusiastic, self-confident, proud, ambitious, and someone who "knows himself" (p. 527). Though 25 respondents described him as "gay," with labels ranging from "stereotypical homosexual male" to "flaming," only five respondents described Jack as "feminine, very feminine," or "the woman of the relationship" (p. 528). Again, the association of gay masculinity and femininity may not be as automatic as some critics have conjectured. Cooper notes that "the responses to the question of how Jack is portrayed indicate audience willingness to view Jack as a multidimensional figure. That avid and frequent viewers are considerably less inclined to see Jack as the most frequent butt of humor may similarly be interpreted as the capacity to see both sides of Jack's trickster personality" (p. 529).

The research performed by Linneman and Cooper is important, because in both cases they found evidence that challenges the audience conjectures about the meaning of the show made by the studies of *Will & Grace* discussed so far. The phenomenal texts produced through their exercise of professional vision were not the same as those produced by unpaid critics. Linneman's and Cooper's findings about the conjectured meaning of *Will & Grace* as a text also give us reason to question the conjectured *effects* of viewing the show; namely, that it reinforces heterosexism and heteronormativity. But while there is reason to doubt such a conjecture, is there any evidence to support the counterconjecture or hypothesis that viewing *Will & Grace* could *decrease* sexual prejudice? To find out, Peter Gregg, Dean Hewes, and I collaborated on a research project to explore what sorts of attitudes were associated with viewing *Will & Grace*.

Study 5: Textualist and Audience Analysis, Take Three

In May 2002, we surveyed 245 university students about their attitudes and beliefs concerning *Will & Grace*, its characters, and gay men in general (Schiappa, Gregg, & Hewes, 2006). Ninety-eight percent reported their sexual orientation as heterosexual. In addition to basic demographic information, the survey included items to assess how much social contact participants have with nonheterosexual individuals, viewing frequency of *Will & Grace*, attitudes toward gay men and lesbians, and items concerning the four main characters. The survey was administered before *Will & Grace* went into syndication and became available for daily viewing.

In survey research no less than traditional textual analysis, one must constitute a phenomenal text. As should be clear from the previous discussion of Linneman's and Cooper's studies, the types of questions posed by the researchers make certain features of the text salient to participants while ignoring others, and this study is no different in that respect. In a sense, our questions were designed to prompt our participants to think of their experience of *Will & Grace* as a whole, to think of each character as a distinct person, and to indicate their attitudes toward gay men in general. To ascertain whether participants view the overall content of the show as positive or not, the following items were included: "*Will & Grace* has encouraged me to think positively about homosexuals," "*Will & Grace* provides a negative view of gay men," "*Will & Grace* is an important step forward in TV situation comedies because it features gay men in major roles," "*Will & Grace* is *not* an important TV show." We also included two items to ascertain whether participants shared Battles and Hilton-Morrow's (2002) beliefs about how Jack and Karen are represented; for each character, participants were asked if she or he "represents a refreshing challenge to 'normal' conceptions" of their gender, and whether the two act "like a child or buffoon who is not to be taken seriously." Unless specified otherwise, all nondemographic survey items were measured with a seven-point Likert-type scale anchored with "strongly disagree" and "strongly agree." We also included a single item explicitly on heteronormativity: "The only normal sexual relationships are heterosexual relationships."

To assess our participants' level of prejudice toward gay men and lesbians, we used the 10-item version of Gregory Herek's (1984, 1988, 1994) well-known Attitudes Towards Lesbians and Gay Men (ATLG) scale. The ATLG scale makes a series of statements about gay men and lesbians to which participants may strongly disagree, disagree, slightly disagree, be undecided, slightly agree, agree, or strongly agree. By summing the point values for each answer, one can create a relative prejudice score that ranges from highly prejudiced to very low (or highly accepting). Typical statements on the ATLG scale include "Homosexual behavior between two men is just plain wrong" and "I think male homosexuals are disgusting" and reverse-scored items such as "Male homosexuality is a natural expression of sexuality in men." Herek's scale has been in use for over 20 years and is regarded as a useful and reliable tool for measuring prejudice toward gay men and lesbians (Herek, 1987, 1988, 1994; Herek & Glunt, 1993; Herek & Capitanio, 1996).

Of the 245 participants, 69% reported that they watched the show "every once in a while" or more frequently. Accordingly, some results are reported by categorizing participants as "viewers" ($n = 170$) versus "nonviewers" ($n = 75$). Overall, viewers perceived portrayals of the gay characters in *Will & Grace* to be positive. Answers to content-related questions include: 73% disagreed that *Will & Grace* "provides a negative view of gay men"; 81% of viewers agreed (from slightly agree to strongly agree) to the statement that the show is an important step forward in television situation comedies because it features gay men in major roles. Responses to the second statement correlated positively with viewing frequency ($r = .25$, $p = .001$). Sixty percent of viewers agreed (from slightly agree to strongly agree) to the statement that the show "has encouraged me to think positively about homosexuals." Again, responses were correlated with frequency of watching the show ($r = .29$, $p < .01$).[4] That is, the more frequently they watched the show, the more likely they were to state that the portrayals of Jack and Will are positive.

Nearly 60% of viewers did *not* agree with the statements that Jack and Karen act like children or buffoons who are "not to be taken seriously." Furthermore, 65% agreed to the statement that Jack represents a refreshing challenge to "normal" conceptions of masculinity, and 56% agreed that Karen represents a refreshing challenge to "normal" conceptions of femininity. Viewing frequency correlated positively to responses to this statement both for Jack ($r = .33$, $p < .001$) and Karen ($r = .26$, $p = .001$); that is, the more often they watched the show, the more likely they were to find Jack's and Karen's transgressiveness refreshing.

Though not reported in the published version of the study, it is worth noting that 54.6% disagreed with the claim that feminine appellatives are insulting, while 27.4% had no opinion, and only 17.9% agreed. Furthermore, when asked explicitly whether they consider Will masculine or feminine, viewers disagreed that he is feminine and on average "slightly agreed" with the statement that he is masculine.

As we had hypothesized, the more often viewers watched *Will & Grace*, the lower they scored on the sexual prejudice scale toward gay men ($r = .36$, $p < .001$). Furthermore, the more frequently they watched the show, the less likely they were to agree with the statement on heteronormativity ($r = .35$, $p < .001$). With respect to the heteronormativity item, 71% of *Will & Grace* viewers disagreed (from slightly to strongly) to the statement that heterosexual relationships are the only normal sexual relationships, compared to 45% of nonviewers. Contrary to the conjectures made by Battles and Hilton-Morrow (2002) and Mitchell (2006), *Will & Grace* does not encourage or reinforce heterosexism; indeed, the opposite appears to be the case.

If *Will & Grace* does promote lower prejudice toward gay men, then we hypothesized that the effect would be stronger for those who did not have significant interpersonal contact with gay men in the "real world" than for those who had gay friends or close coworkers. This hypothesis was confirmed as well. In fact, the strongest correlation between viewing frequency and lower levels of prejudice were found for those with no gay acquaintances at all ($r = .48$, $p < .01$), and there was not a statistically significant correlation for those reporting having more than three gay friends. In short, for those viewers with the fewest direct gay contacts, exposure to *Will & Grace* appears to have the strongest potential influence on reducing sexual prejudice, while for those with many gay friends, there is no significant relationship between levels of prejudice and their exposure to the show.

Given our reliance on correlation data and a nonrandom sample consisting solely of college students, the results of this study cannot prove the causal claim that "watching *Will & Grace* encourages more tolerant attitudes toward gay men." The results are intriguing nonetheless, and they certainly give reason to doubt the claims of those who fear the show does the opposite. Though self-reports must be used with caution (McCroskey, 1984), it is noteworthy that 60% of viewers agreed with the statement that *Will & Grace* "has encouraged me to think positively about homosexuals," and that such answers correlated with frequency of watching the show ($r = .29$, $p < .01$).

An alternative interpretation of the results could hypothesize that television viewers with more favorable attitudes toward gay men are more likely to watch the show and enjoy its gay characters. Is it reasonable to suppose that most or all of the variation found in our results is explained by self-selection and little to none by viewing frequency? Though a definitive answer cannot be provided by this study, there are reasons to doubt that most or all variation is due to self-selection. To be sure, viewers with strongly held negative attitudes about homosexuals are unlikely to watch *Will & Grace*, just as they are unlikely to seek out interpersonal contact with homosexuals (Herek & Capitanio, 1996). Thus a model that assumes a *reciprocal* relationship between television contact and reduced sexual prejudice is more plausible than a "one-way" model that attempts to explain all of the variance implied with either viewing or preexisting attitudes by themselves.

If *all* viewing variation was explained by attitudes toward gay men, then we should not have found the marked difference between the strength of the correlations between those with no gay contact and those with many gay friends. If attitudes toward gay men predicted *all* viewing frequency, then the subgroup with the most gay contact and lowest prejudice scores should have had the *highest* correlation between viewing frequency and prejudice scores among the subgroups rather than the *lowest*. Thus while it may be unreasonable to attribute *all* of the variation in prejudice scores to viewing frequency, it is equally unreasonable to attribute *all* of the relevant variation to prior attitudes toward gay men. It would seem prudent to infer that viewing frequency of *Will & Grace* and attitudes toward gay men are at least mutually reinforcing, and that the show contributes to reducing prejudice among some viewers.

The most important finding of this study was that for those without "real-life" opportunity to interact with gay men, this show may have made a difference in reducing their level of sexual prejudice. In the next chapter, I discuss three more studies that support what I call the "parasocial contact hypothesis," which helps explain why *Will & Grace* decreased prejudice. Before that, however, I want to discuss two more studies concerning *Will & Grace* that focus explicitly on the relationship between the two title characters.

Study 6: Textualism Revisited

Helene A. Shugart (2003) suggests that *Will & Grace* and recent films featuring a gay man and straight woman "couple" recode and "normalize" homosexuality in their representations, with the result that gay male identity is "defined by and renormalizes heteronormativity" (p. 67). Specifically, Shugart argues that the relationship is acceptable because the gay male lead character is "heterosexualized" in two ways. First, a romantic subtext underlying the relationship persists (p. 73). Second, the leading gay male is normalized by being juxtaposed with an "outrageously flamboyant, stereotypical gay male" (p. 76). In *Will & Grace,* Jack is the obvious foil, and Shugart reads Will, in contrast to Battles and Hilton-Morrow, as "conventionally masculine" (p. 77). Thus "heteronormativity is restabilized against the conventionally heterosexual performances that the gay male leads engage" (p. 80). Shugart also argues that sexist patriarchy is reinforced, because the gay male maintains sexual access to the female lead and frequently acts paternalistically toward her, and the female leads are "parodic stereotypes of women" (pp. 80–88). The cumulative effects of such pairing are to "naturalize and reproduce heteronormative politics" (p. 89).

Shugart notes that the "features" of the text that she has coded and highlighted "are manifest primarily in subtexts," and that the strategy of heternorming the gay male leads is "dense and complex" (pp. 87–88).

This may be another way of saying that it is highly unlikely that the meanings she has conjectured would be recognized by an untrained audience. A two-step process is at work here: First, the representations of Will, Grace, and Jack are coded/highlighted in a particular manner (such as "Will is conventionally masculine"). Second, based on that coding/highlighting, Shugart contextualizes those representations in a larger ideological and cultural context to argue for certain negative effects. Even if it is not reasonable to expect researchers to measure the amount of sexism or patriarchal thinking caused by a particular film or television show (step two), it *is* reasonable to ask whether audiences share a critic's receptions of particular characters and relationships (step one). Would viewers agree that there is a romantic subtext in the show between Will and Grace, and if they did, would they think of Will as "less gay" as a result? Would they agree that Jack functions merely as a "foil" to make Will seem straight? How do we reconcile the claims of textualists who read Will as feminine with those who read him as masculine? Would they agree with the description of Will's behavior toward Grace as "paternalistic," or would they describe it as "big brotherly" or simply a "well-meaning but meddlesome friend"? Would they agree that Grace is a parodic stereotype of a woman? Obviously, we will not know unless we ask.[5] I believe the audience research discussed earlier suggests either that they do not interpret the show as Shugart does or that other textual "features" are at work that counterbalance them, because the weight of the evidence from audience research suggests that *Will & Grace* decreases heternormativity rather than increases it.

Study 7: Back to Audiences, Once More

The final study I discuss also focuses on the relationship between Will and Grace, but in a manner quite different from Shugart. Michelle Ortiz and Jake Harwood (2007) draw from Albert Bandura's social cognitive theory to hypothesize that straight viewers who watch the show would witness a positive relationship between Will and Grace and, in effect, would learn to like Will (and, by extension, gay men in general), just as Grace does. Bandura (2002) suggests that viewers internalize cognitive, emotional, and behavioral responses they observe occurring in response to situations they otherwise might not directly experience. In this case, the logic is one of "I like Grace, I observe that Grace likes Will, therefore I like Will." In addition to Bandura's theory, one can see this three-sided relationship (viewer, Grace, Will) as a classic example of balance theory at work (Heider, 1946). Balance theory assumes that people prefer consistency, and it would create dissonance if they liked one person but disliked that person's best friend.

Gathering data from 253 students, Ortiz and Harwood found empirical support for their hypothesis: Viewer identification with Grace significantly predicted lower levels of anxiety about gay men in general and more willingness to interact with gay men. Furthermore, the more viewers perceived Will as typical of gay men, the lower their unwillingness to interact with gay men. While the researchers did not gather the sort of data that would allow us to know precisely how their participants understand the relationship between Will and Grace, in a sense it does not matter, since Ortiz and Harwood's results directly challenge the idea that the relationship promotes heteronormativity. Quite the contrary, since in their study exposure to *Will & Grace* was associated with lower social distance toward gay people.

I end this chapter by summarizing its key arguments. First, there is no such thing as pure textual analysis, nor is there such a thing as pure audience research. All pop culture analysis involves phenomenal texts and the reception of audience members. There is nothing to talk about without constituting a text. Even empirical audience research involves the constitution of one sort of text or another, whether the unit of analysis is a speech-act like shebonics, or characters, a relationship between characters, or one's reaction to the memory of a show as a whole. All audience research is guided by *salience*—what the researcher thinks is important about the text.

At the same time, all such scholarship ultimately is about audience reception. The only question is, *which audience?* What passes for textual analysis is better understood as the receptions of a specialized sort of elite or professional audience. It is a very different sort of audience than most of the millions who watch broadcast television or go to the movies. Academic media critics have more time to contemplate a text, more analytical tools, a richer theoretical vocabulary, an above-average education, and a deeper-than-average ideological commitment. The typical viewer does not stop to count the number of times a shebonic reference occurs.

Of course, this is not to say that textual critics are always wrong, or that textual analysis should be abandoned. However, care must be taken if we are to avoid ending up with what Justin Lewis calls "a number of aberrant decodings" passing for "the preferred reading" (in Hall, 1994, p. 267). The case of *Will & Grace* throws sharply in relief the need for critics to test their audience conjectures with nonpeer viewers. It is telling that textualist analyses virtually unanimously declared *Will & Grace* regressive or negative in various ways once properly decoded by the gaze of professional vision. I believe this to be a function of the political economy of textual criticism of popular artifacts, which rewards readings that are as provocative and as different from the "popular" or dominant readings as possible. In contrast, those who tested such conjectures with audience research found reason to believe that *Will & Grace* has decreased prejudice toward gay men.

It is worth noting that other audience conjectures set forth by textual critics also have been called into question by subsequent audience research. Michele Ramsey, Paul Achter, and Celeste Condit (2001) tested critical claims based on textual analysis (Grey, 1999), that reviews of the controversial book *The Bell Curve* inadvertently increase racism by reiterating racist views and ways of thinking. Ramsey and colleagues' analysis of qualitative and quantitative audience reactions failed to find evidence of such a link and instead found that audience members were adept at integrating new information with preexisting beliefs. Condit and colleagues (2002) utilized survey and focus group data to test academic critics' claims about the relative desirability of "recipe" and "blueprint" as competing metaphors used in popular media to describe the role of the human gene. Their research challenges the claims of academic critics, that the "blueprint" metaphor is understood as more deterministic and authoritarian than the metaphor of "recipe."

The bottom line is that if we want to make audience conjectures, we must have a broader notion of audience than looking in the mirror.

PART 2

Interventions

So far I have argued that critics of popular media should avoid the double binds associated with Representational Correctness because the aspirations of *orthê mimêsis*—purity, innocence, and simultaneity—cannot be met by any particular representation. There is no question that the popular media have done a great deal of harm, historically, in terms of perpetuating stereotypical beliefs (pejorative overgeneralizations) about women and minorities. However, the effects may not be as large as we assume sometimes, and when dealing with an *individual* popular text, we should operate with presumption of negligible effects until adequate evidence can be produced to show otherwise.

I argued that there is a trade-off between efforts to undercut essentializing identity and difference beliefs and normative beliefs associated with androcentrism, Whiteness, and heterosexism. An emphasis on *difference* can be read as reinforcing essentialism and polarization, while an emphasis on *similarity* can be read as reinforcing the false universalism of androcentrism, Whiteness, and heteronormativity. How we decide which popular media to valorize, therefore, depends on what sort of belief and attitude change we think is most urgent for a particular group at a specific historical moment.

In chapter 2 I argued for the advantages of audience research. In a good deal of popular media criticism, an argument is made that a given text *means* such and such (whether the meaning is obvious or subtle, conscious or unconscious, explicit or subtextual) to mainstream audiences, and that such meanings *influence* those who experience them. Such claims constitute what I called "audience conjectures" that would be far more persuasive if supported with evidence garnered through audience research. My position does entail the conclusion that all media scholars must become audience researchers and eschew textual analysis but simply suggests that *if* critics are interested in advancing audience conjectures *then* various forms of available evidence could help such critics make a stronger case.

At times I treat "textual analysis" and "audience research" as self-evident categories, but of course matters are more complicated than that. In the profession of media studies, it is not difficult for scholars to self-identify with one approach or the other (or both). At the same time, we need to recognize that all media scholars, regardless of their professed methodology, must constitute texts—whether their objects of analysis are films, songs, television shows, or the perceptions, comments, and beliefs expressed by audience members. Put another way, a survey response is just as much a text requiring interpretation as a film is. At the same time, it also is useful for media scholars to see all scholarly engagement of popular media as a form of reception analysis. The only question is *which* audience reception is the focus of a scholarly argument. Accordingly, in chapter 3 I described professional textual analysis as a special kind of reception analysis that relies on the exercise of professional vision. We fully expect professional decodings and receptions to be different from unpaid decodings and receptions, and we expect that what professional critics find *salient* in popular media texts will be different from what unpaid audiences find important. However, the very gap in receptions justifying membership in the knowledge class of professional critics sometimes can lead us into missing important cultural work that unpaid receptions are doing. At least I am convinced that this is what happened with competing decodings and receptions of *Will & Grace*.

Part 2 of this book attempts to chart possible directions for evaluating representations found in popular media in a way that avoids the problems identified in part 1. Let me be clear that they are not the *only* directions in which media scholars might go. They represent efforts to practice what is preached in part 1, no more and no less. Chapter 4 represents a *theoretical* intervention, chapter 5 a *critical* intervention, and chapter 6 a *pedagogical* intervention.

As foreshadowed in part 1, a different way to analyze the representations of social groups in popular media is to ask what sort of judgments unpaid audience members are making about the characters they encounter and to ascertain what sort of attitudes and beliefs are reinforced or challenged by such judgments. Critics often focus on plot or what they believe to be the moral or ideological lesson of popular media texts, but arguably a unit of analysis of at least equal importance is how *characters* are understood and judged. Potentially of far greater importance than the ability to identify a specific action that could be deemed "stereotypical" are the larger judgments that audiences make about the likability, perceived similarity, trustworthiness, and attractiveness of individual characters. I argue in chapter 4 that such judgments can influence audience members' attitudes and beliefs about the social groups that individual characters represent. What we call "parasocial contact" can reproduce the proven effects of direct interpersonal contact between majority and minority group members, as majority group members learn about the minority group attributes and form more positive attitudes and beliefs about them.

Chapter 5 offers a critical intervention by engaging Michael Crichton's novel, *Disclosure*. Among other things, our analysis attempts to chart the rhetorical work performed by Crichton's novel by noting how certain gender-based attributes and behaviors are rewarded or punished in the text. This process can be described as "vicarious operant conditioning," as audience members are encouraged or discouraged by the descriptions and fates of various characters to imitate or avoid particular attributes and behaviors. Again trying to practice what is preached in this book, my collaborator and I augment our reception of the text with audience research to check whether our reception of characters' gender portrayals and social desirability was consistent with unpaid audience members.

Lastly, because many media scholars teach undergraduate courses that involve analyzing popular media, in chapter 6 I offer a pedagogical intervention through a description of a course I have taught on "Masculinity & Film." Aside from describing the intent, design, and films featured in the class, I also report what sort of beliefs and attitudes such a class can be reasonably expected to influence.

Throughout these chapters, I also try to practice what is preached in part 1 by integrating humanistic and rhetorical approaches with theories and methods associated with social scientific research. I am convinced that our work can make more of a difference, in and outside of academia, if there was more interaction among progressive scholars in cultural studies, psychology, sociology, and critical media studies.

CHAPTER 4

Learning from Television
The Parasocial Contact Hypothesis

The primary purpose of this chapter is to describe a theory advanced in a series of studies I coauthored with Peter Gregg and Dean Hewes (2005, 2006), which we call the "parasocial contact hypothesis." A secondary purpose is to illustrate a different way for popular culture critics to think about the work that popular texts perform. As Stuart Hall notes, cultures include conceptual "maps of meaning" that classify and organize the world (in Jhally, 1997). As pejorative overgeneralizations, stereotypes can be thought of as a dysfunctional part of a conceptual map that we use to make sense of the world. As critics, we need to think about how popular media can challenge and change a conceptual map in a manner that decreases social and individual prejudice.

As noted in the previous chapter, our research on *Will & Grace* found that viewing frequency was most strongly correlated with lower levels of sexual prejudice toward gay men among our participants who had the *least* direct, personal contact with gay men. This fact struck us as prima facie evidence for the ability of the show to influence beliefs and attitudes, a conviction that is strengthened when one encounters anecdotes such as the following, relayed by a heterosexual mother who participated in one of Thomas Linneman's focus groups:

> I've watched the show [*Will & Grace*] with teenage daughters, and I've noticed that they've changed since [the] beginning [of] watching the show. At the beginning, we started watching it a bit last year, mainly reruns and things like that, and they would laugh

a lot at the humor. And then when Jack would come on that would be this moment of real entertainment, and sometimes they would react . . . and they would say, "Oh that's disgusting!" or "Oh that's ridiculous!" or "Oh he's really," you know, some kind of degrading adjective that they would apply to him. And then it took no more than two or three episodes before they started saying, "Oh, I just *love* Jack. I hope they have Jack as the center story" or something like that. And one of the daughters, I noticed that— we have joint custody and when she would watch it at her house— that she would watch it sometimes and call me up and say, "Did you see it tonight? It was really funny." And before she knew it she was talking to me about having two or three homosexual friends at school and taking flack from classmates for befriending these students. And I *know* this child would not have defended her homosexual friends the year before, so it seems to suggest that it had loosened boundaries that she had previously had. Even if it was humorous at first it became very real and very important to her later on. (Linneman, 2002)

What is going on here? How could a mere sitcom, considered "just entertainment" by most, have the potential to change viewers' levels of prejudice? One attempt to answer that question involves a synthesis of two theories, one from social psychology and one from mass communication research. One of the most important and enduring contributions of social psychology in the past 50 years is known as the contact hypothesis (Dovidio, Gaertner, & Kawakami, 2003). Credited to Gordon W. Allport (1954), the contact hypothesis, or intergroup contact theory, states that under appropriate conditions interpersonal contact is one of the most effective ways to reduce prejudice between majority and minority group members. Coincidentally, two years after Allport's book, *The Nature of Prejudice*, was published, Donald Horton and Richard Wohl (1956) argued for studying what they dubbed "parasocial interaction": "One of the most striking characteristics of the new mass media—radio, television, and the movies—is that they give the illusion of [a] face-to-face relationship with the performer" (p. 215).

Put these two theories together and you have the parasocial contact hypothesis (PCH). If people process mass-mediated communication in a manner similar to interpersonal interaction, then it is worth exploring whether the socially beneficial functions of intergroup contact have an analogue in parasocial contact. To make this case, I first summarize the key components of each theory, then put them together and explain the experiments we conducted to test the PCH.

Intergroup Contact Theory

After decades of research, many explanations and models attempt to explain stereotypes, social categorization, intergroup bias, and how contact can decrease prejudice (Brewer & Brown, 1998; Hewstone, Rubin, & Willis, 2002). The reduction of prejudice through intergroup contact is best explained as the *reconceptualization of group categories*. Allport (1954) understands prejudice as a result of a hasty generalization made about a group based on incomplete or mistaken information. The basic rationale for the contact hypothesis is that prejudice can be reduced as one learns more about a category of people that corrects mistaken beliefs. Psychologists Myron Rothbart and Oliver John (1985) describe belief change through contact as "an example of the general cognitive process by which attributes of category members modify category attributes" (p. 82). A person's beliefs can be modified by that person coming into contact with a category member and subsequently modifying or elaborating the beliefs about the category as a whole.

Categories are formed based on learning the relevant functional, perceptual, or other sorts of attributes that members of a category share. To be meaningful and useful, categories must include items and exclude others, thus humans acquire social categories by learning a set of "similarity/difference relationships" that demarcate one category from another (Schiappa, 2003). If majority group members believe that people defined by a category are different from them in ways they believe are unpleasant, detrimental, or otherwise negative, then the attitudes they hold toward such a group constitute prejudice (whether invidious or not). Prejudicial attitudes toward a category of people, such as "Arabs" or "gay men," may be based on a negative experience, mass-mediated messages, or socialization from family, friends, or other sources.

Gregory Herek (1986, 1987) suggests that such attitudes perform a sense-making, categorizing (or "experiential-schematic") function that is part of a person's knowledge about the world. Past experience, direct or otherwise, with members of a group category guides subsequent interactions with or about that group. Researchers such as Marilynn Brewer and Rupert Brown (1998) and Michael Leippe and Donna Eisenstadt (1994) contend that an important part of the willingness to adjust one's beliefs about a category of people depends on the dissonance that new information about a group creates (Festinger, 1957). Herek (1986) notes that attitudes serving an "expressive" function are more resistant to change; for example, if the belief that homosexuality is immoral is an important part of a conservative Christian's self-identity, then changing such a belief would create more dissonance than would ignoring information that challenges it. Accordingly, a good deal of attention has been paid to the conditions under which intergroup contact is more or less likely to influence prejudicial attitudes.

Because avoidance of members of specific groups is a form of negative social behavior that is consistent with negative attitudes (Brewer & Brown, 1998, p. 578), positive contact can create a sense of dissonance that can lead to attitude change. The contact must be sustained and non-superficial in order to create a dissonant condition in which negative beliefs come into conflict with new beliefs resulting from positive experiences. Additionally, group members must feel of equal status, share common goals, and not be opposed by a salient authority (Allport, 1954; Williams, 1964). If any of these conditions are not met, then prejudicial beliefs may increase (if the groups are in competition, for example), and any dissonance can be resolved without changing prejudicial attitudes.

Following Thomas Pettigrew (1998), it is most useful to concentrate on the process of change that happens through contact, since (as argued later) the process can be reproduced through mediated contact. Pettigrew describes these processes as learning about the minority or "out-group," changing behavior, generating affective ties, and majority or "in-group" reappraisal.

Learning about an out-group was conceived by Allport (1954) as the major way that intergroup contact has effects, and the benefits of such learning have been clearly demonstrated (Gardiner, 1972; Stephan & Stephan, 1984). Rothbart and John (1985) have qualified intergroup contact theory by arguing that disconfirming evidence alters stereotypes only if (1) the minority group members' behavior is inconsistent with their stereotype, (2) contact occurs often and in various contexts, and (3) the minority members are judged as typical. If majority group members have rewarding interactions with minority group members and learn sufficient new information through repeated contact, then the dissonance between "old prejudices and new behavior" can be resolved by revising one's attitudes (Pettigrew, 1998, p. 71). For such dissonance to be sufficient motivation for attitude change, the contact must be successful in generating some sort of intimacy or affective tie toward minority group members (Amir, 1976; Pettigrew, 1997a, 1997b, 1998). In short, contact changes the manner through which in-group members categorize out-group members. The category may still exist (such as "Arabs" or "gay men"), but the salient traits (category-attributes) and the perceived similarity/difference relationships will be modified if the contact experience has been sufficiently positive to change attitudes (Hewstone, Rubin, & Willis, 2002, pp. 589–93; Oakes, Haslam, & Reynolds, 1999, p. 64).

One way to think of such a change is that a stereotype (understood as a pejorative overgeneralization) is turned into a relatively benign "social type." As noted earlier, humans rely on categories to make sense of the world. Even though categories are unavoidable, we hope that certain categories used to differentiate human beings will wither away and die. Much as we would hope otherwise, the chances of such categories as gender, ethnicity, and sexual orientation falling out of use anytime soon are slim to none. In the meantime, the task is to keep such categories from doing harm. Intergroup contact combats stereotypes by making majority group members' understanding of social categories less pejorative and more differentiated (thus less of an overgeneralization).

Extensive empirical research supports intergroup contact theory. Thomas Pettigrew and Linda Tropp's (2006) meta-analysis of over 700 independent samples confirms the contact hypothesis for a variety of minority groups and conservatively estimates the average correlation between contact and prejudice as $-.215$ ($N > 250,000$, $p > .0001$) (see also Pettigrew & Tropp, 2000). Interpersonal contact has proven to be an effective means to reduce prejudice toward homosexuals, in particular. Applying the contact hypothesis to heterosexuals and homosexuals, Herek (1987) found that college students who had pleasant interactions with a homosexual tend to generalize from that experience and accept homosexuals as a group. Herek and Eric Glunt's (1993) national study of interpersonal contact and heterosexuals' attitudes toward gay men found that contact "predicted attitudes toward gay men better than did any other demographic or social psychological variable" (p. 239); such variables included gender, race, education, age, geographic residence, marital status, number of children, religion, and political ideology. Herek and John Capitanio (1996) found that contact experiences with two or three homosexuals are associated with more favorable attitudes than are contact experiences with only one individual. Pettigrew and Tropp's (2006, p. 764) meta-analysis of contact hypothesis studies included 42 studies involving attitudes toward homosexuals and found a significant negative relationship, $r = -.27$, between contact and sexual prejudice ($n = 12,059$, $p < .001$).

Given the fact that interpersonal contact has proven to be a successful means of reducing prejudice, it is worth investigating whether mediated or "parasocial" contact has the same potential.

Parasocial Interaction as Parasocial Contact

Horton and Wohl (1956) introduced the phrase "parasocial interaction" to suggest that communication media can provide viewers with "an apparently intimate, face-to-face association with a performer" (p. 228). The human brain evolved many thousands of years before electronic media came along. When we meet a new person, we process the various sense-information we receive about them quickly and automatically. Because the human brain processes media experiences similarly to how it processes "direct experience," people typically react to televised characters as they would to real people (Kanazawa, 2002). The idea that "mediated life" is equivalent to "real life," at least as far as people's cognitive and behavioral responses are concerned, is the central claim of what Byron Reeves and Clifford Nass (1996) call the "media equation."

In a media-rich environment, people come to "know" more people parasocially than through direct interpersonal contact. Few people have direct contact with the president of the United States, but virtually everyone in the world has strong opinions about the person holding that office. Most media users form attitudes and beliefs about many politicians, athletes, journalists, and entertainers with whom their contact has been exclusively through the mass media. In addition to parasocial contact with "real" individuals, people also have parasocial contact with fictional characters (Auter & Palmgreen, 2000). Obviously human beings are *capable* of making a distinction between a fictional character on a television program and people we know in the real world; however, most of the time while watching television or a movie we do not make the effort to do so.

Mass communication research arguably has overworked the concept of "parasocial interaction," or PSI, to the point that its use as a measure has outstripped theoretical understanding (Schramm, Hartmann, & Klimmt, 2002). Scholars recently have argued that PSI is undertheorized, treated as unidimensional by some and multidimensional by others, and used to describe an antecedent, a process, and an outcome (Auter & Palmgreen, 2000; Cohen, 2001; Giles 2002; Rubin & Rubin, 2001). Parasocial interaction has been used to describe disparate responses of affinity, interest, friendship, identification, similarity, liking, or imitation. The lack of theoretical precision regarding Parasocial interaction is reflected in how survey instruments to assess it have been constructed (Giles, 2002; Schramm et al., 2002). Parasocial interaction is typically measured with Likert scale responses to items such as "I think my favorite TV personality is like an old friend," or "My favorite TV personality seems to understand the things I know." Factor analyses by Peter Gregg (2005) suggest that almost all standard parasocial interaction scale items "load" (are subsumed by) interpersonal variables such as social attraction (likability) or perceived similarity when included in the same survey instrument. Accordingly, it makes sense to interpret most measures of PSI in the literature as documenting a variety of specific parasocial *responses* to mediated contact.

Thus PSI can be treated simply as *contact* or *exposure* and can use the phrase *parasocial response* as shorthand for the cognitive and affective reactions we have to such contact. When we experience televised characters, we form impressions, make judgments about their personality, and develop beliefs about them. As mass communication scholars Rebecca B. Rubin and Alan M. Rubin (2001) note, PSI is "grounded in interpersonal notions of attraction, perceived similarity or homophily, and empathy" (p. 326). People use the same communication-related cognitive processes for both mediated and interpersonal contexts, and "people and media are coequal communication alternatives that satisfy similar communication needs and provide similar gratifications" (Perse & Rubin, 1989, p. 59). Just as people form positive or negative attitudes toward other people in "real life," television viewers develop positive or negative attitudes about the characters they watch on television (Conway & Rubin, 1991). And, just as interpersonal interaction can lead to various sorts of interpersonal responses and relationships, parasocial interaction can lead to various sorts of parasocial responses and (one-sided) relationships. As Sonia Livingstone suggests, "The traditional separation of interpersonal and mass communication" theory that is assumed in most media criticism "is untenable" (1993, p. 8).

Researchers have documented the formation of parasocial relationships for viewers of local television newscasters, soap opera characters, celebrities appearing in commercials, talk radio hosts, characters in situation comedies, sports celebrities, and favorite television personalities (Giles, 2002; Gregg, 2005). Watching certain types of television has the same effect on subjective satisfaction with friendship status as having more friends and socializing with them more often (Kanazawa, 2002). Viewers *describe* and *evaluate* television personalities, neighbors, and friends in functionally equivalent ways (Koenig & Lessan, 1985; Gleich & Burst, 1996). A group of research subjects responded to a hypothetical parasocial "breakup" in similar ways as they would to interpersonal breakups (Cohen, 2004). As reported in a meta-analysis of 30 parasocial interaction studies by Schiappa, Allen, and Gregg (2007), three qualities strongly associated with parasocial contact are the social attractiveness or likability of the characters, their perceived realism, and their perceived similarity.

The analogy between parasocial and interpersonal interaction has encouraged researchers to explore the relevance of interpersonal communication theories to understand the kinds of relational judgments viewers make about televised characters. Drawing from uncertainty reduction theory (Berger & Calabrese, 1975), Elizabeth Perse and Rebecca Rubin (1989) report in their study of soap opera viewers that length of acquaintance is positively related to predictability (attributional confidence) for both interpersonal and parasocial relationships. Rubin and McHugh (1987) suggest that both interpersonal and parasocial contact over time lead to a reduction of uncertainty about others, allowing for increased social and task attraction (cf. Rubin & Step, 2000). In short, the analogies between interpersonal and parasocial interactions and interpersonal and parasocial relationships have sufficient support that it is worth exploring whether mediated forms of contact could influence attitudes about minority groups.

The Parasocial Contact Hypothesis

Parasocial contact can provide the sort of experience that can reduce prejudice, particularly if a majority group member has limited opportunity for interpersonal contact with minority group members. Perse and Rubin (1989) claim that viewers formulate impressions of televised characters to reduce uncertainty about social behavior, and that "*people*" constitute a "construct domain that may be sufficiently permeable to include both interpersonal and television contexts" (p. 73). If we can learn from televised characters representing distinct social groups, then it is possible that parasocial contact could influence attitudes about such groups in a manner consistent with the influence of direct intergroup contact. Such a possibility is anticipated by Allport's recognition of the importance of mass media in forming beliefs about minorities (1954, pp. 200–202) and by Rothbart and John's (1985) inclusion of the media as sources of images that can instill stereotypical beliefs about minorities (p. 83).

The research on parasocial relationships suggests that the processes involved in positive intergroup contact as described by Pettigrew (1998) can be reproduced through mediated contact. One can learn about a minority group from mediated messages and representations, and if one has a positive experience, then one's behavior is altered in that one normally will seek out additional (parasocial) contact rather than avoid it. One can develop affective ties with persons known only through mediated communication, and, whether one reappraises one's beliefs about one's in-group or not, the resulting parasocial relationships could encourage a change in prejudicial attitudes about the out-groups to which minority characters belong.

Previous research can be interpreted as providing support for the PCH. When direct contact is minimal, television can play an influential role in viewers' attitudes about minority group members, and such influence may increase or decrease prejudice (Armstrong, Neuendorf, & Brentar, 1992; Fujioka, 1999; Tan, Fujioka, & Lucht, 1997). Support for the influence of parasocial contact was found in our survey of college student reactions to the popular television show *Will & Grace*, discussed in the previous chapter (Schiappa, Gregg, & Hewes, 2006). First, a significant correlation was found between viewing frequency and measures of parasocial involvement, suggesting that repeated exposure to the show increased viewer involvement with the characters. Second, there was a correlation between lower levels of prejudice toward gay men and greater viewing frequency, and between lower levels of prejudice and greater parasocial involvement. Third, the correlation between less prejudice and parasocial involvement was strongest—an impressive .65 ($p < .05$)—for those students reporting few or no gay acquaintances, and was not significant for those with three or more gay friends. This last finding strongly suggests that for those viewers who already had extensive interpersonal contact with gay people, exposure to *Will & Grace* was not associated with any lower levels of prejudice. Contact has done its job already, so to speak. But for those with little to no interpersonal contact with homosexuals, the association between parasocial interaction and lower levels of prejudice was quite marked. Such data strongly suggest that parasocial contact may function in an analogous manner to interpersonal contact.

The optimal conditions specified under the contact hypothesis require a certain amount of translation to a mass-mediated context. As noted earlier, participants must feel of equal status, share common goals, have sustained and nonsuperficial contact, and not be opposed by a salient authority. All of these factors potentially influence the dissonance that positive contact can produce. While sustained and nonsuperficial contact is obviously relevant to parasocial contact, it is not clear that such factors as feeling of equal status, sharing common goals, and opposition of a salient authority are particularly relevant to viewing television (with the exception of children viewing television with authority figures such as parents or teachers).

The question then becomes, what sort of parasocial contact with mass-mediated characters is necessary to influence attitudes toward minority groups? That is, what are the minimal conditions under which parasocial contact may influence prejudicial attitudes? Direct interpersonal contact has proven to be an effective way to reduce prejudice when majority group members are exposed repeatedly to diverse (typical and atypical), likable, explicit representatives of a minority group (Pettigrew, 1998; Simon, 1998). If the analogy between interpersonal and parasocial interaction is taken seriously, then it follows that parasocial contact has the potential to decrease prejudice when majority group viewers are exposed repeatedly to diverse, likable, and clearly identifiable representatives of a minority group. To determine whether a particular set of viewing experiences provides the requisite sort of exposure, several questions are relevant: Does the exposure provide enough information about minority characters for viewers to form distinct opinions about them? In particular, are viewers able to form judgments about how the characters act (predictability or "uncertainty reduction"), whether they find the characters interpersonally attractive, and have a sense of how similar or dissimilar the characters are from themselves? Based on the analogy with the contact hypothesis, the argument is that without the ability to form such specific judgments about characters that represent a minority group, parasocial contact would not provide the sort of sustained and nonsuperficial contact required to influence attitudes toward minority groups. Furthermore, viewers need to be able to form distinct judgments about all central characters (both minority and majority group members) if they are to be confident that the parasocial contact with minority group characters is *relatively* nonsuperficial.

Exposure to minority group representatives must not only be sufficient for viewers to form discrete judgments about them, but those judgments must be relatively positive. That is, if viewers decide that minority group representatives are socially unattractive, totally unlike them, unpredictable, unreliable, and so forth, then obviously prejudice toward the category of people that the character represents is unlikely to decrease. The literature in intergroup contact theory consistently stresses that majority group members must reach a certain level of "intimacy" or develop "affective ties" with minority group members for there to be sufficient dissonance to lead to attitude change. As a minimal condition for parasocial contact to promote a change in attitudes, the judgments made of minority group characters must be at least as positive as the judgments made of majority group characters.

Obviously, whether a particular portrayal is "positive" or "negative" is a matter of perception. In our studies, the idea of a positive response was operationalized as one or more of the following parasocial responses: predictability, similarity, likability, trustworthiness, and physical attractiveness.

Viewers must consider minority group characters sufficiently likable or admirable to provide motivation for attitude change. Such motivation has been documented in the contact hypothesis literature as stemming from social attraction, or likability, as well as from "respect" or task attraction (Kiesler & Goldberg, 1968) that results from working cooperatively to pursue common goals. Liking and trustworthiness (task competence) can be mutually reinforcing as long as a competent person seems "human" and fallible (Aronson, Willerman, & Floyd, 1966). Given that likability and positive social judgments often are correlated with physical attraction (Dion, Berscheid, & Walster, 1972), it also is possible that physical attraction could provide the needed dissonance with prejudicial attitudes to induce attitude change.

As noted previously, attitude change involves a reappraisal of how the majority group member understands the category to which minority group members belong. The similarity/difference relationships that demarcate the out-group minority category from the majority member's own in-group are revised when prejudice is reduced, so that the common humanity of both groups is recognized, and perceived differences are reduced (Pettigrew, 1998). Five studies reported in a meta-analysis of parasocial interaction literature by Schiappa, Allen, and Gregg (2007) note that parasocial contact is positively correlated with perceived similarity ($r = .48, p < .05, N = 614$).

To summarize the argument thus far, I have identified two key preconditions for parasocial contact to influence attitudes: First, there must be *enough* contact for viewers to form discrete judgments about characters representing a minority group. Such judgments could include the following: Are the characters reasonably predictable? How similar or different do they seem from me? Are they likable? Do they seem trustworthy—people on whom I could count? Are they physically attractive? Second, such contact must be relatively positive, meaning that judgments about characters representing minority groups are not consistently worse than those made about characters representing majority groups.

If these preconditions are met, based on the PCH one could predict that positive portrayals of minority group members will lead to a decrease in prejudicial attitudes. Obviously not everyone can be influenced in such a manner. A member of the Ku Klux Klan (KKK) is unlikely to be swayed by *Roots*, for example. At the other end of the spectrum, there appears to be an upper limit, or "ceiling effect," to the influence of intergroup contact. That is, while having interpersonal contact with more than one representative of a minority group provides added opportunity for gaining information about their group and can thus reduce prejudice more than contact with only one representative, it has not been demonstrated that a measurable linear relationship extends past having interpersonal contact with two or three minority group members (Herek & Capitanio, 1996). It follows, therefore, that the possible beneficial effects of parasocial contact with minority characters would be strongest with those viewers with the least direct interpersonal contact with the minority group and have less or no effect for those with a great deal of interpersonal contact with that minority group.

In what follows, I describe three studies we conducted that explore and test the PCH. I have omitted most of the statistical details to make the descriptions more accessible, but these are readily available (Schiappa, Gregg, & Hewes, 2005). The studies are guided by two key questions: Can parasocial contact by majority group members with minority group members lead to a decrease in prejudice? Are the effects of parasocial contact moderated by previous interpersonal contact with minority group members?

Study 1: *Six Feet Under*

Six Feet Under is a critically acclaimed television series that averaged 5.7 million viewers for its first two seasons and during its 5-year run earned a number of Emmy awards, Golden Globes, and a Peabody Award. *Six Feet Under* is described by HBO (2003) as providing a "darkly comic look at the Fishers, a dysfunctional family who own and operate an independent funeral home in Los Angeles. Patriarch Nathaniel Fisher is no longer living (except in the hearts and visions of his family). So his wife Ruth, sons Nate and David, and daughter Claire are left to cope with the routine and not-so-routine aspects of life in the grief-management business."

During the first season of *Six Feet Under*, a prominent story line dealt with David Fisher coming to terms with his homosexuality and gradually coming out to his family, friends, and church (Bunn, 2002). Keith Charles is a gay, African American police officer who is described by HBO as "the love of David's life." As a member of the Fisher family, David is a central character. Keith is a supporting character that appears in most of the first season's episodes and has been featured regularly on the *Six Feet Under* HBO Web site as a regular cast member. David and Keith are explicitly identified as gay yet are quite different in terms of personality; Keith is an assertive police officer and "out," while David is a deferential funeral home director and, at least during the first season, keeps his homosexuality confidential. I would note that the characters and plot lines in *Six Feet Under* stand in contrast to *Will & Grace*, since the latter is a light comedy. Furthermore, David and Keith are shown engaging in sexual acts, unlike Will and Jack in *Will & Grace*.

Participants consisted of 174 college students between the ages of 18 and 36 enrolled in an undergraduate course titled "Television Studies: *Six Feet Under*" in the spring semester of 2003. The course description and syllabus emphasized that the course would use *Six Feet Under* as a common text for discussion in order to introduce students to various rhetorical and communication theories as they apply to television. The course met once a week for 3 hours for 15 weeks. On the first night of class, all students present completed one of two surveys. Seventy-four students were randomly assigned to a pretest group to complete a survey that included standard demographic questions, an item assessing previous exposure to *Six Feet Under*, Gregory Herek's (1984, 1988, 1994) Attitudes toward Lesbians and Gay Men scale (ATLG), and a number of questions about the media that were unrelated to the study. The remaining students completed a survey unrelated to this study about death attitudes, since a major theme of *Six Feet Under* is, of course, death. This second group (posttest only) did not complete the ATLG instrument until after all episodes were viewed ($n = 100$). The sample was split into two groups in order to allow us to test for instrument sensitization for those completing the pretest. That is, we wanted to be sure that the mere fact that some students answered the items on the ATLG scale did not influence their answers later.

Over a period of 5 weeks, students were shown 10 episodes of the 13 aired in the first season of *Six Feet Under*. Short clips were shown and a brief summary provided only for the three episodes not shown in full during class so that students could keep up with various plot narratives; the other 10 episodes were shown in full. The average number of episodes viewed by participants was 10.4, as a number of students became sufficiently interested in the show to rent the episodes not fully shown in class. During the 5 weeks of viewing, there was *no* in-class discussion of the show. After attendance was taken each class meeting, one episode was shown, followed by a 15-minute break, then a second episode was shown. No discussions were held concerning the shows during class until the experiment was concluded. The episodes of *Six Feet Under* were discussed throughout the remainder of the semester in the context of television research in general.

All participants completed a 200-item posttest after viewing 10 episodes of the show *Six Feet Under*, consisting of basic demographic questions, the ATLG scale, and subscales measuring degrees of predictability (uncertainty reduction), likability, physical attractiveness, trustworthiness (task attractiveness), and perceived similarity for the six main characters.[1] Items were reversed on half of the surveys administered to prevent biasing results from respondent fatigue and question order. An item asked how many gay acquaintances participants had ("I do not know any gay, lesbian, or bisexual people personally," "I am acquainted with a few gay, lesbian, or bisexual people, but not as friends," "I have one or two gay, lesbian, or bisexual friends or close coworkers," "I have more than two gay, lesbian, or bisexual friends or close coworkers").

The postviewing survey included questions specifically tailored to solicit judgments about six main characters from the first season. Four of the six are members of the Fisher family: Ruth, the mother of the family, sons Nate and David, and daughter Claire. The other two characters included in the survey were Keith Charles, described earlier, and Brenda Chenowith, Nate Fisher's love interest in the first season.

The predictability or "uncertainty reduction" scale contained five items adapted from Kathy Kellerman and Rodney Reynolds (1990) that assess how well the participant feels he or she knows each individual character (e.g., "How well do you think you can predict X's feelings and emotions?"), with answers ranging from "very well" to "not well at all." Likability, trustworthiness, and physical attraction were assessed using the well-established interpersonal attraction measures described by

James McCroskey and Thomas McCain (1974). The likability scale was composed of items that examine how desirable social interaction with the character would be (e.g., "I think X could be a friend of mine"). The physical attraction scale was made up of items that explore how the participants feel about the character's physical appeal (e.g., "X is very attractive physically"). The trustworthiness or "task attraction" scale consisted of items examining how the participants feel about working with the character (e.g., "I have confidence in X's ability to get the job done"). The perceived similarity scale was adapted from that developed by McCroskey, Virginia Richmond, and John Daly (1975). It consisted of five items that explore how similar or different the character is from the participant ("X perceives things like I do," "X is similar to me," "X and I share similar attitudes").

As described in the last chapter, the Attitude toward Gay Men subscale is part of Herek's (1984, 1988, 1994) Attitudes towards Lesbians and Gay Men (ATLG) instrument. Previous research conducted by Herek and his colleagues has shown that higher levels of prejudice, as measured by the ATLG scale, correlate significantly with high religiosity, lack of contact with homosexuals, adherence to traditional sex-role attitudes, belief in a traditional family ideology, and high levels of dogmatism (Herek, 1987, 1988, 1994; Herek & Glunt, 1993; Herek & Capitanio, 1996). The Attitudes towards Gay Men (ATG) short form consists of five statements concerning gay men (such as "Homosexual behavior between two men is just plain wrong"). The Attitudes toward Lesbians (ATL) subscale consists of five statements concerning lesbians (such as "Female homosexuality is a sin").

We only used data from surveys completed by students who reported that they had *never* seen an episode of *Six Feet Under* prior to the course, yielding a pretest group ($n = 56$) and a posttest group ($n = 126$) with no prior exposure to the content of the series. The first thing we did was ascertain whether our two preconditions had been met. First, did the viewers have enough exposure to the six main characters to make discrete, individual judgments about each of them in terms of predictability, likability, trustworthiness, similarity, and physical attractiveness? Without going into the details of the multivariate repeated-measure ANOVA test we conducted, the short answer is yes. Viewers were able to form judgments about each character for each of the factors, and their judgments differed for each character. In short, the viewers got to know each character well enough to judge each as a distinct individual.

The literature on the contact hypothesis suggests that the potential to decrease prejudice improves with contact with noticeably different representatives of a minority group (Rothbart & John, 1985). Accordingly, we also ran a statistical test (paired *t*-test) with all scales between the two gay characters, David and Keith, to assess the distinctness of participants' judgments about them. Significant differences were found on all measures. It is clear that participants formed distinct judgments about each gay character in terms of the dimensions assessed.

The second precondition was that representations must be relatively positive, meaning that judgments about the gay characters David and Keith needed to be at least as positive as the majority group characters. To determine whether this was the case, we basically calculated a score for each factor (predictability, likability, trustworthiness, similarity, and physical attractiveness) and compared the average score of the straight characters with that of the gay characters. There were no statistically significant differences for four of the five factors. The one exception was trustworthiness or "task attraction," where David and Keith scored *more* trustworthy than the straight characters. In sum, parasocial contact with the main characters of *Six Feet Under* was of sufficient *quantity* and *quality* that viewers were able to form distinct and discrete positive judgments about the minority group characters.

Having met the two preconditions, we predicted that parasocial contact with the gay characters in *Six Feet Under* would lead to a decrease in prejudicial attitudes. When we compared the pretest and posttest scores for the ATG test, we did, indeed, find that the level of prejudice had decreased, and that the change was statistically significant—12%. That this decrease is probably due to the parasocial contact with gay men in *Six Feet Under* is supported by the fact that there was *no* change in participants' scores on the ATL test, which makes sense given that none of the regular characters on the show is represented as a lesbian. Such a result is consistent with prior research, indicating that positive attitudes toward lesbians do not consistently result in positive attitudes about gay men (Herek, 1988).

It is impossible to sort out *exactly* what emotional or cognitive factors might have led to this change of attitude. Given that Ortiz and Harwood (2007) found that identification with a straight character (Grace) could lead to increased willingness to interact with gay men, it is possible that one explanation for the change was the fact that the straight characters, especially the lead character Nate, treat the gay characters with respect and affection, but not deference. We also found that viewers found the two gay characters, David and Keith, physically attractive, and that the level of attractiveness correlated with lower prejudice. For Keith, in particular, participants' positive judgments about his likability, trustworthiness, and similarity correlated with lower prejudice. Thus the more positive the parasocial response, the more likely prejudice would be lower.

We also predicted that the more gay acquaintances and friends the participants said they have the weaker the influence of parasocial contact would be on prejudicial attitudes. We divided the participants into two groups, those with little to no gay contact ($n = 50$) and high contact (one or more gay friends, $n = 75$). To test this prediction, the correlations between the five parasocial response measures on one hand and ATG on the other were calculated for the high contact and low contact groups. These pairs of correlations were done separately for ratings of David and Keith, yielding a total of 10 paired correlations. We predicted that these correlations would be greater for the low contact group than for the high contact group, but the difference did not turn out to be statistically significant. Thus our second prediction was not supported.

The findings from Study 1 offer general support for the parasocial contact hypothesis. When parasocial contact is of sufficient quantity and quality to allow the sort of judgments to be made about mass-mediated characters that people make with direct interpersonal contact, prejudicial attitudes may be reduced.

Study 2: *Queer Eye for the Straight Guy*

We conducted a second study to test the PCH, for four reasons. First, *Queer Eye for the Straight Guy* provides an unusually rich program that at the time of our study was not widely watched by college students (who often lack cable TV access). The show is a reality-based makeover show featuring five gay professionals assisting a heterosexual male, as the title suggests. Accordingly, it provides viewers with contact with five different men who are explicitly identified as gay. Increasing contact with a category or social group "enables one to make finer and finer discriminations within the category"; the greater the "diversity and volume of contact," the greater the potential of such contact to decrease prejudice (Taylor, 1981, p. 102). Second, because the show is an example of "reality TV," it allows us to examine the parasocial responses to another genre of television programming. Third, we felt it important to employ an experimental design that was superior to the *Six Feet Under* and *Will & Grace* studies so we could strengthen the ability to draw causal inferences and reduce the chance of confounding factors. Accordingly, we used what is known as the Solomon (1949) four-group design for Study 2.

The fourth reason is a bit more theoretical. We planned to show three episodes of *Queer Eye*, which is a bit more than 2 hours of programming. During each episode, there is almost always at least one gay man on screen, and often more than that. With five different gay characters, the parasocial contact would provide a rich environment for learning about the category of gay men. This seemed an ideal opportunity to explore whether the reduction of prejudice through intergroup contact can be explained as the reconceptualization of group categories.

Rothbart and John (1985) argue that contact facilitates the cognitive process by which attributes of *individual* category members modify perceived attributes of the category *as a whole.* As Shelley Taylor (1981) notes, "A stereotype is usually characterized as a set of trait adjectives that describes a social group" (p. 102). As "trait adjectives" (category-attribute beliefs) are modified, the similarities and differences used to categorize people change, as do our attitudes toward such categories. For example, if someone believes that all gay men are highly feminine and flamboyant (all Xs are Y_1 and Y_2) but learns from parasocial contact that this is not always the case, then that person's understanding of the *category* of gay men has changed (some Xs are Y_1 and some not Y_1, some Y_2 and some not Y_2). The greater the diversity of gay men one gets to know, the more complex and differentiated one's category of gay men will be. As Allport puts it, "A differentiated category is the opposite of a stereotype" (1954, p. 173). That is, the richer one's understanding of any category of people, the less likely one would maintain negative, overgeneralized beliefs about them.

Thus in this study, in addition to testing the same two predictions we made in the *Six Feet Under* study, we also predicted that parasocial contact with minority group members will result in changes in category-attribute beliefs about the minority group as a whole, and that changes in levels of prejudice about a minority group will be associated with changes in category-attribute beliefs about that minority group. In other words, we predicted that the more participants learned about gay men's diverse attributes, the more their prejudice would be reduced.

Queer Eye for the Straight Guy debuted in 2003 and became the "hottest show of the summer" (Giltz, 2003). After some initial reshuffling of cast members, the show features a team of gay makeover advisors: Jai Rodriguez on culture, Thom Filicia on interior design, Carson Kressley on fashion, Kyan Douglas on grooming, and Ted Allen on food and wine. In each episode, the self-described "Fab Five" team descends on the living quarters of a heterosexual male and attempts to change his lifestyle, appearance, and living quarters for the better. In this study, the episodes shown were selected on the basis of convenience, as we relied on episodes available on DVD and on the sampling of shows generously provided by Scout Productions, the company that produces *Queer Eye.*

Our participants consisted of 160 students between the ages of 18 and 57 recruited from the undergraduate population during the summer session 2004. Participants were randomly assigned to one of four groups. Two of the groups were "control" groups that did not watch *Queer Eye*—one group completed the same pretest and posttest that our experimental group did, but without watching *Queer Eye*, the other completing only the posttest. The other two groups were shown *Queer Eye*, but again, one group completed both a pretest and a posttest, and the other completed only a posttest. The reason for such a complex arrangement is that it allows a number of careful comparisons to be made that help rule out other possible explanations for the attitude change we predicted. For example, because we did not have a control group in the *Six Feet Under* study, one could argue that the subsequent reduction in prejudice was not due to watching *Six Feet Under* but may simply have been the result of college students learning greater tolerance over the course of the semester. Furthermore, by dividing participants into those who only completed a posttest and those who completed both a pretest and a posttest, we were able to determine whether or not taking the pretest by itself "sensitized" the participants into thinking about gay men differently.

Participants assigned to the two pretest and posttest groups completed the pretest at least 2 weeks prior to the actual experiment and were given a room number, date, and time to return for a "television viewing session." The pretest consisted of standard demographic items, a measure of number of gay acquaintances (described in Study 1), the ATLG instrument, and three 30-item "Personality Inventories" (described next).

At the viewing sessions, participants assigned to a control group were administered the study posttest including the ATLG and Personality Inventories. Participants assigned to the experimental groups were shown three episodes of *Queer Eye* for a total of 135 minutes of program content. After viewing the episodes, the participants then completed the posttest, including the ATLG, Personality Inventories, and various parasocial response measures.

The Personality Inventories consisted of a series of "trait adjectives" (Taylor, 1981) as category-attribute statements for three social groups: heterosexual men, homosexual men, and heterosexual women. The items were drawn from the short-form version of Bem's Sex Role Inventory (Bem, 1974, 2004) and were worded as category-attribute statements, such as "In general, male heterosexuals are affectionate." Participants responded to each item using a 7-point scale response, ranging from strongly agree to strongly disagree. For each of the three categories, 10 statements used trait adjectives categorized by Bem as stereotypically masculine ("aggressive," "assertive," etc.), 10 as feminine ("affectionate," "compassionate," etc.), and 10 as gender-neutral or "undifferentiated" ("conscientious," "reliable," etc.). The degree of change in beliefs was measured by comparing pretest and posttest scores on each item of the Personality Inventory for Male Homosexuals and then summing the absolute values of the different scores. That is, if one person scored an item with a 2 on the pretest and a 6 on the posttest, and another scored that same item as a 7 on the pretest and a 3 on the posttest, then both would be scored as a change of 4. No change in beliefs whatsoever about the group would = 0, whereas the maximum possible change in beliefs would produce a score of 180, since the maximum score was 6 for each of a total of 30 items. This particular test can only be applied to the two pretest/posttest groups.

The posttest also included a series of items to assess parasocial responses to the show. It was judged impractical to ask items about each of the five main characters separately, so instead a series of items assessing likability, physical attractiveness, trustworthiness, and perceived similarity was posited about the group as a whole, such as "The Fab Five perceive things like I do."

As predicted, after viewing the three episodes, the participants in the experimental groups scored significantly lower on the ATG test (this time about 11%) than they did in the pretest and compared to the control groups. Similar to what we found in the *Six Feet Under* study, there was no significant change in scores on the Attitudes toward Lesbians scale, which again strengthens the argument that the change resulted from the program content. As part of our assessment of how positively the characters were viewed, and to determine whether such judgments were related to changes in attitudes, we focused on the pretest and posttest experimental group. We examined the incremental *change* in ATG scores with our five parasocial response scales and found that three factors correlated significantly to ATG change scores: likability, trustworthiness, and perceived similarity. Once again, positive judgments about televised gay characters were generalized to less prejudice toward gay men in general. All of these correlations, like those in the *Will & Grace* study, were in the .30 range, which is three times larger than the average documented in Shanahan and Morgan's (1999) meta-analysis of the average correlations in television cultivation studies.

We also predicted that the more gay acquaintances and friends the participants said they have, the weaker the association will be between televised contact with minority characters and lower levels of prejudice. This time, the results were as predicted. The number of gay contacts correlated to the ATG change scores so that the more gay interpersonal contacts a person reported, the smaller the change in the ATG score. The ATG change scores for those with low direct, personal contact were higher than those with high contact, and the difference was statistically significant.

We predicted that parasocial contact with minority group members would result in changes in category-attribute beliefs about the minority group as a whole. As expected, the experimental group showed a much greater degree of changed beliefs than did the control group, and the difference was statistically significant. In contrast, we also summed the absolute values of the different scores for all items in the Personality Inventory for Male *Heterosexuals* and found no significant difference between the treatment and control groups. Last but not least, we predicted that changes in levels of prejudice about a minority group would be associated with changes in category-attribute beliefs about a minority group. That is, we thought the more changes in how participants understood the category of "gay men," the more likely it was that prejudicial attitudes would be reduced. As anticipated, for the pretest and posttest experimental group, changes in the ATG score were significantly correlated to changes in beliefs about gay men ($r = .38$, $p < .05$). That is, the more participants' beliefs about the category changed—regardless of the direction of any particular change—the more their prejudice was decreased.

It is worth noting that when we pulled out just the feminine attributes as one set and just the masculine attributes as another set, we found that we could not generalize that participants saw gay men as more or less feminine or more or less masculine as they did in the pretest. Nonetheless, there were enough overall changes in specific category-attribute beliefs to do significant category work and to encourage lower levels of prejudice. This finding is particularly significant, since it tells us that what critics may find highly salient, such as a specific behavior we code as feminine or masculine, may not be as important to sexual prejudice and attitudes toward gay men as is sometimes assumed.

Study 3: Eddie Izzard, Transvestite Comedian

Given that the PCH received support in the first two studies, a third study was undertaken to test the generalizability of the PCH to another stigmatized minority group. In a study I describe in chapter 6, my colleagues and I (Schiappa, Gregg, & Lang, 2004) report that qualitative and quantitative data gathered in a class on "Masculinity and Film" indicate that students' attitudes about male transvestites changed in a more favorable direction after watching comedian Eddie Izzard's (2002) *Dress to Kill*. Accordingly, in this study we used an experimental design to test the PCH with respect to the category of male transvestite. Specifically, we tested the prediction that prejudice would be decreased and would be associated with measures of positive parasocial responses; that parasocial contact with minority group members will result in changes in category-attribute beliefs about the minority group as a whole; and that changes in levels of prejudice about a minority group will be associated with changes in category-attribute beliefs about a minority group. We anticipated that too few participants would know male transvestites to test our prediction regarding prior interpersonal contact.

Dress to Kill is an Emmy Award-winning comedy special featuring stand-up comedian and transvestite Eddie Izzard. In his routine, performed while dressed in women's clothing, Izzard notes that transvestites are heterosexual (as opposed to gay drag queens) and suggests that there are all sorts of transvestites, ranging from "Executive Transvestites" to "Weirdo Transvestites." Most of the 80-minute comedy routine is not about transvestitism, however, as Izzard's topics range from European history to the growing pains of adolescents.

Our participants consisted of 61 college students between the ages of 18 and 38 recruited from the undergraduate population during the summer session of 2004. Participants were randomly assigned to a treatment or control group. All participants completed a pretest that consisted of basic demographic questions, Herek's ATLG instrument, five category-attribute statements about male transvestites, and an Attitudes toward Transvestites (ATT) scale. Control group members were given a lecture on public speaking and then completed a posttest consisting of the five category-attribute statements about male transvestites and the ATT instrument. Treatment group members watched Eddie Izzard's *Dress to Kill* and then completed a posttest consisting of scales measuring predictability, likability, physical attractiveness, trustworthiness, perceived similarity, and ATT. All participants also were asked if they knew anyone who was a male transvestite. The survey items for the parasocial response measures were worded to be statements specifically about Eddie Izzard, such as "I think Eddie Izzard could be a friend of mine." The category-attribute statements prompted by Izzard's routine included the following: "'Transvestites' and 'drag queens' are pretty much the same thing," "Other than what they wear, transvestites are generally like everyone else," "Most transvestites are heterosexual." The degree of change in beliefs was measured by comparing pretest and posttest scores on each category-attribute item and then summing the absolute values of the different scores. No change in category-attribute beliefs would = 0, while the maximum possible change in beliefs would = 30. The ATT scale consisted of 10 evaluative items that were adapted from the wording of Herek's ATLG instrument, such as, "The idea of men wearing women's clothing is ridiculous to me," "Transvestites are sick," and "Men wearing women's clothing is just plain wrong."

We predicted that exposure to positive portrayals of minority group members would lead to a decrease in prejudicial attitudes. For the treatment group, posttest scores showed a change in the ATT score that indicated less prejudice toward male transvestites, compared to the pretest scores, and the change was statistically significant (14%). The pretest and posttest scores for the control group were not significantly different. We also predicted that the level of prejudice would be related to levels of uncertainty reduction, or perceived similarity, or social, physical, or task attraction for minority group characters. Posttest ATT scores did correlate strongly and significantly with likability, physical attraction, and perceived similarity.

We predicted that parasocial contact with minority group members would result in changes in category-attribute beliefs about the minority group as a whole. As expected, the treatment group showed a greater degree of changed beliefs than did the control group, and the difference was statistically significant. Lastly, but importantly, we predicted that changes in levels of prejudice about a minority group would be associated with changes in category-attribute beliefs about a minority group. As anticipated, changes in ATT scores significantly correlated to changes in beliefs about transvestites ($r = .44$). Once again, the more participants learned about the category, the more differentiated it became, and the more prejudice was decreased.

Cumulatively, the studies reported here provide support for the PCH for two minority groups and across three television genres. The PCH has significant theoretical and social implications. For decades, mass communication researchers have insisted that mass media and television, in particular, can influence viewers' beliefs about the world. Research on parasocial contact and the relationships that such contact produces is significant, because it suggests that one form of learning from television is about individuals and categories of people.

To be sure, there are limitations to the inferences that can be drawn from the three studies reported here. First, the participants were all college students. In Study 1, because students voluntarily enrolled in the course, they are not a random sample and cannot be assumed to be representative even of all college students. This process effectively mirrors the practical reality of television behavior, since virtually all television viewing is a matter of self-selection. The practical constraints of using a course made it impossible to have a randomly assigned control group. The absence of a control group, however, means that factors apart from the experiment could have influenced students' attitudes during the weeks involved. The consistent results across the different studies and experimental designs, however, strongly suggest the PCH works as predicted.

Second, though our key findings were statistically significant, there is no way to know what sort of *practical* significance reductions of 11% to 14% on paper and pencil tests of prejudice would have in the real world. There is ample evidence to support what is known as the "theory of reasoned action," which suggests that we think of attitudes as behavioral intentions (Fishbein & Ajzen, 1975; Sheppard, Hartwick, & Warshaw 1988). In other words, thoughts typically do correspond to deeds, and our actions are guided by our attitudes. A decrease in prejudicial attitudes will result, overall, in a decrease in prejudicial actions. But by how much? Certainly we should not think of this as turning bigots into saints. At the same time, we should not be too hasty in dismissing the potentially important contributions parasocial contact can make. In the anecdote reported at the beginning of this chapter, positive parasocial contact with Will and Jack led a teenager to develop interpersonal contacts, and as Herek and Capitanio's (1996) research has shown, positive contact reduces prejudice, which leads to more positive contact reducing prejudice, and so on.

When I was a teenager, calling a guy a "homo" was about the worst insult one could utter. I am sure that if I had been asked, my attitudes about male homosexuality would have been highly prejudiced. In college, I acted in a play in which two of the characters were gay (or at least bisexual), and one was played by the first "out" gay man I ever knew (as far as I knew). Prior to that time, my only contact with gay men had been parasocial, and the only example I can still remember were the two gay assassins in the James Bond movie *Diamonds Are Forever*. My collegiate theatre experience was a textbook example of the contact hypothesis at work: We were of equal status as actors, united toward a common goal of a successful play, and unopposed by any authority figure. Though we did not become close friends, the experience was enough to change my habits of thought about gay men for the rest of my life. In our studies, we found change resulting from as little as 80 minutes of viewing time. If just a small amount of parasocial contact can produce a marked decrease in one's prejudice toward a minority group, as our studies show, then there is little doubt that popular media can be the catalyst for important and progressive attitude change.

Third, only further research can establish whether parasocial contact with other minority groups would have the same results that were found in these studies with respect to gay men and male transvestites. The influence of incremental parasocial contact may be quite different for groups for which there is already considerable media exposure, such as for African Americans. In their research on racial attitudes of Midwestern Whites, Robert Entman and Andrew Rojecki (2000) report that none of their interviewees referenced learning *favorable* evidence about Blacks from the media, but some did cite negative evidence learned from the media, even if it conflicted with their personal experience (pp. 28–29).

Future research should not only test the PCH with respect to other minority groups but should also seek to understand the quantity and quality of mass-mediated content required to induce attitude change. For example, how many episodes of programming are necessary to influence attitudes? Is comedic, dramatic, or reality programming more likely to induce change? What sorts of interactions between majority and minority characters within the programming are most productive of attitude change? Additional research also should investigate how parasocial responses change over time with continued contact, and whether or not attitude change, such as what we have documented, persists over time.

It should be stressed that it is unlikely that there is *a* single aspect of parasocial contact that can be identified as causally related to attitude change. As the review of the literature on the contact hypothesis indicated, dissonance and attitude changes result from a combination of factors, including new information about a minority group and a sense of trust, respect, or attraction with representatives of a minority group. In Study 1, we found associations between lower prejudice levels and four parasocial response measures with respect to one gay character, but only one such association for the other character. In Study 2, attitude change correlated to likability, trustworthiness, and perceived similarity, but not physical attraction. In Study 3, three parasocial response measures were associated with higher posttest ATT scores, but none significantly correlated to the *amount* of change. Contrary to our expectations, none of the three studies found an association between attitude change and character predictability. While we did not test for it, we also suspect that the positive responses to gay characters by majority group representatives in the programs also contributed to favorable parasocial responses by our participants, as social learning and social comparison theory would suggest (Festinger, 1954; Ortiz & Harwood, 2007; Wood, 1989). Further research will allow greater elaboration and specification of the most important elements of parasocial contact for encouraging attitude change.

Implications for Media Critics

I certainly am not advocating that all media critics drop what they are doing and focus exclusively on conducting experimental media effects research. Nonetheless, for those critics interested in how popular media influence attitudes and beliefs—especially those concerned with heteronormativity, racism, sexism, and classism—I hope that this chapter encourages an engagement with multiple theories and multiple methodologies. Even the critic who wants to make "big picture" claims about the role of hegemonic media in U.S. culture cannot help but make assumptions about how individuals and groups think, feel, and act. That is, all critics write with an implicit theory of social psychology.

In particular, the studies described here begin to point the way to a different approach to thinking about stereotypes and Representational Correctness. What is important about minority group representation is not that it be perfect, which is impossible, but that it be diverse and positive. And these studies mark some progress toward clarifying what we mean by "diverse" and "positive." "Diverse" in this context means diverse *attributes*: the more complex and multidimensional the character(s), the greater the opportunity for representations to do important category work. As critics, we should never underestimate the importance of recognizing that *a differentiated category is the opposite of a stereotype* (Allport, 1954, p. 173). "Positive" in this context depends on the audience's response, not an abstract ideal. Though other formulations certainly are possible, in our studies we defined positive as audience judgments that the characters are at least as likable, trustworthy, and physically attractive, and/or whose common humanity is perceived as similar as the primary majority group characters are.

How can we tell, then, whether a particular performance should be damned with the label "stereotype"? Not surprisingly, I suggest that the answer depends on a judicious combination of textual and audience research. While a *category* can be deemed stereotypical if it is a pejorative overgeneralization, an *individual performance* (what lawyers would call the instant case) cannot be judged as promoting stereotypical *meaning* or *effects* in isolation. Indeed, an individual performance is a silent text until constituted by particular audiences. How that text is constituted and given meaning depends in part on the intratextual and intertextual representational ecology for a particular social group. Just because Gay Male Character X can be described as "flaming" does not make him a stereotype, it just makes him a member of a recognizable social type. To predict what sort of "meaning" X has for viewers requires one to situate his performance not only in the context of show but also in the larger context of other available, mainstream representations of gay men. Furthermore, to predict the sort of category work that a given performance may have for an audience would depend on (1) the audience's prior familiarity with the social category X represents, and (2) the sorts of judgments audience members make about X.

Accordingly, we are now in a better position to consider the competing critical assessments of *Queer Eye*. Indeed, academic media critics have been divided over what to make of the show and offer contradictory conjectures about audience effects. Dana Heller (2004) reads the show fairly positively and suggests that *Queer Eye* "is the lens through which the nation attempts to review and reinvent masculine subjectivity" (p. 349). Liz Morrish and Kathleen O'Mara (2004) conclude that "one joy of this show is its ability to challenge the idea of a hegemonic masculinity by allowing different variations to proliferate even within gay male identity" (p. 352). David Weiss (2005) examines the language used by the gay characters in *Queer Eye* to argue that their utterances perform "conflicting, fluid, and uncategorizable—that is, 'queer'" identities that challenge stereotypes (p. 73). In contrast, E. Michele Ramsey and Gladys Santiago (2004) argue that *Queer Eye* conflates male homosexuality with femininity in such a way to leave hegemonic definitions of gender and sexuality intact. Comparing Carson Kressley to "Jack" on *Will & Grace*, they suggest that viewers laugh *at* his humor rather than *with* him and that the show helps "sustain a heteronormative society" (p. 354). Similarly, though they acknowledge certain positive aspects of the show, Hilton-Morrow and Battles (2004) conjecture that the show works to reinscribe and recuperate hegemonic masculinity in a manner that is "relentlessly heterosexist in its effects." Robert Westerfelhaus and Celeste Lacroix (2006) describe how *Queer Eye* functions "as a mediated ritual of rebellion that domesticates Queers, contains Queer sexuality, and places straight men at the sociosexual center. The series thus supports the very heteronormative order it seems to challenge" (p. 426).

To be sure, it would be hard to make the case that *Queer Eye* provides any sort of direct challenge to the "heteronormative order" any more than M*A*S*H challenged the military industrial complex or *The Cosby Show* challenged institutional racism. As I have argued previously, this is an unreasonable burden to put on *any* entertainment television program. At the same time, our research suggests that such shows *can* influence individually held beliefs and attitudes. The sexual prejudice questions we asked included items that directly tapped into the idea of heteronormativity, such as "Male homosexuality is a natural expression of sexuality in human men," and "Male homosexuality is a perversion." Furthermore, in one study (discussed in chapter 6) in which we used a scale designed explicitly to assess attitudes toward heteronormativity (including such items as "The only normal sexual relationships are heterosexual relationships," and "Heterosexual sex is the natural way to have sex"), we found that participants' answers were highly correlated ($r = .84$, $p < .001$) with their answers to the items on the Attitudes toward Gay Men scale. What this means is that when sexual prejudice is reduced, participants *also* indicated a reduction on their commitment to heteronormativity. Thus for viewers for whom viewing *Queer Eye* reduced prejudice, heteronormativity also was decreased.

In the most blistering review that I found, Terry Sawyer in popMatters.com (2003) equates *Queer Eye* to "minstrelsy," arguing that the show depicts gay men as "materialistic vamps, style clowns with cock-centered worldview." *Queer Eye* "portrays gays as moral savages who live their entire lives in pagan adoration of high-end hair product." Claiming that the show's stereotypes "simply reify and subtly reinforce the incoherent category of oppression that corralled everyone together in an ill-fitting noose in the first place," Sawyer rhetorically asks, "How exactly could this representation 'improve' the position of gays in mainstream culture?"

The answer is that not all viewers agree with Sawyer's interpretation. When a critic labels a particular performance "stereotypical," that critic is engaging in category work of his or her own. He or she says, in effect, what *I* find salient about this performance is that I see it as similar to (name of established stereotype). The difference, however, between a recognizable but benign social type and contributing to a pejorative overgeneralization is in the mind of the beholder. Calling a performance "stereotypical" does not make it so unless one can prove that the performance is carrying out *stereotypical* (pejorative overgeneralizing) *category work*. In the case of *Queer Eye*, the evidence points the other way.

In an online poll hosted by Advocate.com (2004), most who criticized the show simply used the terms *stereotype* or *stereotypical* without identifying specific traits. Those who did identify attributes described as stereotypical included "have fabulous taste" and are "thin," "young," "materialistic," and "campy." However, the vast majority of those who responded were favorable toward the show, describing it as "funny, witty, and smart," "gives visibility to gay men," shows "positive interaction between the straight and gay guys," and demonstrates that "we have talent and are honest people." Of the 1,157 who responded to the poll—most of whom presumably were gay, given the primary audience for *The Advocate*—almost 68% agreed that *Queer Eye for the Straight Guy* is "a step forward for the gay rights movement," with 22% disagreeing and 10% remaining undecided.

Obviously I agree with those who see the show as a step forward. The point for critics is that one way to break through the stereotype debate is to explore what audiences actually learn about gay men from watching the show and how such information can change or reinforce attitudes. How does a particular film or television show influence audience members' understanding of the *category attributes* associated with specific social groups? What sort of *social judgments* (likability, respect, attraction, perceived similarity) do audiences make about pivotal characters? Especially for those viewers who have little to no direct, personal contact with gay men, the show can reduce heteronormative prejudice because it provides diverse and positive depictions of gay men. That is a praiseworthy achievement. Personally, my primary concern about the show is not about its representation of gay men but about the fetishizing of a product-driven lifestyle (cf. Sender, 2006), but that seems a fair criticism of most, if not all, commercial television (Jhally, 1987). For those who fault *Queer Eye* for not representing *enough* diversity, let us acknowledge the positive cultural work that the show has performed while also agreeing that there is plenty of such work left to be done.

CHAPTER 5

Context Matters

Antifeminism in Michael Crichton's *Disclosure*

By the mid-1990s, writer Michael Crichton seemed to embody modern popular culture, literally and figuratively. In 1993, Crichton authored four of the nine longest-running mass-market paperback best-selling novels: *Jurassic Park, Rising Sun, Congo,* and *Sphere.* All four were made into major motion pictures. In 1994, Crichton continued his growing multimedia success with *Disclosure.* The novel, ostensibly about role-reversed sexual harassment in the corporate workplace, spent 22 weeks on the *New York Times Bestseller List.* For 20 weeks, *Disclosure* was on the *Publisher's Weekly* 1994 longest-running hardcover best seller list, at number one for five of those weeks. In paperback, *Disclosure* ran for 25 weeks as one of the *Publisher's Weekly* 1994 mass-market best sellers, 8 weeks as number one. The film version of *Disclosure* was released just in time for Christmas 1994. As soon as the film debuted, the paperback shot back up to the top slot of best sellers for 4 more weeks in early 1995. Sixteen weeks after its release, *Disclosure* had grossed an impressive $82.1 million at the box office, placing it in the top 20 grossing films during that time period.

Video rentals of *Disclosure* were significant. By its third week of availability, *Disclosure* became the number one video rental in its category. It stayed at number one for 3 weeks and remained in the top 10 for 8 more weeks. Perhaps even more notable were *Disclosure's* initial laser disc sales (remember laser discs?). At $39.98 a disc, *Disclosure's* sales were in the top 10 in its category for 11 consecutive weeks in late summer 1995. Having

---

Originally written with Valerie S. Terry.

run on cable via Home Box Office (HBO) and aired on prime-time network television, there is no doubt that Crichton and *Disclosure* have had tremendous exposure to a diverse mass audience in the United States and around the world and thus have the potential for significant influence upon these audiences.[1] This widespread exposure and the social significance of the issue that *Disclosure* engages—sexual harassment—justify this text for critical analysis. My purpose in this chapter is to investigate the possible rhetorical consequences of *Disclosure's* depiction of gender roles. The focus is primarily on the book version of *Disclosure,* since that is the text over which Crichton clearly has direct control; nonetheless, most of the observations also apply to the movie treatment.[2]

Despite being framed an "egalitarian feminist" exploration of the power dynamics of sexual harassment, *Disclosure* can be read as an antifeminist backlash characteristic of some mainstream popular culture of the late 1980s and 1990s. Consequently, Crichton's argument for an egalitarian feminist perspective of sexual harassment is made less effective by the patriarchal ideology of antifeminism that his story perpetuates. Four primary claims support this contention: First, the "category work" that Crichton's characters perform in *Disclosure* reinforces a negative stereotype of U.S. female executives and promotes a traditional, patriarchal perspective. Second, the story's framing of traditional women's roles in society undermines major tenets of feminism, such as equality and sex and gender blindness. Third, by tying the success of the lead male character to the "taking on" of traditional masculine characteristics, *Disclosure* reinforces social myths about men and success. And fourth, Crichton's use of an impersonal narrator to promote reader sympathy for and identification with the lead male character—who is cast in the role of "victim"—functions to marginalize the harassment experience of women. Other explicit attacks on feminism and feminist agendas further reveal *Disclosure's* antifeminism. Professor Terry and I were guided in our reading of the text by Sandra L. Bem's (1974, 1993) and James Mahalik and colleagues' (2003, 2005) sex-role research concerning how dominant culture normatively defines sex-role expectations, Bonnie J. Dow's (1990, 1996) analysis of cultural hegemony and feminism, Kathleen Hall Jamieson's (1995) work on "double binds" that perpetuate sexual discrimination, and Wayne Booth's (1983) writings on the rhetoric of fiction, in particular, the use of the impersonal narrator.

Crichton's Postfeminism in *Disclosure*

Crichton describes his gender politics as "egalitarian feminism," a stance that says "men and women are equal and should have equal opportunity." He contrasts this position with "protectionist feminism," which asserts that "women have special needs and special requirements" (in Getlin, 1994,

p. E6). Crichton (1990) has stated, "The best way to think about men and women is to assume there are no differences between them" (p. 92). He contends that "men and women are equally good, equally bad, equally stupid, equally smart" (in Span, 1994) and he concludes, "women are no better than men" (in Goldner, 1994, p. 6). Crichton's political position is compatible with a sex and gender-blind "postfeminism." In an ideal post-feminist, "humanist" society, issues are not characterized by gender; ac-cordingly, "women's issues" and "men's issues" are misnomers for areas of social interest. According to Mary Douglas Vavrus (2002b), mainstream news coverage largely assumes a postfeminist perspective. She argues that news accounts of political women in major stories in the 1990s promoted a postfeminist politics that encouraged women's private, consumer life-styles and middle-class aspirations, while it discouraged public life and political activism.

Several explicit claims intended to identify Crichton's humanism appear in the book. The fly page of *Disclosure* offers two quotations that frame and contextualize the story that follows. The first is from Title VII of the Civil Rights Act of 1964:

It shall be an unlawful employment practice for an employer: (1) to fail or refuse to hire or to discharge any individual, or oth-erwise to discriminate against any individual with respect to his compensation, terms, conditions, or privileges of employment because of such individual's race, color, religion, sex, or national origin or (2) to limit, segregate, or classify his employees or applicants for employment in any way which would deprive or tend to deprive any individual of employment opportunities or otherwise adversely affect his status as an employee, because of such individual's race, color, religion, sex, or national origin. (fly page)

While Title VII of the Civil Rights Act of 1964 had not yet fully incorpo-rated gender-neutral terminology, the overriding notion of the act is clear and provides the umbrella theme for *Disclosure*: Equality for all, with no exception, based on "race, color, religion, sex, or national origin." The law describes the goal of a successfully feminist and humanist society where sex and gender no longer have explanatory power. What does explain behav-ior for Crichton is *power*. Crichton frames his story with a second quotation on *Disclosure's* fly page, this one from Katharine Graham: "Power is neither male nor female." Graham's quote offers the thematic thread that con-nects the explicit postfeminist notion of sex blindness to the sexual harassment case presented in *Disclosure*. Louise Fernandez, the female attorney for the male victim in the story, summarizes this connection:

> Harassment is about power—the undue exercise of power by a
> superior over a subordinate. I know there's a fashionable point of
> view that says women are fundamentally different from men, and
> that women would never harass an employee. But from where I
> sit, I've seen it all. . . . Personally, I don't deal much in theory.
> I have to deal with the facts. And on the basis of facts, I don't see
> much difference in the behavior of men and women. At least,
> nothing that you can rely on. (Crichton, 1994, pp. 147–48; sub-
> sequent text quotations are by page number only)

To punctuate this point, Fernandez's colleague comments: "Power protects power. And once a woman gets up in the power structure, she'll be
protected by the structure, the same as a man . . . power is neither male
nor female. Whoever is behind the desk has the opportunity to abuse
power. And women will take advantage as often as men" (p. 268). In an
exchange between the story's hero and harassment victim Tom Sanders
and Bob Garvin, the chief executive officer of DigiCom, the company
where they work, the ideals of Title VII and Graham's precept are woven
into the story's fabric: "'We have an obligation to attain equality,' Garvin
said. 'Fine. But equality *means* no special breaks,' Sanders said. 'Equality
means treating people the same'" (p. 60).

As noted later, few critics were willing to embrace Crichton's ideological prescriptions. Why? Not because of any features intrinsic to the
text but rather because of the meanings audience members are likely to
construct in response to the movie in their particular cultural and historical context. As cultural critic Lawrence Grossberg notes, "An event or
practice (even a text) does not exist apart from the forces of the context
that constitute it as what it is. Obviously context is not merely back-
ground but the very conditions of possibility of something" (1997,
p. 225). As a historical matter, we still live in a society sufficiently satu-
rated with patriarchal attitudes, behaviors, and structures so that a move
to egalitarian (post)feminism seems, at best, premature and, at worst, an
impediment to social change (Coppock, Haydon, & Richter, 1995; see
also Modleski, 1991, pp. 3–22). The key assumptions of postfeminism are
demonstrably false (Hall & Rodriguez, 2003). As a recent slogan among
some feminists suggests, "I'll be a postfeminist in postpatriarchy." The
objective here, however, is not to engage in an extended debate about
the merits or problems of postfeminism but rather to explore the specific
ideological work advanced rhetorically in Crichton's text. The goal is, as
Dow (1996) puts it, "to understand the implications of postfeminist
rhetoric" circulating in various cultural products (p. 96). Indeed, regardless of his political intentions, as a rhetorical matter Crichton's text

perpetuates patriarchal beliefs that contribute to antifeminist backlash on the subject of sexual harassment. I now turn to the four specific arguments in support of such a reading.

Argument 1: Perpetuation of Negative Perceptions of Female Executives

Crichton claims that "the behavior of the two antagonists mirrors each other, like a Rorschach inkblot. The value of a Rorschach test lies in what it tells us about ourselves" (p. 405). With this claim in mind, the question is what Crichton's story informs us about the persistent stereotypes (pejorative overgeneralizations) concerning female executives that continue to permeate our society and, if *Disclosure* is any indication, our popular literature. Much of the subsequent analysis of Crichton's *Disclosure* is based on the way he portrays gender-specific behavior. The argument is that in addition to explicit critiques of feminism and his framing of sexual harassment in a way that undercuts the sexual politics involved, Crichton's characters send the androcentric message that masculinity is the norm. As noted in chapter 1, a good deal of evidence indicates that gender is still understood in the United States in largely dichotomous fashion, and the combination of androcentrism and gender polarization does much to perpetuate patriarchal beliefs and behaviors. Work by Sandra Bem (1974, 1993) and others indicates that we often categorize behavior along gendered and dichotomous lines, such as: aggressive/gentle, ambitious/compassionate, competitive/yielding, independent/loyal, forceful/affectionate, individualistic/sensitive to needs of others, has leadership abilities/loves children. Despite a good deal of social and legal progress, pejorative overgeneralizing about gender persists (Lueptow, Garovich, & Lueptow, 1995).

Particularly with respect to *leadership roles*, which are central to *Disclosure*, men are still expected to act in traditionally masculine ways and women in traditionally feminine ways. Managers, leaders, and other professionals are encouraged to be assertive, independent, rational, strategic, tough, and aggressive—and so are men (Morgan, 1997, p. 191; Smeltzer & Watson, 1986). In contrast, the communal characteristics of deference, inclusivity, and cooperation that women are socialized into usually are associated with subordinate roles (Miller, 1986, p. 61). When women leaders in particular act in a manner that is incongruous with stereotypical expectations, the odds are that such behavior will be judged negatively:

> [P]erceived incongruity between the female gender role and leadership roles leads to two forms of prejudice: (a) perceiving women

less favorably than men as potential occupants of leadership roles and (b) evaluating behavior that fulfills the prescriptions of a leader role less favorably when it is enacted by a woman. One consequence is that attitudes are less positive toward female than male leaders and potential leaders. Other consequences are that it is more difficult for women to become leaders and to achieve success in leadership roles. Evidence from varied research paradigms substantiates that these consequences occur, especially in situations that heighten perceptions of incongruity between the female gender role and leadership roles. (Eagly & Karau, 2002, p. 573)

In early research on sex stereotyping, Rosabeth Kanter (1977) identified four negative social roles for women in work environments and three positive social roles for men:

Women	*Men*
Sex object	Sturdy oak
Mother	Fighter
Child	Breadwinner
Iron maiden	

It is not a difficult stretch to see how Crichton's characters fit these roles. The only successful executive women in his novel are "iron maidens" who are conventionally unfeminine: independent, ambitious, directive, competitive, and tough (Garlick, Dixon, & Allen, 1992). However, as Alice Eagly and Steven Karau (2002) point out, it is just such gender-bending women who are likely to be socially sanctioned for their stereo-typically gender-inappropriate behavior.

One might be tempted to praise Crichton for offering portrayals of women that run counter to stereotypes and thus, as argued in chapter 1, challenge essentialism and gender polarization, even if he is promoting androcentrism. However, such portrayals only work if they are *positive.* Typically the enjoyment of media content is a function of a viewer's emotional disposition toward characters and the outcomes experienced by those characters as a narrative unfolds (Raney, 2004). If gender-role violating women are one-dimensional and not likable, then readers are unlikely to enjoy such characters and root for their success. If women leaders are unlikable, valued only when acting like a man, or if there is not *some* effort to provide a positive portrayal of *men* successfully violating stereotypical expectations, then masculine-acting women will not challenge stereotypical norms. Patriarchy, and thus Men, will continue to rule supreme. The almost deafening roar of androcentrism almost certainly will drown out any message that challenges gender-based expectations. In Crichton's world, to be successful executives, women must be like men. But they should not expect to be liked. To be happy, women in the book apparently must follow traditional paths. Sanders, we will see, wins once he "acts like a man."

The lead female character, the "harasser," and two pivotal supporting female roles are drawn with characteristics that perpetuate negative social types. The characters are portrayed in ways that reinforce what Jamieson (1995) describes as the "femininity/competency" double bind: "We still confront a bind that expects a woman to be feminine, then offers her a concept of femininity that ensures that as a feminine creature she cannot be mature or decisive" (p. 120). Crichton's female characters, we contend, are predominantly portrayed as feminine *or* competent. As a result, Crichton fosters a decidedly patriarchal perspective. According to Dow (1990), "The point of a hegemonic perspective [is that] the medium adjusts to social change in a manner that simultaneously contradicts or undercuts a progressive premise . . . 'inoculating' the dominant ideology from radical change by incorporating small amounts of oppositional ideology" (p. 263). While the role-reversal technique in *Disclosure* attempts to "incorporate" the notion of postfeminist "oppositional ideology" (i.e., sex blindness) into its story about sexual harassment, by perpetuating negative social types of female executives we argue that *Disclosure* exhibits a traditional patriarchal perspective and undercuts its own potentially progressive message when engaging not only sexual harassment in particular but the roles of men and women in modern American business in general. By showing women who are acting counter to traditional fashion in less than flattering terms, *Disclosure* still manages to sustain the gender polarization that contributes to sexual inequality in American social life.

Meredith Johnson is one of two lead characters in *Disclosure*. She is female, and she is the "harasser." In the story, Crichton constructs Johnson, first, as physically beautiful but lacking in technical expertise and professional knowledge: "She didn't really have any deep knowledge, but she didn't need to. She was good-looking, sexy, and smart, and she had a kind of uncanny self-possession that carried her through awkward moments" (p. 27); "She used to cross her legs whenever she was asked a question she couldn't answer. 'She could always use sex to distract people. She's good at that'" (p. 279). Crichton adds an additional stereotypical element about beautiful women in executive positions in his description of Johnson about to give a major presentation to some corporate "heavyweights": "In her dark blue suit, she looked the model of corporate correctness, but she was strikingly beautiful. At the podium, she put on horn-rimmed glasses and lowered the conference room lights. . . . 'Now, if I can just work this thing . . .'" (p. 57). Crichton implies that to be taken seriously, Johnson has to "uglify" herself by putting on "horn-rimmed glasses." Further, she is compelled either to feign ignorance of how to work the presentation equipment to gain the sympathies of the predominantly male audience, or Johnson is truly befuddled by a lack of the required technical expertise. Exacerbated by the "exception" that she represents a "model of corporate correctness, *but*... beautiful" (p. 57, emphasis added), the stereotype of the weaker, less technically oriented but ornamental sex also is advanced as another character remarks about Johnson: "[She's] the demo queen. She started out doing demos. Appearance has always been her strongest point" (p. 58). And later, following a detailed exchange with Tom Sanders involving a highly technical matter, Sanders remarks to Johnson: "All that gobbledygook about controller chips and read heads. You don't know what you were talking about" (p. 125).

Because his story is set in a high-tech firm, Crichton engineers opportunities to demonstrate Johnson's lack of the technical expertise she should have to be "Vice President for Advanced Operations and Planning" (p. 26). For example: "Because you see, all this raises a related question . . . having to do with executive judgment. To be frank, I've [John Conley, vice president of the firm looking to merge with Johnson's company] heard some rumblings in the division about her [Johnson's] appointment. In terms of whether she really has a good enough grasp of the issues to run a technical division" (p. 221). In fact, it is a highly technical matter that ultimately contributes to Johnson's downfall in the company. Granted, a lack of such required expertise would, or at least should, contribute to *any* individual's dismissal, but in the figure of a woman who has been characterized as using her sexual acumen and physical attractiveness to achieve her executive position in the first place, such incompetence compounds the stereotype.

Crichton also characterizes Johnson as vindictive, conniving, and manipulative, not only in her daily standard of operation in the workplace ("everybody in the company knows that Meredith is a shark. Meredith Manmuncher, they call her. The Great White" [p. 193]) but, as just mentioned, in the way in which she eventually attained her high-ranking executive position:

> Garvin [CEO of DigiCom, where Johnson and Sanders work] was smiling [in the family portrait], his hand resting lightly on his [now-dead] daughter's shoulder, and she was tall and athletic-looking, with short, light blond, curly hair. . . . Meredith [shown in a photograph early in her professional association with Garvin] wore her hair short, in a curly, informal style. . . . There was no doubt about what she had done. (p. 190)

This is another example of a negative perception of professional women resorting to tricks and schemes in order to get what they want. Such a depiction might have supported an egalitarian feminist premise for *Disclosure* if Johnson had been a competent manager forced to overcome the institutionalized prejudice against women in high-ranking executive positions through wiles because her capabilities alone were not sufficient for her success. However, because Johnson is shown to be unqualified to hold that executive position, as exemplified in the following commentary from Sanders, the negative perceptions about her are reinforced:

> Meredith didn't think the [technical] changes would matter, because she didn't know anything about production. She was just cutting costs. But she knew that the changes at the plant would eventually be traced back to her, so she thought she had a way to get rid of me [Sanders], to make me quit the company [by accusing Sanders of sexually harassing her]. And then she would be able to blame me for the problems at the plant. (p. 378)

Just as Dow (1990) discusses paternalism and how it served to undercut the independence of the Mary Richards character in the television situation comedy *The Mary Tyler Moore Show*, so paternalism plays a similar role between Garvin and Johnson in *Disclosure*. The implication is not only a reinforcement of the manipulative nature of Johnson, as described in the just-quoted passage, but of negative perceptions about successful female executives and their relationships with male mentors or, more accurately, male protectors: "Bob has decided that Meredith Johnson is going to head up the division" (p. 25); "Bob has placed her [Johnson] in direct line for succession, when he steps down as CEO sometime in the next two years" (p. 26); "I think Bob sees himself in her . . . And I tell you, she plays it. . . . He crosses his arms, she crosses hers. He leans against the wall, she leans against the wall. . . . And from a distance . . . she looks like him" (p. 173); and, regarding Garvin's "unswerving support" (p. 168) of Johnson, "For years, Garvin had had a blind spot for Johnson. Whenever criticisms of Johnson arose, Garvin would somehow change the subject, shift to something else. There was no reasoning with him" (p. 168).

Though Crichton provides Garvin with an effective soliloquy advocating the need for "more women in high corporate positions" (p. 168), it comes directly after the discussion of Garvin's "unreasonable" support of Johnson for such a position, thus negating, or at best neutralizing, the legitimacy of the speech. Here Crichton is acknowledging the imbalance of males to females in high-level executive positions, but the issue is rendered impotent from making a greater impact on the "dominant ideology" that contributes to the imbalance by the incompetence of Johnson and the suspect nature of Garvin's "unswerving" support of her.

When Johnson is ultimately dismissed from her job, Stephanie Kaplan, DigiCom's chief financial officer, is chosen to replace her. While this would seem a triumph for feminists, a close inspection of the characterization of Kaplan proves the contrary. Kaplan does not escape the "femininity/ competency" double bind, nor is she particularly personable or likable—a fact that reduces the potential value of her character as a gender-bending role model. She is described as "a tall woman with prematurely gray hair and a notably silent manner . . . known as Stephanie Stealth, or the Stealth Bomber—the latter a reference to her habit of quietly killing projects she did not consider profitable enough" (p. 43). Crichton further distinguishes Kaplan as follows:

> Garvin didn't really like her [Kaplan]. . . . Colorless, humorless, and tireless, her dedication to the company was legendary; she worked late every night and came in most weekends. When she had had a bout of cancer a few years back, she refused to take even a single day off . . . the episode seemed to have increased Kaplan's relentless focus on her impersonal domain, figures and spreadsheets, and heightened her natural inclination to work behind the scenes. In her own way, she was mysterious—and potentially dangerous. (p. 53)

Kaplan also is described as "plodding and unimaginative" (p. 345), "silent and intense . . . competent, but disliked by many in the company" (p. 13). Her appointment to replace Johnson at the end of the story reinforces the negative beliefs about the type of woman it takes to succeed, one whose characteristics are traditionally coded as masculine: objective, a rational, nonemotional thinker, action oriented, and strong. Crichton adds a dose of paternalism even to this already less-than-flattering representation of successful women executives by noting that Kaplan "owed her position" in the company to Max Dorfman, a former male DigiCom director (p. 198).

Sanders's attorney in his sexual harassment suit against Johnson and their company is Louise Fernandez, another recognizable social type—almost a caricature—in *Disclosure* of a successful female executive. Fernandez is described as "a tall woman in her thirties, with straight blond hair and a handsome, aquiline face. . . . She had a direct manner and a firm handshake" (p. 134). As with Kaplan, the characteristics of Fernandez are more traditionally masculine, even to the use of the word "handsome" to describe her face. Additionally, having been described to Sanders as "sweet and demure" (p. 98) by another character, Sanders's reaction upon meeting Fernandez is one of surprise: "She wasn't at all what he had expected. She wasn't sweet and demure at all. And certainly not Hispanic" (p. 134). Fernandez's manner "was more than clinical, more than professional . . . she was in some deep way detached, and very cold" (p. 138).

Fernandez appears to be the sole pivotal female character in *Disclosure* who is successful in her own right, based on her competence and capabilities: Fernandez "is just lethal on these discrimination cases. Lethal. Got the jury to award our client nearly half a million. That Fernandez can work the case law like nothing you've ever seen. She's won fourteen of her last sixteen cases" (p. 98). Fernandez does not escape hegemonic constraint by Crichton, however. Though Crichton incorporates a successful and competent female character into his story in the figure of Fernandez, arguably, to support his postfeminist premise, the character is constrained from making a strong, positive impact from this perspective by her predominantly masculine characteristics, unfeminine qualities that make her less likable (clinical, detached, cold), and an ethnicity that is cloaked.

Crichton's depiction via role reversal of a case of sexual harassment in *Disclosure* functions in an antifeminist manner because of the negative perceptions about female executives that it perpetuates. Characterizations of at least three of the pivotal female characters in the story are almost caricatures; that is, two (Kaplan and Fernandez) would pass as men if not for the biological female sex Crichton bestowed on them. The third and lead female character, Johnson, is the stereotypical epitome of the "woman scorned" (p. 161) in her acts of vindictiveness, connivances, and manipulations. She also represents the negative social type of female executive who is professionally incompetent and involved in a paternalistic relationship with a male mentor. The implication of these double-bind representations is that if a woman has the traditionally acknowledged masculine traits of independence, objectivity, action-orientation, and strength, and the ability to think rationally and unemotionally, then she can succeed in the workplace but lose her claim to femininity (Jamieson, 1995, pp. 120–45), a role violation for which she risks social sanction (Eagly & Karau, 2002).

On its face, of course, there is nothing necessarily wrong with employing recognizable, even if negative, social types in a story. Just as humans *must* make sense of the world through categories, fictional stories often must rely on easily recognizable social types or "stock characters" (McKee, 1997). However, in a contested representational ecology in which negative perceptions and pejorative overgeneralizations (stereotypes) about women in leadership roles persist, it is fair and appropriate to challenge the sort of category work that *Disclosure* performs. The category work identified so far is very far from egalitarian or any other kind of feminism.

Argument 2: Traditional Women's Roles in Society

Disclosure frames other supporting female characters as either subservient to men in their professional and/or personal lives or aggressively dominant in these same relationships. Additionally, the only female characters in *Disclosure* who appear happy or content and who retain some traditional feminine characteristics are those depicted in subordinate roles. These characterizations aggravate the double bind described by Jamieson (1995) as "womb/brain": "Throughout history, women have been identified as bodies not minds, wombs not brains. The distinction is captured in the clichés of our culture. Where men think, women feel. The man is the head of the family, the woman the heart" (p. 53). Such characterizations reinforce the patriarchal perspective that was just discussed and that the female executives represented in *Disclosure* demonstrate.

Cindy Wolfe is Tom Sanders's assistant. She places herself or is placed in a subordinate professional position to the men at DigiCom. Cindy, as she puts it, "works for Tom" (p. 71). She refers to the chief executive officer of DigiCom as Mr. Garvin: [speaking to Sanders] "Mr. Garvin was just here, looking for you" (p. 15). Further exemplifying her position relative to that of Sanders's, another character states, "Cindy? Mr. Sanders is going to be unavailable for a few minutes" (p. 39). Identified as an assistant, Cindy is later referred to as "beautiful" (p. 73) and an all-knowing secretary ("And the secretaries always know everything, don't they?" [p. 72])—a cliché of subordinate women's roles in the workplace. Cindy also is a caregiver, another traditionally feminine role: "[Sanders] glanced up. Cindy was standing in the doorway, looking concerned. 'Tom, do you want coffee?' . . . She lingered at the door. 'You want a bagel? Have you had breakfast?'" (p. 31); "[Sanders] felt as if she was treating him like an invalid. . . . As he hurried down the stairs to the third floor, he felt relieved at the distraction. Cindy was right to get him out of the office" (p. 34). Though a minor character, Crichton seems to emphasize Cindy's history of romantic relationships with men: [Cindy speaking to Sanders] "'Nine years ago? . . . I think I was with my boyfriend in Europe.' 'Not your present boyfriend?' 'No . . . This guy was a real jerk'" (p. 32). Though subtle, this inferred reliance on or need for a man further frames Cindy in a subordinate woman's role. Additionally, even Cindy's name connotes subordinate status, as it is commonly associated with young girls. Cindy's contentment with her current situation is implied. She is supportive of and loyal to Sanders, and she appears generally as a happy character: "Tom, I just want you to know, I don't believe what they are saying" (p. 182), and "Cindy was turned away, laughing on the phone" (p. 77). Cindy's happiness and contentment seem to be byproducts of her playing a traditional woman's role in the workplace and in her personal relationships.

Adele Lewyn is a housewife and mother. She is characterized as "one of those wonderfully calm, almost phlegmatic women who could talk on the phone while her two kids crawled all over her, tugging at her, asking her questions," and "in a similar fashion, Adele just let Lewyn [Mark, her husband] rage while she went on about her business" (p. 197). Adele is thus framed as a contented and satisfied woman exhibiting the traditionally defined feminine characteristics of passivity, deference, and subordination to her husband and children.

Mary Anne Hunter is head of Data Telecommunications at Digi-Com. She is described as "petite and intense" (p. 42) and somewhat compulsive: "She never ate lunch, but ordinarily went on a five-mile run after each [staff] meeting" (p. 42). She is outspoken and confrontational, traditionally considered masculine characteristics: "What's this? If Garvin brought in some guy from Microsoft to run this division, nobody'd say he must be fucking somebody" (p. 44), and "What is this conversation really about? It's about the fact that you're all pissed off because now you have to report to a woman" (p. 45). What femininity Mary Anne exhibits is framed in a trivializing way: "She had changed into a skirt and blouse, and she was smiling broadly, as if she had just left her lover" (p. 50). Though not designating the gender of the supposed lover, this reference implies that whatever pleasure Mary Anne was experiencing must have been derived from some sexual encounter, again more traditionally depicted as a masculine trait. While Mary Anne is married, her only other "feminine" characteristic—her small stature—is framed as a detriment: "[Sanders] watched [Mary Anne] walk away, a slender, compact figure in exercise clothes, carrying a leather briefcase. She was barely five feet tall. The men on the ferry were so much larger. He remembered that she had once told Susan that she took up running because of her fear of rape" (p. 215). Mary Anne's positive attributes are framed as a consequence of her masculine tendencies compensating for her feminine weaknesses. She does not successfully escape the femininity/competence and womb/brain double binds.

Susan Handler is Tom Sanders's wife. Unlike Adele, Susan is a part-time attorney who is drawn as being successful in the workplace but not as a wife and mother. Crichton's depictions concerning her care of her children appear less than flattering. Referring to her 4-year-old daughter, Susan says, "She's old enough to help out" (p. 7); parental neglect is implied by this passage: "Sanders sat down, wiped Matt's face, and began to feed his son. The boy immediately stopped crying, and swallowed the cereal in big gulps. The poor kid was hungry" (p. 9). Further, Susan "was not good at managing the routine at home" (p. 6); "He'd [Sanders] told Susan a dozen times he didn't want the kids to get diet drinks. They ought to be getting healthy food. Real food. But Susan was busy, and Consuela [Susan's house-helper] indifferent. . . . It wasn't right. It wasn't the way he had been brought up" (p. 107). Crichton implies that Susan has not properly balanced her career and home life. Sanders castigates Susan and, by implication, other professional women who neglect their "womanly" duties at home: "How are you oppressed? You never wash a load of clothes. You never cook a meal. You never sweep a floor. Somebody does all that for you. You have somebody to do everything for you.

You have somebody to take the kids to school and somebody to pick them up. You're a partner in a law firm, for Christ's sake. You're about as oppressed as Leona Helmsley" (p. 105).

Along with her apparent deficiency as a traditional wife and mother, Susan is framed with masculine characteristics of aggressiveness and driving ambition. In their sexual relationship, Susan is the aggressor with Sanders: "'Can't you please feed them? Pretty please?' Teasing, she ruffled his hair, and her bathrobe fell open. She left it open and smiled. 'I'll owe you one . . .'" (p. 7), and "[Susan] snuggled up against him, pressing her face against his neck, and threw her leg over his side. This was her invariable overture, and it always annoyed him. He felt pinned down by her heavy leg" (p. 103). Professionally, Susan's success is evidence of her ambitious drive: "Her practice in Seattle was successful; she had spent many years building it" (p. 132); "[Susan] was sitting up in bed, reading, with legal files and papers scattered across the bedcovers" (p. 99); and, "[Susan] ran her finger down her appointments. 'I can move that . . . And . . . conference call . . . Yes . . . Yes. I can leave for a few days'" (p. 159).

One way the rhetorical work of a dramatic text can be charted is by the consequences that result from characters' choices. If characters who behave in a traditionally gendered manner are rewarded for such a choice, and characters who behave in an untraditional manner are either portrayed in an unlikable fashion and/or are punished for their choices, then the message is clear. We might describe this sort of fictive strategy as vicarious operant conditioning. Recall that young viewers exposed to successful counterstereotypical sex-role portrayals are more likely to change their beliefs about available career choices than those who are not (Miller & Reeves, 1976). Though not specifically a study of gender, the most in-depth research on television and violence found that viewers who identified with "successful" (unpunished or rewarded), aggressive behavior by televised characters in their youth were more likely to engage in aggressive behaviors themselves in later life (Huesmann, Moise-Titus, Podolski, & Eron, 2003). In short, there is at least some solid evidence that what I have described as vicarious operant conditioning *works*, for better or for worse.

By framing supporting female characters as either content because they are in traditional and subordinate female roles or successful in business because they are not, *Disclosure* compounds its traditional patriarchal perspective, perpetuating the gendered double binds facing American female executives. Also, by depicting even minor female characters as requiring traditionally masculine characteristics to excel in the workplace, or traditionally feminine ones to be content as subordinate, *Disclosure* invites the assessment that its "postfeminist" politics are decidedly antifeminist.

Argument 3: Manly Men and Success

Characteristics traditionally coded as masculine include being aggressive, being dominant, exercising power over women, being self-reliant, and being in control of one's emotions (Mahalik, et al., 2003). However, throughout most of *Disclosure*, Tom Sanders displays primarily those characteristics coded as traditionally feminine, including being passive, deferential, and emotional. It is not until Sanders takes on masculine characteristics that he ultimately triumphs over the circumstances that have controlled him throughout the story. Such a plot device functions as vicarious operant conditioning to encourage "men to be men."

Sanders's passivity and deferential habits often result in domination or abuse by those around him, especially females: In the book's opening scene, Sanders avoids confrontation with his wife about feeding their children breakfast and subsequently is late for work on the day he expects to be promoted (pp. 6–10); "When he picked up Matt [Sanders's 9-month-old son], his towel slipped off, and he clutched at it. Eliza [Sanders's 4-year-old daughter] giggled. 'I see your penis, Dad.' She swung her foot, kicking it" (p. 8); "He was the peacemaker. . . . He knew how it would go: he'd get up first, fix her a cup of coffee, and take it to her in bed. Then he'd say he was sorry, and she would reply that she was sorry, too. They'd hug, and he would go get dressed for work. And that would be it" (p. 108). Sanders's passivity and subordination seem to be particularly evident in his sexual relations: "'Susan, damn it. I'm not in the mood.' [Susan speaking to Sanders] 'We hardly ever have sex anymore, as it is.' 'That's because you're [Susan] always traveling.' It just slipped out. 'I'm not "always traveling."' 'You're gone a couple of nights a week'" (p. 104); "instantly there was nothing but his desire, hot and angry, more intense for the fact that he didn't really want to be there, that he felt she [Meredith Johnson] had manipulated him to this place . . . she smiled at him, a knowing, victorious smile" (p. 94). Upon hearing that he has not gotten the promotion that he had expected, Sanders's reactions are primarily emotional, with physical manifestations: "Sanders wasn't going to get a promotion. He broke into a light sweat and felt suddenly dizzy as he walked along the corridor. He leaned against the wall for a moment. He wiped his forehead with his hand and blinked his eyes rapidly" (p. 19). Sanders's reaction also is deferential: "'I'm just trying to get along,' Sanders said. 'I want to be here when the division goes public'" (p. 67). A combination of Sanders's passiveness, deference, and emotion is exhibited in a business meeting in which Johnson is purposely baiting him in front of several top DigiCom executives and those from the company with which DigiCom plans to merge:

> [Johnson speaking to Sanders] "When you and I spoke about
> Twinkle [a DigiCom project], Tom, I understood you to say that
> the problems were quite serious." "They are, yes." "Well, I don't
> think we want to be covering anything up here." He [Sanders]
> said quickly, "I'm not covering anything up." The words came out
> almost before he realized it. He heard his voice, high-pitched,
> tight. . . . He knew he sounded defensive. But he couldn't help
> it. (p. 123)

Immediately following the meeting, in another encounter with Johnson,
Sanders again demonstrates a traditionally "feminine" physical reaction
to confrontation: "He bit his lip, trying to control his anger" (p. 125).

Even in taking action against Johnson, Sanders's reluctance for confrontation and use of aggression is evident: [Louise Fernandez speaking to
Sanders] "'Mr. Sanders, I misjudged you. I had the impression you were a
timid man.' 'They're forcing me to do this'" (p. 175). In a conversation with
Max Dorfman, Sanders's mentor to whom he has gone for advice about the
sexual harassment suit, Dorfman goads Sanders for his passivity and lack of
aggressiveness: "'You have let her [Johnson] define the game, Thomas.' 'I
had to do something. She broke the law.' 'She broke the law,' Dorfman
mimicked him, with a sarcastic whine. 'Oh me, oh my. And you are so de-
fenseless'" (p. 202). One hundred twenty-eight pages later, Dorfman again
chides Sanders about the incident with Johnson: "You wanted this confrontation, Thomas. . . . You're not a victim. You call yourself a victim because you don't want to take responsibility for your life. Because you are
sentimental and lazy and naive. You think other people should take care of
you" (p. 330). This is a turning point for Sanders. From this point to the
end of the story, Sanders takes charge of his situation; that is, Sanders sheds
the passive, deferential, emotional characteristics that he has demonstrated
throughout the book and becomes the aggressor. Sanders takes Dorfman's
advice and begins to control his emotions to think "objectively": "'Solve the
problem,' Max had said" (p. 343). Sanders eventually does this, figuring out
a way to get information from DigiCom's new virtual reality simulator that,
coupled with other evidence (pp. 350–85), exposes Johnson as being incompetent and a liar: "'Meredith's problem is that she lies,' Sanders said.
'She's smooth, and she gets away with it. She's gotten away with it her whole
life. I'm going to see if I can get her to make a single, very big lie'" (p. 379).
Sanders aggressively confronts Johnson in a meeting of high-level DigiCom
executives and executives from the company seeking to merge with Digi-
Com with the evidence he has gathered: "Meredith looked concerned.
'Tom, we all know that you're extremely competent. How could this have
happened?' Sanders hesitated. This was the moment. 'It happened because
the line was changed,' he said. 'The specifications were altered.' 'Altered?

How?' 'I think that's something for you to explain to this group, Meredith,' he said. 'Since you ordered the changes'" (p. 382).

As a result of Sanders's confrontation with Johnson and the evidence he compiles against her, Johnson is fired from the organization, and the sexual harassment case is dropped. Sanders wins. Winning, making work primary, taking risks, controlling emotions, being self-reliant, and exercising power over women are all dominant masculine norms (Mahalik, et al., 2003). The implication is that not until Sanders becomes aggressive, controls his emotions about the problem he has to solve to save his career and his reputation, and is willing to confront Johnson and her supporters is he able to prevail over his circumstances, to take charge of his life. These traditional masculine characteristics allow Sanders to overcome the inadequacies personified in the traditional feminine characteristics that he formerly exhibited.

Argument 4: Creation of Character Sympathy through Impersonal Narration

In addition to negative stereotypes of female executives, stereotypes of women in society, and hegemonic stereotypes of men and success, in *Disclosure*, author Crichton uses what Wayne Booth (1983) describes as "impersonal narration" to elicit reader sympathy for Sanders. Because this is a role-reversal story, Crichton, a male, may have felt his authorial silence was important to the credibility of his narrative. Nonetheless, the choice by Crichton to tell the story in an impersonal manner functions rhetorically to encourage sympathy for his male protagonist: "By the kind of silence [an author] maintains, by the manner in which [an author] leaves his [or her] characters to work out their own destinies or tell their own stories, the author can achieve effects which would be difficult or impossible if [s/]he allowed himself [or herself] or a reliable spokes[person] to speak directly authoritatively to us" (Booth, 1983, p. 273).

One of these effects is *sympathy*. According to Booth (1983), authors may choose to be silent because their "central intelligence is of the kind that will seem most sympathetic if presented as an isolated, unaided consciousness, without the support that a reliable narrator or observer would lend" (p. 274). This, is the approach Crichton takes in *Disclosure*. Further, if a "central intelligence" is "convincingly decent . . . we usually find our emotional and intellectual reactions to him [her] as a character affecting our reactions to the events [s/]he relates" or in which he or she is involved (Booth, 1983, pp. 273–74). Thus, through the persona of the impersonal narrator, Crichton creates reader sympathy not just for Sanders but for the circumstances in which he is involved, including the harassing incident. In this way, Crichton sidesteps the critical issues of authorial intent (first persona), implied audience (second persona), and, perhaps most troublesome, the negated or marginalized audience (third persona; see Turner & Ryden, 2000). Crichton's purpose as an author ostensibly is to present an egalitarian feminist perspective of sexual harassment to an implied audience comprised of the mainstream reading public. The previous analysis describes, however, the dramatic and rhetorical tactics that Crichton uses that function to reinforce certain beliefs about the sex-role propriety of that audience. The neglected audience of Crichton's *Disclosure* is the important segment of society that suffers most from the phenomenon of sexual harassment: women.[3]

Sanders's author-created isolation in *Disclosure* is established in the book's opening scene and is enhanced in two other situations. First, after Sanders told Susan the details of the harassing incident involving Johnson, Susan leaves town with their children to avoid publicity associated with the sexual harassment suit that Sanders has filed against Johnson. "Walking back to his office, [Sanders] suddenly realized how alone he felt.... He was on his own now. He had imagined he would feel relieved, free to act without restraint, but instead he felt abandoned and at risk" (p. 160). Second, "sitting in the deserted law offices [of his attorney, Louise Fernandez, the night before a scheduled mediation session with Johnson], Sanders [has] the feeling that he [is] all alone in the world, with nobody but Fernandez and the encroaching darkness ... this person he had never met before today was fast becoming a kind of lifeline for him" (p. 207).

Booth (1983) also notes that

> [a sympathy effect] is possible ... only when the reflected intelligence is so little distant, so close, in effect, to the norms of the work that no complicated deciphering of unreliability is required of the reader. So long as what the character thinks and feels can be taken directly as a reliable clue about the circumstances [s/]he faces, the reader can experience those circumstances with him [or her] even more strongly because of his [or her] moral isolation. (p. 274)

From the opening pages of the book, Sanders is the focal point of the story and enacts the "norms of the work." He is a mid-level management executive at a high-tech firm in Seattle. He has a wife, two children, a home in a bedroom community from which he commutes to work by ferry, and he is getting too old to play touch football. By portraying Sanders in this way, Crichton creates a character that many readers feel is reliable, because they can identify with him. Booth describes the relationship between reliability and identification as follows:

The peculiar intensity of such an effect [i.e., sympathy] depends . . . on a static character. The changes which go to make up the story are all changes in fact and circumstance and knowledge, never in the essential worth or rightness of the character herself [himself]. [She]he must be accepted at her [his] own estimate from the beginning, and that estimate must, for greatest effect, be as close as possible to the reader's estimate of his [her] own importance. (pp. 276–77)

To this end, the events of the story take place in 4 days, from Monday through Thursday of 1 week. By virtue of such a short time frame, the reader can be reasonably sure that the moral character of Sanders is static. Thus once Sanders's "worth or rightness"—or his "decency"—is established, it does not change, even if his behavior might. So, Booth contends, readers can identify with Sanders, be sympathetic to him, and consider him reliable. And if reliable, states Booth, the reader can experience Sanders's circumstances that much more intensely because of his moral isolation. While Sanders seems to be a man at the mercy of his circumstances, his "decency" and "worth and rightness" are evidenced in *Disclosure* just as sympathy is, as an effect of impersonal narration. That is, in *Disclosure*, the isolated Sanders can do for himself "what no other narrator could possibly do for [him]. Very little heightening of [his] character is needed to make us unite with [him] against the hostile world around [him]; simply because [he] is the only sensitive person visible . . . [he] wins us irresistibly" (Booth, 1983, p. 276). As a further result, the backlash against the relatively unlikable female characters is heightened.

From the book's opening scene, to Sanders's lost promotion, to the harassing incident, to the functioning of the legal system, until the point when he acts to take advantage of the lucky string of incidents that will eventually substantiate his version of the harassment, Sanders appears as a victim of circumstance. Because his decency also is apparent, the reader's sympathy for him is encouraged, even though initially Sanders is unable to control what is happening to him and around him. Though not in direct conflict with the main tenet of a postfeminist vision—sex blindness—this sympathy is created in favor of the male character involved in the sexual harassment suit. Does having a sympathetic male protagonist make *Disclosure* antifeminist? Not by itself, though two qualifications are important. First, despite Crichton's belief that the "advantage of a role-reversal story is that it may enable us to examine aspects [of sexual harassment] concealed by traditional responses and conventional rhetoric" (p. 405), the sympathetic focus on a male victim of harassment diverts attention from the fact that the vast majority of sexual harassment is perpetrated by men against women (Keyton, 1996, pp. 119–22). The late-in-the-story discovery of a tape recording of the sexual harassment incident may work well as a plot device, but it again trivializes how it is often difficult for women to bring successful action against sexual harassers. Second, how that character is portrayed in contrast to other characters, especially women, becomes crucial. As we have emphasized, feminists are among Sanders's victimizers. As conservative columnist George Will (1994) declares, "Many men feel put upon by feminism" (p. A23). To the extent that the use of impersonal narration encourages us to identify and sympathize with Sanders, Crichton may be asking us as well to feel put upon by feminism. As the preceding analysis contended, the manner in which Crichton tells a man's sexual harassment story functions rhetorically and ideologically to normalize an already dominant masculinist perspective on sexual harassment and to marginalize a feminist perspective.

Audience Judgments of Character Attributes

The persuasiveness of the claims made through the preceding textual analysis of Crichton's *Disclosure* depends on whether or not the passages from the book offered as evidence to you, the reader, are sufficient to warrant assent. By highlighting certain passages from the book that we believe to be rhetorically salient, it has been argued that the way he portrays gender-specific behavior functions to foster gender stereotypes and antifeminism. The claims about the meaning of such passages may or may not be persuasive to those professional critics who share our theoretical and ideological commitments, but the question remains as to whether a wider, general readership would interpret the character portrayals as conjectured.

It was not judged practical to test the reading of the novel's characters by trying to have a controlled experiment in which participants would read the entire novel in a single, uninterrupted session. Instead, a survey was constructed containing passages from *Disclosure*, including all of the passages cited earlier. The purpose was to explore the question, do other readers share our interpretations of how the characters are portrayed? As argued previously, the question is not whether critics can label a characterization as a stereotype or negative social type but whether the relevant audiences of a work make such a judgment. To answer the question, it is necessary to ascertain how readers categorize the gender attributes of the characters, as well as how readers *evaluate* such characters.

Building on Sandra Bem's (1974) work, psychologists describe the way most people categorize sex roles as follows: (1) *sex typed*: a male who possesses predominantly masculine traits and behaviors or a female who possesses mostly feminine characteristics; (2) *cross typed*: high feminine and low masculine traits and behaviors for males and the inverse for females; (3) *androgynous*: those who possess high levels of both masculine and feminine traits and behaviors; (4) *undifferentiated*: those who possess low levels of both masculine and feminine characteristics (Spence, Helmreich, & Stapp, 1975; Fecteau, Jackson, and Dindia, 1992). When constructing her Sex Role Inventory (BSRI), Bem (1974) found that "for both males and females, the mean desirability of the masculine and feminine items was significantly higher for the 'appropriate' sex [sex typed] than for the 'inappropriate' sex [cross typed]" (p. 157). Thus the categories of sex typed, cross typed, and androgynous are particularly useful for categorizing Crichton's character descriptions. Given Bem's findings and Crichton's characterizations, it was hypothesized that participants would find the cross-typed characters less socially desirable than the sex-typed or androgynous characters. In other words, characters portrayed as acting in ways traditionally appropriate to their biological sex would be considered more socially desirable than those who violated such norms.

Forty-nine college students were given selected passages from *Disclosure* and asked to identify the basic sex-role type of the character portrayed, and to rate the social desirability of those characters. The survey was administered to students from several classes in the fall semester of 1996. Obviously the use of a nonrandom sample hinders the ability to generalize about the results, but the prediction was sufficiently consistent with previous work on sex-role stereotyping to regard our rhetorical reading of the text either as bolstered or challenged by our findings.

Sex-role typing was operationalized in the survey using three categories: sex typed, cross typed, and androgynous. The survey consisted of seven sets of character descriptions encompassing five of the major female characters described earlier and two categories of the lead male character taken first from early in the book, then from later passages. For each character at least two descriptions were given in order to give subjects a reasonably manageable sampling of how the character is depicted in the novel. After each of the seven sets of character descriptions, subjects were asked to classify the character as either (1) sex typed, (2) cross typed, or (3) androgynous.

The variable of social desirability was measured by a single-item scale adapted from Bem's (1974) discussion of how she selected items for the BSRI. Once participants classified each character as sex typed, cross typed, or androgynous, they were asked to rate the social desirability of that character on a seven-point scale of social desirability, ranging from "very socially desirable" to "very socially undesirable."

To reduce the risk of influencing the participants' responses, a colleague not involved in the textual analysis of *Disclosure* administered the survey.[4] Our colleague gave students a brief definition of the different sex-role types and of the term *socially desirable* (or *appropriate*). Subjects also were told that in determining sex-role type they should draw on whatever the terms *masculine* and *feminine* meant to them, as well as whether *they* felt the characters were socially desirable rather than society in general.

As predicted, cross-typed characters are rated significantly lower in social desirability than either sex-typed or androgynous characters.[5] Thus if Crichton intended such characters as Kaplan and Fernandez to be viewed positively, then he was unsuccessful. Such a finding supports the contention that the most positively portrayed characters are those who conform to traditional gender expectations, given that participants rated sex-typed characters as more socially desirable than either androgynous or cross-typed characters. The preferred characters were Sanders when he acted manly and the female characters who acted in a stereotypically feminine manner. It might be argued that the results are more a reflection of the degree of socialized sexism among our participants than a result of Crichton's characterizations. If that is the case, then it still suggests that Crichton was *so* unsuccessful in advancing "egalitarian feminism" that he ended up reinforcing the normative force of sex-role stereotypes instead of challenging them.

Might the participants have come to a different conclusion had they read the whole book? Maybe, but it remains an untested hypothesis. At the very least, the results suggest that the interpretation of how the key characters are portrayed in this chapter was shared by a contemporary audience made up of unpaid critics.

Explicit Antifeminism in *Disclosure*

Despite being framed as an "egalitarian feminist" exploration of the power dynamics of sexual harassment, *Disclosure* functions ideologically as an antifeminist backlash characteristic of some mainstream popular culture of the late 1980s and 1990s. Four primary arguments supported this claim: First, *Disclosure* perpetuates negative social types of American female executives that promote a hegemonic patriarchal perspective; second, the story's framing of traditional women's roles in society undermines major tenets of feminism, such as equality and sex and gender blindness; third, by tying the success of the lead male character to the "taking on" of traditional male characteristics, *Disclosure* reinforces social myths about men and success; and, fourth, Crichton uses an impersonal narrator to create reader sympathy for and identification with the lead male character, who is cast in the role of "victim," negating the female reader (and viewer) audience.

Though it is impossible to determine whether *Disclosure* actually changed any attitudes or beliefs about sexual harassment in the mid-1990s, it could only have helped the backlash to feminism and feminist political agendas, including efforts to decrease sexual harassment against women. A far more socially useful novel and movie would have been a story that dramatizes in an equally powerful manner the power dynamics that occur when men harass women, as they all too often do. Most, though obviously not quite all, of the plot twists and intrigue of the high-tech story told by Crichton could have been preserved in such a story. As the story was told, however, it functions to perpetuate the sorts of attitudes that prevent, rather than facilitate, Crichton's egalitarian feminist future.

Additional explicit attacks on feminism and feminist agendas further reinforce a reading of Crichton's *Disclosure* as antifeminist. The first of four examples is a conversation that takes place early in the story, when Sanders has just learned that he has lost out on a long-awaited promotion to Johnson. Sanders is talking to Mark Lewyn, a character who is later described as someone "you could never take too seriously" (p. 197). Further, "Lewyn liked being angry. Sanders had known him a long time . . . everyone just let Lewyn rage, because everyone knew that, in the end, it didn't mean anything" (p. 197). Apparently, in this scene, Lewyn is "just raging" about Johnson's appointment over Sanders:

> "Pale males eat it again. I tell you. Sometimes I get so sick of the constant pressure to appoint women," Lewyn said. "I mean, look at this design group. We've got forty percent women here, better than any other division, but they always say, why don't you have more. More women, more—"
>
> "Mark," [Sanders] said, interrupting. "It's a different world now."
>
> "And not a better one," Lewyn said. "It's hurting everybody. Look: when I started in DigiCom, there was only one question. Are you good? If you were good, you got hired. If you could cut it, you stayed. No more. Now, ability is only one of the priorities. There's also the question of whether you're the right sex and skin color to fill out the company's HR profiles. And if you turn out to be incompetent, we can't fire you. . . . Because no one's accountable anymore. No one is responsible. You can't build products on a theory. Because the product you're making is real. And if it stinks, it stinks. And no one will buy it." (p. 67)

This passage implies the seeming reasonableness of Sanders by contrasting his comments with the "ragings" of Lewyn. The potential effect of making Lewyn's remarks seem objectionable may be tempered, however, because the reader is not made aware of Lewyn's tendency to "rage" and "not be taken seriously" until 130 pages later. Additionally, the analogy of a "theory" that "stinks" and consequently that "no one will buy" easily could be read as a reference to Title VII. Contrasting a mandated system of equality with one based solely on ability, the former is discredited in a way unchallenged by any character in the novel.

A second example of antifeminist ideology in *Disclosure* occurs when Bob Garvin, DigiCom's CEO, takes a stand for the equality of women in "Corporate America" on behalf of Johnson: "Corporate America is rooms full of men. And whenever I talk about putting a woman in, there's always a 'But Bob' that comes up. The hell with it. . . . We've got to break the glass ceiling sometime" (p. 168). When reminded that DigiCom has two female executives, Garvin responds:

> "Sure, let the CFO [chief financial officer] be a woman. Let a couple of the midrange execs be women. Throw the broads a bone. The fact remains. You can't tell me that a bright, able young woman starting out in business isn't held back by a hundred little reasons, oh such good reasons, why she shouldn't be advanced, why she shouldn't attain a major position of power. But in the end, it's just prejudice. And it has to stop. We have to give these bright young women a decent opportunity." (p. 169)

While espousing pro-feminist ideas, Garvin's endorsement of Johnson is undermined by the suspect nature of the relationship he has with her, as noted earlier. The notions of equality and affirmative action are evident in Garvin's comments, but his sincerity is suspect due to the doubts raised about his motivations. Overall, Garvin is not presented as a particularly likable, competent, or credible character, which facilitates an easy dismissal of his feminism.

A third example of an antifeminist sentiment in *Disclosure* involves the negative portrayal of the female character Constance Walsh. Walsh is "a regular columnist at the Post-Intelligencer [the local newspaper]. . . . Feminist perspectives, that kind of thing" (p. 215). Walsh is described by Louise Fernandez as "a bitch. . . . Very unpleasant and very capable" (p. 224). Walsh writes a scathing column entitled "Mr. Piggy at Work" (p. 213), a thinly veiled commentary on the incident involving Sanders and Johnson. Walsh's "feminist perspective" in the commentary is openly hostile toward the male and not entirely accurate in reporting the facts as they have been presented to the reader:

> The power of the patriarchy has revealed itself again. . . .
> [Company X] has appointed a brilliant, highly competent woman

to a major executive position. But many men in the company are doing their damnedest to get rid of her.

One man in particular, let's call him Mr. Piggy, has been especially vindictive . . . he has been running a bitter campaign of innuendo inside the company to keep it from happening. When that failed, Mr. Piggy claimed that his new boss sexually assaulted him . . .

Some of you may wonder how a woman could rape a man. The answer is, of course, she can't. . . . [Rape] is exclusively a crime of males, who use rape . . . to keep women in their place . . .

For their part, women simply do not oppress men. Women are powerless in the hands of men. (pp. 213–14)

Walsh also is depicted as being unfair to another key character in the story, Louise Fernandez: [Walsh speaking to Fernandez] "Look. Maybe you've got some kind of a technical legal case here, and maybe you don't. But as far as I'm concerned, you're just another minority woman trying to get ahead with the patriarchy by getting down on her knees. If you had any self-respect you wouldn't be doing their dirty work for them" (p. 286). Thus the one character who is explicitly denoted a "feminist" is characterized very negatively and as noncredible. Additionally, the views she espouses are portrayed as partial and dogmatic. The implication is that Crichton's postfeminist perspective is, in contrast, impartial and nondogmatic.

The fourth example in *Disclosure* that displays Crichton's antifeminism occurs when he contrasts men's perspectives with that of women's in the "contemporary climate" (p. 218). The "chilly climate" long documented for women in professional settings and the dangerous climate of domestic violence for women in many homes are largely ignored by Crichton. Instead, we learn of the "chilly climate" that feminists have created for men in society. In this environment, "men were assumed to be guilty of anything they were accused of" (p. 218):

Don't smile at a child on the street, unless you're with your wife. Don't ever touch a strange child. . . . If Susan [Sanders's wife] saw a child crying on the street, she picked the kid up. She did it automatically, without thinking. Sanders would never dare. Not these days. . . . And it was prudent to be careful around your own children, too, because if your marriage went sour, your wife might accuse you. . . . Sanders knew men who would not take a business trip with a woman, who would not sit next to a female colleague on an airplane. . . . This was a world of regulations and penalties entirely unknown to women. (p. 218)

It is a tough world for men these days, Crichton implies, and feminists are largely to blame. Thus Crichton's self-declared egalitarian treatment of a feminist perspective can be read as a backlash to such a perspective. From a critical perspective, regardless of Crichton's claimed political intentions, as a rhetorical matter his text functions ideologically to perpetuate patriarchal beliefs that contribute to an antifeminist backlash on the subject of sexual harassment.

CHAPTER 6

Quitting "Man"

Masculinity, Film Criticism, and Pedagogy

Some years ago I was asked by the chair of the Women's Studies Department at our university to offer a course that would provide a feminist perspective on masculinity and film. At that point in time, courses that focused on masculinity were rare, and we felt that examining a popular culture medium would be attractive to students. So far I have taught the class five times over a period of 8 years, each time providing a feminist perspective to analyze portrayals of sex and gender in film with a particular emphasis on how men and masculinity can be represented. In this chapter, I describe the course and its theoretical orientation, and I report the results of qualitative and quantitative data gathered on several occasions.[1] I offer this chapter as an example of what has come to be called the "scholarship of teaching and learning" (SOTL). Typically associated with suggestions made in Ernest L. Boyer's (1990) *Scholarship Reconsidered*, SOTL is viewed as an intervention into the usual research and teaching dichotomy in order to broaden notions of scholarship while encouraging an enrichment of teaching practices.

The course, titled "Masculinity & Film," meets once a week for 3 hours. Class begins with a lecture of about 60 minutes, followed by a short break, followed by a film viewing. Films are shown on a fairly large screen with the room darkened to imitate the experience of attending a movie theatre. Students write a short reaction paper about each film (due the following week) that focuses on gender representation and what are described as the rhetorical functions of the film. Students also take a midterm and final exam that cover the readings and lecture material.

Students are encouraged to consider, first, how films construct different notions of gender. Over the first weeks of class, students are assigned the whole of Sandra L. Bem's book *The Lenses of Gender* (1993). Coupled with lectures that contrast an essentialist understanding of gender to a social constructionist approach, the initial goal of the course is to encourage students to reflect on what the words "masculine," "feminine," "undifferentiated," and "androgynous" mean to them and to contemporary U.S. society. To aid in this process, students are introduced to masculine and feminine items on Bem's (1974) Sex Role Inventory (SRI), as well as the gender norms identified in the Conformity to Masculine Norms Inventory and the Conformity to Feminine Norms Inventory (Mahalik et al., 2003, 2005). The point of taking a social constructionist approach is to emphasize that gender norms are fluid and historically situated. Examples range from historical examples (makeup and wigs were once common for upper- and middle-class men, knitting was men's work, etc.) to cross-cultural comparisons (social acceptability of men crying, for example) to recent research indicating that most study participants no longer view many of Bem's SRI items as gendered (Hoffman & Borders, 2001). The idea of "hegemonic masculinity" is introduced, but students are taught about Toby Miller's assessment (1998) that the idea of hegemonic masculinity should be set aside in favor of more specific, historical analyses of how masculinity and sexuality are performed and responded to.

Given the fluidity and historical contingency of cultural understandings of gender, the role of popular media, such as film, in depicting gender becomes salient. Students are encouraged to note how leading and important supporting characters are developed with respect to their performance of, or resistance to, gender norms. That is, are men rewarded or punished by acting in traditionally masculine ways? As noted in chapter 5, the enjoyment of media content is usually a function of a viewer's emotional disposition toward characters and the outcomes experienced by those characters as a narrative unfolds. While there are obviously important exceptions, most viewers tend to enjoy a film when good things happen to sympathetic characters and bad things happen to villains. My contention, developed in lectures and described in the previous chapter as vicarious operant conditioning, is that it is the interplay among character attributes, choices, and consequences presented in film that functions rhetorically to encourage or discourage particular gender norms. As argued in the previous chapter, for example, the main character of *Disclosure* is portrayed sympathetically. When he "acts like a man" in the film's last act, he succeeds and—if the film has been successful in promoting our identification with the protagonist—the audience enjoys and symbolically shares in his success. The persuasive message might be glossed as "act like a man," but students are encouraged in their papers to identify the specific masculine norms promoted by the film, such as making work primary, controlling one's emotions, winning, exercising power over women, taking risks, and being self-reliant. Gender messages also can be negative, such as when characters are unsuccessful or even punished for violating particular gender norms. Vicarious operant conditioning can be culturally progressive by rewarding gender bending and tolerance, for example, or culturally regressive by punishing gender bending or rewarding intolerance.

Next, students are encouraged to explore *how* the film succeeds (or fails) in making the key characters appealing or unappealing, that is, which elements of the story's structure, dialogue, actions, and characterizations succeed (or fail) in "coaching" a particular response from the audience? Material from sources such as Robert McKee's influential book *Story: Substance, Structure, Style, and the Principles of Screenwriting* (1997) is particularly useful in this regard.

Finally, students are encouraged to think of themselves as critics. That is, with an increased range of analytical and theoretical tools, along with the practice they gain by writing weekly papers, students are encouraged to see themselves as critics who can make thoughtful and persuasive claims about the rhetorical, aesthetic, or ethical dimensions of popular film. In addition to empowering the students directly, I also emphasize that many of them will become (if they are not already) parents who have a responsibility to teach their children critical media literacy. As part of the process of seeing themselves as critics, the idea that the "same" film text can be read in multiple, even contradictory, ways also is taught. In particular, with several films the student's task is to make an argument for one of two contrary readings, as I explain later.

The course has three goals that are made explicit in the course syllabus: first, to enhance students' understanding of basic principles of film theory and criticism, including an introduction to classical and contemporary theories of how film influences viewers and different critical positions that can be taken toward socially relevant film; second, to enhance students' understanding of basic theories of gender representation, including an introduction to essentialism versus social constructionism as theories and as modes of representation, and third, to influence students' attitudes. As a feminist I do not simply want students to learn what "hegemonic masculinity" means—I also want students to think that it is a bad idea because certain traits traditionally coded as masculine encourage destructive and oppressive behavior. Furthermore, drawing from Susan Faludi's *Stiffed* (2000), I make it clear that men are harmed by masculine stereotypes as well.[2] In short, I want to deconstruct an essentialized notion of masculinity, encourage students to recognize that coding behavior by gender is a socially and historically contingent

practice, and increase students' acceptance of a range of gender performance and sexual preferences. My goals are in the spirit of Barry Brummett's suggestion that "the business of rhetorical scholars is to teach
people how to expand their repertoires for making experience and to
show that the awareness that expanded repertoires must entail are subversive" (1991, p. xxiii).

I should make it clear that "no students were harmed in the making
of this class." The syllabus makes the feminist and social constructionist
themes of the course explicit. By providing fair notice of the goals of the
course, students whose religious beliefs (for example) might be in conflict with such themes understand what they will be hearing if they decide
to take the course. Students are treated respectfully if they disagree with
statements made in lecture or discussion. Papers are not graded on the
basis of ideological conformity but on how well a student makes *case* for
a particular reading or position. The feedback I have received over the
years suggests that students do not feel browbeaten or preached to. At
the same time, I suspect I am cut slack because I am a straight male. The
same words coming from an apparently gay male or from a female probably would face more resistance than I have encountered thus far.

A Sample List of Films

Because the list of films watched varies from semester to semester, a brief
description of a particular semester's offerings is in order. I describe the
films shown in the fall semester of 2003 because, as will be discussed
later, it is the semester in which I gathered data about students' attitudes.

With one exception, I attempt to select films for the class that are not
stereotypically macho films. My assumption, which students have supported when asked, is that they are already quite familiar with various
icons of filmic masculinity, such as John Wayne, Bruce Willis, or Arnold
Schwarzenegger. Rather, the persistent theme of the course was that
"masculinity" is not a fixed idea or set of norms, and that a range of masculinities is performed in any given culture at any given time. We began
by viewing *The Thin Man* (1932) to feature William Powell's suave but
playful Nick Charles. Powell's character is easily coded as "masculine," but
it is a performance of masculinity quite different than, say, Humphrey
Bogart's Sam Spade of *The Maltese Falcon* (1941). The second film viewed
was *High Noon* (1952), which is the one film chosen precisely because
Gary Cooper's portrayal of Will Kane is traditionally masculine. At this
point in the course the students are introduced to Bem's (1974) Sex Role
Inventory and the Conformity to Masculine and Feminine Norms Inventories (Mahalik et al., 2003, 2005). These lists of attributes provided the
class with a common vocabulary with which to discuss masculinity without

oversimplifying the concept or treating it ahistorically. By using the 20 items scored as "Masculine" on the BSRI, for example, students had a ready-made set of norms with which they could compare and contrast different performances of masculinity in subsequent films.

The other films viewed are listed here with a brief rationale for why they were included. *Shane* (1953) was used to introduce psychoanalytic film theory and was the first of several films that was open to a "queer" reading. During lecture, a brief case was made for a queer reading by contrasting Alan Ladd's almost feminine appearance with the contemporaneous appearance of Gary Cooper in *High Noon*, as well as providing a brief reading of various scenes as homoerotic. Typically this is the point in the semester when even the bored students become engaged, as they have the opportunity in their reaction papers to amplify or *critique* a queer reading. It is a pivotal, empowering moment when the idea of "contested readings" becomes concretized for them.

Some Like It Hot (1959) was used to introduce the idea of gender performance, cross-dressing, and gender bending, plus it is a terrific film. Students are encouraged to ponder whether the central characters, played by Tony Curtis and Jack Lemon, become better *persons* as a result of adapting their behavior to pass as women in their cross-dressing experience. Early in the film, both characters objectify and try to manipulate women; by the end, arguably, they are less traditionally masculine but better human beings. Students also have the option of writing their papers to analyze the famous last two lines of the movie, in which Jack Lemon's "Jerry" tries to persuade Joey Lewis's character, Osgood, that he cannot marry him. Jerry: "Oh, you don't understand, Osgood! Ehhhh . . . (pulls off his wig) I'm a man." Osgood's expression does not change as he shrugs slightly and says, "Well, nobody's perfect."

Boyz N the Hood (1991) was used to discuss the intersections between race and masculinity. The pre-film lecture describes stereotypes of Black men and women in film, and television and cultivation theory is introduced to frame a description of empirical research that has been done on the effects of past representations (Entman & Rojecki, 2000). For this film's paper, students are encouraged to explore the film's linkages of Black masculinity and violence and gender and fatherhood and to use this opportunity to analyze how they themselves perform gender and race.

After viewing the documentary *Bowling for Columbine* (2002), students were encouraged to write reaction papers in the form of a memo to filmmaker Michael Moore about how a consideration of masculinity would have enhanced his analysis of violence in the United States. I have since replaced this film with a fascinating documentary made by local filmmaker Emily Goldberg, *Venus of Mars* (2003), which chronicles the life of a local rock musician who has chosen to remain a pre-op transsexual in order to remain married to his lifelong love. This film has been an excellent addition, in part because the filmmaker is willing to meet with the class after the viewings.

For *Glengarry Glen Ross* (1992), students were encouraged to consider whether the film is a celebration or a critique of "hegemonic masculinity." Students are required to define what they mean by the term and to make a case for their particular reading of the film. The documentary *Crumb* (1995) was used to talk about the influence of childhood on psychosexual development, and on the relationship between pop culture and gender politics.

The Full Monty (1997) is a rich text that facilitates discussion of a number of topics. First, the film was used to introduce Laura Mulvey's (1975) notion of "the gaze," since a good deal of what drives the movie is the discomfort the men experience as they become the object of the gaze. Second, students are encouraged to examine the relationship between gender and fatherhood, in particular, to think about whether traditional norms of masculinity help or hinder men from being a good parent. Third, the film plays with stereotypes, as it is the African Englishman who is most concerned with his penis size, and the best-endowed man in the group is gay. Such portrayals invite viewers to ponder the stereotypical linkage between manliness and penis size.

Fight Club (1999) is a film that engages issues of masculinity in a number of ways. In addition to using the film to discuss "preferred," "negotiated," and "resistant" readings (Hall, 1980), I also use this week to introduce students to a McLuhanesque approach to communication technology. An excellent essay by Robert Brookey and Robert Westerfelhaus (2002) is used to discuss queer readings of mainstream films and the use of DVD technology by film producers to limit resistant readings. *Smoke Signals* (1998) was used to encourage students to consider how different masculinities are performed by "contemporary American Indians." Viewing the film affords an opportunity to introduce students to the ways in which the various indigenous tribes of the Northern Hemisphere have been represented oversimplistically both linguistically (with such generalizing labels as "contemporary American Indians") and through the stereotypical representations common throughout most of the history of film. This film also facilitates a discussion of Whiteness.

The Adventures of Priscilla, Queen of the Desert (1995) was used to discuss homosexuality and transgender issues. The film provides an excellent opportunity to discuss issues of gender nonconformity, myths about the origins of homosexuality, fatherhood and gender, and, above all, gender performance. Alternatively, Vito Russo's (1987) *The Celluloid Closet* provides a useful historical chronicle of gay representations in film, and again there is an opportunity to draw on empirical research regarding the influence of stereotypical representations (Shanahan & Morgan, 1999).

The last viewing was not of a film, but of the Emmy Award-winning HBO comedy special by transvestite Eddie Izzard, titled *Dress to Kill* (1999). This is shown in the last regular class meeting, which also functions as a review for the final exam. The key themes of the class are emphasized: to recognize the complexity of masculinities, to read movies critically, to question essentialism, gender polarization, and androcentrism, and to reconsider an understanding of gender norms. Students are urged to pay attention to the explicit "category work" that Izzard does with respect to the category "transvestites" and to use the last paper to discuss whether they found Izzard disturbing or a refreshing alternative performance of masculinity.

Did the Course Change Attitudes?

Curious about whether the course was actually influencing students attitudes, I decided to gather data from the 98 students enrolled in the class during the fall 2003 semester. Doing so was an eye-opening experience and a reality check on how much difference a one-semester course may or may not make. Though the course provided students with information about a number of subjects, including film, gender, and media theory, the basic research question was this: Does a class that uses film to explore masculinity influence student attitudes about men and masculinity? There were two sets of attitudes that we thought the course might influence: the first included attitudes about specific norms associated with masculinity, the second attitudes about specific categories of people, such as male homosexuals and transvestites.

To measure attitudes concerning specific masculine attributes, I selected the Conformity to Masculine Norms Inventory, or CMNI (Mahalik et al., 2003), because it appeared to be the most comprehensive instrument available, and the wording of the items was easy to adapt for male and female students. The CMNI attempts to measure levels of individual conformity to socially dominant gender role expectations for masculinity. Drawing on reviews of scholarly literature on traditional masculine norms in the United States and focus group research, Mahalik and his colleagues developed 11 subscales that I initially listed in chapter 1. The *Disdain for Homosexuality* subscale consisted of 10 items emphasizing others' perception of the person as straight (such as "It is important to me that people think I am heterosexual"). The *Self-Reliance* subscale consisted of six items emphasizing one's own independence (such as "I hate asking for help"). The *Violence* subscale consisted of eight items emphasizing pleasure from or approval of violent acts (such as "I like fighting"). The *Winning* subscale consisted of 10 items emphasizing the importance of winning (such as "In general, I will do anything to win"). The *Emotional Control* subscale consisted of 11 items emphasizing keeping one's emotions in check (such as "It is best to keep your emotions hidden"). The *Risk-Taking* subscale consisted of 11 items emphasizing dangerous actions as a way to be masculine (such as "Taking dangerous risks helps me prove myself"). The *Power over Women* subscale consisted of nine items emphasizing controlling women (such as "Things tend to be better when men are in charge"). The *Dominance* subscale consisted of four items emphasizing control over others in general (such as "I should be in charge"). The *Playboy* subscale consisted of 12 items emphasizing promiscuity (such as "If I could, I would frequently change sexual partners"). The *Primacy of Work* subscale consisted of eight items emphasizing work's importance to the individual (such as "I am often absorbed in my work"). The *Pursuit of Status* subscale consisted of six items emphasizing the significance of social status (such as "It feels good to be important").

Results from Mahalik and his colleagues (2003) indicated strong internal consistency for all subscales. Furthermore, their research indicated that the CMNI produced results consistent with other measures of masculine norms, including the Brannon Masculinity Scale (Brannon & Juni, 1984), the Gender Role Conflict Scale (O'Neil, Helms, Gable, David, & Wrightsman, 1986), and the Masculine Gender Role Stress Scale (Eisler & Skidmore, 1987). In the data I collected with my colleagues Peter Gregg and Martin Lang, the subscales proved equally consistent.[3]

To assess attitudes toward male homosexuals, we selected the five-item version of Gregory Herek's (1984, 1988, 1994) Attitudes towards Gay Men (ATG) instrument, described in earlier chapters. We also used an unpublished heteronormativity scale (Hetnorm) created by Peter Gregg, which consisted of six items stating or challenging heteronormative beliefs (such as "Homosexual families are unnatural"), derived from previous research on the concept (Connell, 1995; Hird & Jackson, 2001; Kimmel, 1997).[4] Two survey items were devised to assess whether students were able to dissociate transvestitism from homosexuality. These items were "Transvestites are probably just confused homosexuals," and "Men who wear women's clothing want other men to be attracted."[5]

As mentioned earlier, 98 students registered for the class. On the first day of class, the students completed a survey that included standard demographic questions along with the ATG, Hetnorm, CMNI, and transvestitism items described earlier. On the final day of class, the survey was repeated. For each survey, students were asked to provide a special code number based on a combination of digits from their social security and student ID numbers to allow for pairing of pretests and posttests. Apparently, a number of students did not know one number or the other, or could not follow the directions provided, as we were able to match up only 53 surveys from the pretests and posttest (28 females, 23 males, 2 unspecified; average age 21.9).

The student reaction papers were kept by the instructor for this particular semester. The instructor and one of the course's graduate teaching assistants read through the papers to identify passages in which students explicitly discussed their attitudes about masculinity, homosexuality, and transvestitism.

I describe the results of the quantitative data by each survey subscale we used. *Attitudes about Homosexuality* and *Heteronormativity:* Students indicated lower levels of prejudice in the posttest than they did the pretest on the measures concerned with homosexuality and heteronormativity, and the differences were statistically significant. Overall, the students registered less negative attitudes toward gay men when completing ATG items on the posttest than they did in the pretest. Notably, when sorted by sex, our results showed a significant change among the males, but not females. Similarly, students as a whole indicated less heteronormative attitudes on the Hetnorm scale than in the pretest. When sorted by sex, again the results indicated a statistically significant change among males, but not females. *Transvestitism:* The results demonstrated that participants connected homosexuality and transvestitism less in the posttest than did the pretest group. When sorted by sex, significant change was found among males as well as females.

CMNI: When data from the class as a whole were considered, only 2 of the 11 subscales of the CMNI showed change. Quite unexpectedly, the results for the *Violence* scale indicated slightly *more* conformity to the masculine norm of the acceptability of violence in the posttest than in the pretest group. In contrast, the results demonstrated *less* conformity between the masculine norm regarding *Self-Reliance* in the posttest than in the pretest group. Significant changes were not found with any other subscales.

The two statistically significant changes were found when we included data from the class as a whole. Interestingly, when data were analyzed looking only at males or only at females in the class, there were no significant changes between the pretest and posttest results of the CMNI subscales.

Though the papers written by students in the class were, no doubt, crafted in part to please the course instructors, some of their comments are useful in terms of understanding the results just described. In particular, we focused on comments in student papers written in response to two viewings—transvestite Eddie Izzard's *Dress to Kill* and *The Adventures of Priscilla, Queen of the Desert.*

The vast majority of students indicated that they enjoyed Izzard's stand-up routine a great deal. A number of students credited the class for encouraging them to give Izzard a fair hearing. For example, one male student commented, "Before this class started I was not well informed about masculinity in society. If I watched Izzard's stand-up before this, I wouldn't have laughed because of who he is. [With] the knowledge I gained, I was able to look beyond what he looked like and really listen to what he had to say."

Most students' comments in reaction to Izzard's transvestitism can be put into two categories: Some students openly acknowledged his transvestitism and suggested that he influenced their understanding of transvestites, while others maintained that they quickly "forgot" his transvestite status. As an example of the first category, one female student suggested, "Izzard definitely changed my view, I'm sure, on the intellectual and humorous capabilities of cross-dressing comedians." Such an admission is noteworthy, as people are more likely to claim that a particular message persuaded others than they are to admit it may have persuaded them.[6] A male commented, "I think people like Izzard are important in the transformation of society's norms." Another male student commented specifically on Izzard's credibility: "Izzard's rundown of American and world history shows his intelligence and reiterates the fact that transvestites are just like everyone else."

The following comment was typical of the second category: "I really enjoyed Izzard's *Dress to Kill* stand-up routine. I was taken aback a little when he came out dressed like an Asian whore, but after about 10 minutes of laughing my head off at his jokes I didn't see a man dressed as a woman telling jokes, but a comedian telling jokes." A female student noted, "At the end of the film *Dress to Kill*, a comedic stand-up routine, I realized I was never consciously aware that the main character, Eddie Izzard, was performing the entire time in drag." A male student commented, "After about 2 minutes I nearly forgot Eddie Izzard was a transvestite." A female student's comment was typical of many others: "Basically after the initial reaction of Eddie's appearance being unexpected and unfamiliar, you don't think about it."

While the vast majority of students' comments were positive, there were a few dissenters whose comments suggested that they were unpersuaded by the film or the class lectures. One male student stated, "It was very uncomfortable to watch a man dressed like that do stand-up. I rather like the idea of hegemonic masculinity and don't feel that Izzard is a nice alternative."

Students' comments in reaction to *The Adventures of Priscilla, Queen of the Desert* were also strongly positive. As argued in chapter 4, viewing sympathetic or positive portrayals of gay characters can reduce prejudice (see also Riggle, Ellis, & Crawford, 1996). The students' comments suggest that the combination of class content and the viewing of the film may have led to the observed reduction in reported prejudice and heteronormativity described earlier. One male student notes that *Priscilla* "exemplified a number of different constructions of sexual identity and really showed that drag queens aren't necessarily that different from the average person." A female student claimed, "The movie did a great job of making us love characters that are not 100% in the mainstream. . . . A movie like this could even work with someone like my grandfather, someone who has very conservative, old-school beliefs."

Another female student suggested, "The characters made me feel comfortable with them, and that is the reason I was able to let go of inhibitions that I had and see the movie for what it was—a deeper look into how and why homosexuality is such a big part of our culture today. The main characters' battles with their own gender identity pulled me in."

In their reactions to the film, some students drew directly from lecture material concerning Queer Theory and the idea that gender is performed. One female student reported, "The film allowed me to recognize the possibility that gender may only be a performance. Perhaps gender does not exist beyond those 'acts'." Another female student noted, "The movie illustrates a variety of different people acting out their particular gender in different ways. . . . What I learned in lecture is that even [though] I am an actual girl, I am 'performing' my gender the same way the drag queen is."

Reflections

I begin with the data concerned with norms about masculinity as measured by the CMNI. I can only speculate as to why, for the class as a whole, there was a slight increase in conformity to the norm of the acceptability of *Violence*. Though some of the films included antiviolence themes (*Boyz N the Hood*), violence was part of the hero's success in such films as *High Noon*, *Shane*, and *Fight Club*. And, of course, messages about the efficacy of violence as a means to an end permeate our culture, especially during the war in Iraq that dominated 2003. I also can only speculate as to why there was slightly less conformity with the norm of *Self-Reliance*. Certainly many films highlighted the need for cooperation, such as *The Full Monty* and *The Adventures of Priscilla, Queen of the Desert*, but the data are insufficient to attribute any change in attitude to the viewings of these films. From a methodological perspective, clearly the data would have more meaning had we conducted parallel pretest and posttest data from a control group. It also is possible that our limited sample size inhibited our ability to detect changes, since *t*-tests of several items approached but did not reach significance.

I suspect, in retrospect, that the content of the class remained at a level of abstraction that most students did not interpret as a specific challenge to their own views about specific masculine norms. That is, though students may understand that "masculinity" is a socially constructed notion that varies from culture to culture, from time period to time period, such knowledge did not motivate them to reconsider their own conformity to norms of masculinity and femininity. As Herek (1986, 1987) might put it, a change in beliefs about the world, which he describes as serving an "experiential-schematic" function, does not necessarily require changes in beliefs that serve an expressive function of defining one's identity. Put another way, while students may understand that an essentialist approach to gender is flawed, this belief did not "trickle down" to a change in their specific perceptions about what are desirable qualities in contemporary culture. This is a noteworthy realization, because it suggests for classes with a feminist agenda that there is likely to be resistance to efforts to resocialize students as to how they ought to see their own gender performance.

Though in general personal norms about masculinity did not appear to be altered by the class, we find it noteworthy that students' attitudes about specific categories of people *did* change, specifically, their attitudes toward gay men, heteronormativity, and transvestitism and homosexuality. The results in these areas are consistent with the parasocial contact hypothesis, described in chapter 4. Comments in student papers provide anecdotal evidence that exposure to in-class films did, in fact, encourage students to reconsider their beliefs about homosexuality and transvestitism.

I remain hopeful that classes that bring together elements of communication and gender theory with specific popular culture artifacts can not only serve to increase students' critical media literacy (though that certainly would be a worthwhile endeavor by itself) but also can prompt students to reconsider their specific beliefs about appropriate gender norms—if not for themselves, then perhaps for their children. I also am convinced that approaching such classes with a quasi-experimental design (Shadish, Cook, & Campbell, 2001) to assess student outcomes not only generates interesting data but also can become a valuable part of the teaching process itself. To adapt a famous movie line, one has to know one's limitations.

PART 3

Conclusions

CHAPTER 7

Beyond Representational Correctness

Five Suggestions

How do we move beyond Representational Correctness? In this conclud-
ing chapter I want to synthesize the arguments advanced throughout the
book and address relevant issues that I have not yet discussed. I offer
these points as suggestions to those interested in professional criticism of
popular media in general, and to my fellow academics in particular.

1. Avoid unrealistic expectations, and move beyond debates over stereotypes.
   My argument that we should avoid falling into the trap I have labeled
Representational Correctness is not motivated by a belief that representations should not be critiqued—indeed, I firmly believe that they should
be. My point is that the criteria for judging representations cannot be purity, innocence, and simultaneity, which add up to an *omnia perfectissima*
standard that no representation can ever meet. As I suggested in chapters 4, 5, and 6, we need to look at the specific work that popular media
do in specific contexts.
   Other scholars, most notably Stuart Hall, have critiqued Plato's version of RC that is informed by the correspondence theory of truth—a representation is faulty if it does not accurately correspond to, or authentically
depict, how a particular social group "really is." Hall (1992, 1997) is critical
of such an approach to representation, because it assumes that an object,
an event, or a social group has "meaning" that stands outside of human
communication. They do not, he suggests, until represented in visual
or auditory language. As Kenneth Burke would say, the object, event, or social group must be "entitled" *as* an object, an event, or a social group to be

meaningful (1966, pp. 359–79). Or, as Hall puts it, "Representation is *constitutive* of the event" (in Jhally, 1997).

As Hall notes, once one moves to such a "constitutive" approach, the meaning of representations becomes less stable: "Since they're likely to be very different as you move from one person to another, one group or another, one part of society or another, one historical moment and another—just as those forms of representation will change, so the meaning of the event will change" (in Jhally, 1997). Such instability is, of course, the key reason Hall (1980) advanced his influential description of three different decoding positions—preferred, negotiated, and oppositional. To know what sort of political and cultural work a popular media artifact is accomplishing requires audience research to ascertain how such texts are being "read": "It remains for empirical work to say, in relation to a particular text and a particular section of the audience, which readings operate" (Hall, in "Reflections," 1994, p. 265).

If we move away from Representational Correctness, beyond charges of stereotyping, and toward asking questions about category attributes and social judgments prompted by popular media, then we can find a path out of what I think are otherwise irreconcilable differences about individual representations. As an example, I want to return to the clash over representations of African Americans introduced in chapter 1 that can be found in the writings of Donald Bogle and John McWhorter.

Bogle is the author of several enormously influential treatises on popular media representations of African Americans. In *Toms, Coons, Mulattoes, Mammies and Bucks: An Interpretive History of Blacks in American Films*, now in its fourth edition, Bogle (2001b) provides a sometimes depressing chronicle of the persistence of negative stereotypes throughout the history of film in the United States. What is not clear, however, is what would count as a positive representation. Though Bogle praises individual performances, he spends only a paragraph on the book's last page describing the future characteristics of "what goes into the making of a decent, humane black film" (p. 433).[1] As Bogle makes clear in the preface to the first edition, "The thesis of my book is that *all* black actors—from Stepin Fetchit to Rex Ingram to Lena Horne to Sidney Poitier and Jim Brown—have played stereotyped roles. But the essence of black film history is not found in the stereotyped role but in what certain talented actors have done with the stereotype" (1994, p. xxiii, emphasis added).[2] More often than not, "new" representations are described as variations of old, stereotypical themes. Similarly, in his book on African Americans on network television, Bogle (2001a) charts the "fundamental racism" and "misinterpretation of African American life" that underlay "much of what appeared on the tube" (p. 4). As reviewers of *Primetime Blues* noted, despite bright moments of praise, the overall tone of the book is "despairing" (Tucker, 2001), and Bogle appears "torn" between a desire for what I have described as Representational Correctness, on the one hand, and, on the other hand, the acknowledgment that the commercial needs of network television will always lead to compromise (Anderson, 2001).

Conservative critic John McWhorter (2003) argues that Bogle's book *Primetime Blues* pigeonholes "almost every black contribution to series television from 1970 to 2000 into one of several stereotype categories" (p. 116). McWhorter's critique is similar to the argument I advanced in chapter 1, where I noted that some media critics create a double bind that categorizes performances either as inaccurate (or, in this case, "inauthentic") or stereotypical: "The problem with Bogle's framework is that as it is constructed, it is all but impossible for any black performance to pass as kosher. Instead, it becomes a 'damned if they do, damned if they don't' exercise" (p. 118). McWhorter alleges that Bogle creates a number of such double binds: Nurturing Black women are "Mammies," while feisty ones are "Sapphires" (from *Amos 'n' Andy*). Black men who cooperate with White men are either Toms or deracialized, while the alternative seems to be the stereotype of the "Angry Black Man" (pp. 104–37).

Setting aside the politics fueling McWhorter's critique, the point he makes is one that media critics should take seriously. There is a problem with the pattern of inference often employed to make critical claims. One starts with a definition of a stereotype, such as Bogle's description of Bucks: "Bucks are always big, baadddd [n-word]s, oversexed and savage, violent and frenzied as they lust for white flesh" (2001b, pp. 13–14). We learn how to define and use a category through exposure to "prototypical exemplars" (Schiappa, 2003). In the case of media stereotypes, critics learn to recognize a stereotype in part by exposure to an uncontroversial example of the category, such as the characters of Lynch and Gus in *The Birth of a Nation* or characters from the first television show with an all-Black cast, *Amos 'n' Andy*. Once it is established that the category of Stereotype X has a Y attribute, critics can then apply the label "stereotype" to subsequent performances where a character exemplifies a Y attribute. Such reasoning is analogical, of course, since two performances are never identical. The argument is usually that character so-and-so is *like* a previous, uncontested exemplar. It may not take much, therefore, to code a representation in a stereotypical category, such as toms, coons, or bucks for African American males.

For example, if it is sufficient to brand a representation as an instance of the "buck" stereotype when the character is male and (sometimes) violent (X has attributes Y_1 and Y_2), then, along with Bogle, we end up categorizing performances as diverse as Laurence Fishburne's Ike Turner in

What's Love Got to Do with It?, Mr. T as *The A-Team's* B. A. Baracus, and Wesley Snipe's Simon Phoenix in the futuristic sci-fi film *Demolition Man* as "bucks" (Bogle, 2001a, p. 270; 2001b, pp. 272, 408–10). If one attribute is considered a sufficient condition to qualify a performance as stereotypical, then the elasticity of such pejorative categories is such that a "positive" representation becomes almost impossible to identify. Take Black male comedians, for example. J. J. "Dyn-o-mite" Walker on *Good Times* is categorized by Bogle as exemplifying "coonery," Redd Foxx on *Sanford and Son* replayed Kingfish from *Amos 'n' Andy*, Sherman Hemsley's George Jefferson "seemed an update on the exaggerated comic coon" (2001a, pp. 189, 203, 212), and Eddie Murphy's early movies are "essentially coon roles" (2001b, p. 286). Bill Cosby's performance in *The Cosby Show* and Flip Wilson's outrageous character Geraldine are among the few that earn Bogle's approval, but in both cases Bogle is sure to quote criticisms, including one critic's comment that Cosby "no longer qualifies as black enough to be an Uncle Tom" (2001a, p. 295).

To return to the argument made in chapter 3, it is up to critics to decide which attributes and textual features are rhetorically salient in their decoding of particular popular media. My concern is that the combination of (1) elastic categories, (2) argument by (loose) analogy, and (3) a political economy of criticism that tends to value negative assessments more than positive ones can lead to an interpretive flexibility that makes it less likely that critics will ever perceive any progress in representations of minorities. The parasocial contact hypothesis suggests one possible way to move beyond the "Can You Find the Stereotype?" game. The solution may be to look at the category attributes audiences are learning and the social judgments they make to consider the cultural and social psychological work of specific representations.

Moreover, as the studies described in this book suggest, one can examine the relationship between such attributes and judgments and corresponding attitudes about minority groups with *specific* audiences. In general, the word "stereotype" ought to be defined as "a pejorative overgeneralization," and the labels for *particular* categories of stereotypes ought to be used in a more limited fashion to identify (1) a set of specific category-attribute beliefs that (2) we have reason to believe contribute to invidious attitudes.[3] The issue is not a context-free question of what sort of representation of homosexuality is "too gay" or "not gay enough," or what racial representations are "deracialized" or "stereotypical," but an audience-specific question of what sorts of category attributes and social judgments increase or decrease prejudice. Finding the answer will give us an empirical basis by which to distinguish between harmful stereotypes and more benign social types.

2. Seek a productive synthesis of different methods and theories.

Academic media critics trained in semiotic or textual analysis are typically well versed in critical and cultural theory informed by poststructuralist approaches to language and meaning. This has had a somewhat odd, unanticipated result, as noted by Hall. In a discussion of the influence of deconstruction and psychoanalytic theory on critical theory, he notes that such developments expand "our understanding of just how complex meaning really is, and how many different sites of determination are involved in it. So we know a lot more about it, but actually we are less secure in giving that an empirical and demonstrably empirical moment of research. And that is one of the reasons that one of the problems just now is that everybody nowadays is, surprisingly after thirty years, a literary critic" (Hall, 1994, p. 273). The irony, of course, is that the more complex the process of making meaning, the slippery the sign, the *more* need there is for audience research. We need the sensitive readers of texts to which Hall refers, but we also need critics willing to engage in some of the many available methods of investigating how audiences respond to such texts.

I have spent a good deal of time in this book advocating that we need to do more than provide our own readings of popular media texts *if* our ambitions include the desire to advance conjectures involving audiences. My point here is to call for greater dialogue among scholars with various theoretical and methodological orientations who share an interest in the role popular media play in advancing or hindering a more just and humane society. A literary critic of 19th-century American fiction may not need to conduct focus group discussions, craft surveys and interview schedules, or run an occasional regression analysis, but critics of popular media would benefit from such training. I argued earlier that critics should draw more from relevant theories in mass communication or social psychology, but having a dialogue requires at least two parties—those who self-identify as social scientists need greater familiarity with contemporary theory (critical, cultural, feminist, poststructuralist, queer theory, etc.) and more sensitivity to the text via rhetorical and semiotic analysis.

For example, those familiar with social scientific theories of mass communication effects know that the three major theoretical approaches—cultivation analysis, social learning theory, and the uses and gratifications perspective—imply very different visions of the audience. Indeed, advocates of one approach may criticize another approach precisely because the vision of the audience is too passive and pessimistic (cultivation analysis) or too active and optimistic (uses and "grats"). Meanwhile, media critics trained in more qualitative, textual, and humanistic approaches play out a similar debate between the advocates of "hegemony theory," who tend to see the audience as mostly passive and tend to have a pessimistic approach (since challenges to the dominant ideology are ultimately "contained" and absorbed), and scholars who agree with John Fiske (1989b) in seeing audiences as empowered, active agents who put the resources of popular culture to their own particular uses. Yet to my knowledge (and I very well may have missed something), there has not yet been a sustained effort to explore the connections between these two traditions. For example, if we use Hall's (1980) influential encoding/decoding vocabulary as exemplary, one possible (and admittedly highly speculative) mapping would be as follows:

> Preferred readings are to cultivation analysis as
> resistant readings are to uses and gratification theory.

An alternative mapping would vary according to one's object or unit of analysis. For example, part of the clash between textual and audience approaches toward *Will & Grace* discussed in chapter 3 can be understood as a clash between visions of the audience. Other than Linneman's focus on speech acts, the basic objects of analysis of the other studies were *characters* in the show. I think it is fair to characterize Shugart's (2003), Battles and Hilton-Morrow's (2002), and Mitchell's (2006) analyses as informed by hegemony/cultivation theory, which assume a fairly passive view of the audience. The audience studies by Schiappa, Gregg, and Hewes (2005), Ortiz and Harwood (2007), and Cooper (2003) take a more active view of the audience's ability to decode and learn from *Will & Grace*, and thus they fall more in the negotiated reading/social learning approach. It is not so much that audience research is "right" and textual analysis is "wrong" as it is arguably a matter of conceptual "fit." While hegemony/cultivation theory may work well to analyze the "big picture" of recurring plots and values, it may underestimate just how important characters are to people and may fail to recognize that making judgments about characters requires nearly identical cognitive processes as are used when meeting people face-to-face. Arguably, if the critical object of analysis involves the reception of *characters*, then a more active perspective will have greater explanatory power.

Similarly, since the available research suggests that certain attitudes are associated with liking specific genres, such as the association between attitudes about vigilantism and punitive punishment and the enjoyment of crime dramas (Raney & Bryant, 2002), it can be argued that a uses and gratifications approach may be most appropriate for those interested in the cultural work of genres.

In any case, the bottom line is that media critics and social scientists alike are dubious about what could be described as the null hypothesis of media effects; namely, that popular media do not matter at all and have zero influence on audiences' beliefs, attitudes, and behaviors. To the extent that they reject the null hypothesis, it makes sense to have a multifaceted framework that explains how texts do their work and what people do with them.

3. Praise the good stuff.

In part due to the impossible standards of Representational Correctness, critics of popular media rarely allow themselves to celebrate successful, mainstream films or television programs. Praise often is reserved for programs that enact an aesthetic and ideology that critics approve, but which were not successful commercially, such as the often-praised but seldom-seen television show *Frank's Place* (Bogle, 2001a, pp. 322–27) or art house films (especially those foreign produced) that in the United States reach primarily a small, mostly White, liberal, educated audience. I exaggerate, of course, but not by much.

Part of the reason for so few appreciative readings may be a function of the institutional political economy of academic media criticism, if not evolutionary psychology. After all, the evidence is fairly clear that negative information and evaluations, because they potentially represent a larger threat to our survival as animals, tend to generate greater brain activity, increased attention, and longer memory than positive information and evaluations.[4] Just as it would be difficult for me to publish this book if my primary claim was, "Hey, media critics are doing a great job!" it may feel to many media critics that it would be hard to publish laudatory criticism. It is more provocative and better demonstrates the critic's "added value" to engage an apparently progressive popular culture artifact and find fault with it. The more counterintuitive, the better.

Critics need to point to positive examples. If one cannot point to a more progressive direction, then one literally will go nowhere. I have presented some popular culture critics with the catch-22 described in chapter 1 and asked, what would be a good representation? What *should* television and film writers and producers do? The answer I received from some was that it was not their job to come up with an answer. I respectfully disagree. Not only do we need to celebrate socially productive representations, instead of constantly bemoaning how they are "contained" by one ism or another, we also need to be proactive about the direction in which film and television should go. Accounts of the development and reception of programming such as Julie D'Acci's (1994) study of *Cagney and Lacey* need to be multiplied, for example. If one does not like the triad of prejudice described earlier, fine, but one still needs a theoretical framework that explains why some representations are bad and others are *preferable*. We need to be imaginative: How could a television situation comedy encourage mobilization? How can we take advantage of the power of entertainment media to foster prosocial change?

There are, of course, examples of positive assessments offered by scholars of popular media. Interestingly, most of the good news has been about educational programming aimed at children. Programs including *Allegra's Window, Between the Lions, Blues Clues, Cyberchase, Dora the Explorer, Dragon Tales, The Electric Company, Gullah Gullah Island,* and, of course, *Sesame Street* have been proven to provide educational benefits to children viewing them (Fisch, 2004; Fisch & Truglio, 2004). Not all of the positive attention has been limited to children's programming, however, as there *are* critics who have found certain mainstream adult programming worthy of praise.[5]

4. Figure out how to live with capitalism.

I am no apologist for free-market capitalism in general, particularly with respect to the mass media. I concur with critics who note that unchecked capitalism especially in the form of media concentration diminishes political diversity in the drive for obscene profits, and it works against the best interests of a democracy (Bagdikian, 2004; McChesney, 1999). It also is hard to argue with claims that the profit motive of commercial television *generally* (though not *always*) discourages innovation and risk taking (Jhally & Lewis, 1992, p. 143) and privileges entertainment over enlightenment (Postman, 1985), and that a "liberal media" in the United States is a myth (Herman, 1999).

Despite the problems associated with media capitalism, criticism that begins and ends with an anticapitalist rhetoric seems not only naïve but ultimately disempowering.[6] I agree with Celeste Condit's admonition that critics should recognize the material problems facing many citizens, and that we need to advocate "turning the mixed economy to the advantage of those who are less advantaged, protecting the environment in all feasible ways, and understanding and protecting gender, racial, and ethnic diversity" (1996, p. 383). At the same time, we need to avoid what Richard Rorty describes as "the point of view of a detached cosmopolitan spectator" lamenting the evils of "late capitalism" as if "we can just wait for capitalism to collapse" (1998, p. 103).[7] What we need are critical interventions that not only identify the pernicious effects of capitalism but point to reasonable alternatives, and that take note of when the profit motive can be channeled into progressive directions. As Rorty notes, "The public, sensibly, has no interest in getting rid of capitalism until it is offered details about the alternatives" (p. 104). Though I know that some of my critical theorist colleagues may cringe when reading this, I agree with Rorty when he suggests that "the Left should get back into the business of piecemeal reform within the framework of a market economy" (p. 105).

Some analyses of popular culture follow the example of Sut Jhally and Justin Lewis in *Enlightened Racism* (1992), in their judgment, *The Cosby Show*, ultimately because it props up the American Dream that we live in a classless society in which rugged individuals can succeed if they try hard enough. It may have undercut racist essentialist and polarizing beliefs, but that was not good enough for Jhally and Lewis, because for them White privilege is first and foremost an economic privilege; as long as capitalism is intact, so is racism.[8] Lamenting that "the bland repetition of feelgood fantasies makes sound business sense," Jhally and Lewis declare, "Something is rotten in the state of television, and we should do something about it" (1992, pp. 143–44). What that "something" should be, however, is unclear, other than hoping that network executives grow a conscience. As the final sentence of their book says, "We must admit to not being hopeful about the prospects" (p. 144). Fine, but then why bother with a sitcom like *The Cosby Show?* And why conduct dozens of focus groups if the conclusions of the study are predetermined by one's economic theory? I exaggerate, of course, but not by much.

One's critical energy can be spent in better ways. One way is to study politics and economics and make one's voice heard in relevant political venues. Another path for those committed to academic criticism is to look for the ways in which the political economy of mass media can be put to prosocial uses. That is, if we concede that consumer capitalism is not going away, then how can we take advantage of its logic? Consider the example of media representations of "Mr. Mom." As Mary Douglas Vavrus (2002a) documents, positive portrayals of stay-at-home dads are fueled largely by economic factors. However, her account of how such portrayals "normalize male nurturance and domesticity" implies that this may be an example of where (relatively) progressive representations that undercut gender essentialism and polarization are profitable.[9] Though economically motivated, the popular culture construct of "Mr. Mom" can be viewed as a "linguistic crowbar" that helps us open up our concept of appropriate roles for men (Schiappa, 2003, p. 57).

Similarly, Sarah Banet-Weiser (2004) argues that "girl power" programming on Nickelodeon, while obviously part of a market strategy to capitalize on the cultural fad of girl power, nonetheless provides refreshingly different cultural scripts for both boys and girls that challenge conventional narratives. Banet-Weiser concludes that media critics are too quick to dismiss the concept of "girl power" as a media-constructed, consumer-generated tool; rather, she argues, the messages of "girl power," such as *Clarissa Explains It All, As Told by Ginger* and *Nick News*, "represent a range of options and models, and in many ways these images are a refreshing and politically authorizing change from traditional images of femininity" (pp. 136–37).

The point here is both economic and strategic. The economic point is that commercial television in the United States is not going away anytime soon, so we should not expect the entertainment industry to stop trying to sell entertainment. The strategic point is to ask ourselves, how do we as critics balance our disdain for crass commercialism with a respect for the power of popular media to promote desirable ends?

For example, sitcoms work because they are funny and because we get to know and like the characters, so they are going to continue to focus on individuals and the situations in which they find themselves. We cannot expect sitcoms to dispel false consciousness and to bring about The Revolution that frees us from capitalism. Accordingly, it is important to take notice when the genre can and does provide programming that contributes to positive attitudinal changes, such as *Will & Grace* and *The Cosby Show*. It also is vital that critics raise awareness, especially for our students, of popular media that we think escape the constraints of the market to provide provocative and positive images and messages (see text that follows). What we cannot do, or at least should not do, is strike a pose that urges contempt toward the products of an economic system we dislike without making constructive suggestions for improvements or failing to praise progress when it happens.

5. Preparatory pedagogy promotes empowerment.

It is vital that critics of popular media demonstrate their craft in the classroom to promote critical media literacy. It has been my experience that while some students enjoy the tragic pose of the cynical chic, most get turned off if all of the messages they hear in class are pessimistic. As all teachers of popular culture classes probably have experienced, it is a major accomplishment simply to get students past the "it's just entertainment" stage of pop media criticism (Rockler, 1999a). The reason for this is fairly simple: Students become consumers of popular culture from a very young age and come to associate it with pleasure and enjoyment. The resistance that students show to ideological analysis is not so much because they disagree with the theories we teach, but because critique is perceived as sucking the joy out of their pop culture experience. A wicked passage in Jonathan Franzen's 2001 novel *The Corrections* exaggerates the perils of excessive Representational Correctness, but not by much:

"[This whole class] is just bullshit every week. It's one critic after another wringing their hands about the state of criticism. Nobody can ever quite say what's wrong exactly. But they all know it's evil. They all know 'corporate' is a dirty word. And if somebody's having fun or getting rich—disgusting! Evil! And it's always the death of this and the death of that. And people who think they're free aren't 'really' free. And people who think they're happy aren't 'really' happy. . . . Here things are getting better and better for women and people of color, and gay men and lesbians, more and more integrated and open, and all you can think about is some stupid, lame problem with signifiers and signified. Like, the only way you can make something bad out of an ad that's great for women—which you have to do, because there has to be something wrong with everything—is to say it's evil to be rich and evil to work for a corporation, and yes, I know the bell rang." (p. 44)

A fair critique? Not entirely. But it nicely illustrates the fact that if students like popular media and are told that they should not then they will find a way to reduce the resulting cognitive dissonance. I suspect that many of them treat the theoretical and critical content of dissonance-producing class lectures or readings simply as material to be stored long enough to get past the final exam, much like the quadratic equation was for me when I took algebra. Then they forget it, as I did.

Naomi Rockler's (1999a) study of mainstream consumers' dismissals of ideological critiques of *The Lion King* documents four different rhetorical strategies people deployed, including a characterization of "critics" as being hopelessly out of touch with how people relate to popular culture. The question, however, is *why* people are motivated to use such strategies to begin with. Critics informed by hegemony theory tell us that the masses have been manipulated into participating in their own oppression, and such critics are not entirely wrong. But try telling college students that they have been duped and that they are all pawns of the capitalist regime, and most will start treating class as if it were a visit to the dentist.

To overcome such resistance we not only have to make criticism pleasurable, we have to make our own critical interventions persuasive. For example, Rockler (2001b) reports student opposition to Newberger's (1994) allegorical reading of *The Lion King,* just as Sun and Scharrer (2004) report student opposition to a psychoanalytical reading of the original *The Little Mermaid* story and to an allegorical reading of the movie version. Perhaps the problem is not only that students resist critical analysis of Disney movies, but that the critical analysis itself was too easily dismissed as unpersuasive.

I do not mean to imply that we have to sugarcoat class content or take the position that "it's all good." What we need to do is point to both the good and the bad, the positive as well as the negative representations, so that students not only feel empowered to make comparative judgments but also *hopeful.* One of the reasons so many people celebrated the coming out episode of *Ellen* was that it gave them *hope* for better representation of gay and lesbian people in television. While I cannot refute Bonnie Dow's (2001b) award-winning Foucaultian reading of the coming-out episode as a hegemonically contained "confession" that self-disciplines sexuality, I know I *resist* her reading because I feel like it kills the joy and hope necessary to pursue social change. While we have to be careful not to convey to students an attitude of "everything is fine and getting better on its own," we also have to avoid the message that "you may think things are getting better, but in fact they never do."

Given the mess that critical media literacy is in across the United States, especially compared to the United Kingdom, it would require another book to treat the subject with the depth it deserves. Nonetheless, a few points are worth making in this context.

First, there is evidence (though we need more) that critical media literacy does make a difference. Perhaps most relevant to this book is research that suggests that students who have completed a course involving the critical interpretation of mass media and that requires them to engage in the *practice* of media analysis are more likely to be open to critical interpretations of popular media. Emanuelle Wessels (2006), for example, found that students with a previous critical media course were more willing and able to read zombie movies as conveying critiques of gender, corporate, and military institutions than students who had not taken such a class. Students without a sophisticated critical vocabulary tend to see themselves as passive consumers who are less likely to engage the ideological work of a popular text or fall back on a general criticism that a show or film is "unrealistic" (Rockler, 1999b, 2006). Students can and do explicitly resist critical readings of popular culture texts at times, of course (Rockler, 1999a, 1999b, 2001b; Sun & Scharrer, 2004), and a systematic study of how and why some classes succeed and others fail is certainly needed. My own suspicion is that much of our critical media literacy pedagogy still operates in an elitist, "protectionist" framework that students resist because it is perceived to be antipopular culture (Buckingham, 1998; Kubey, 1998, pp. 64–67). Our students comprise a particular *audience*: to understand and influence their reception of popular media requires a particular kind of audience research.

Stuart Hall's approach to contesting stereotypes is to advocate a kind of critical media literacy. That is, rather than try to counter bad representations with good ones, Hall suggests a deconstructive approach through which viewers/consumers have the ability to recognize and resist the cultural work of stereotypes: "The very act of opening up the practice by which these closures of imagery have been presented requires one to go into the power of the stereotype itself and begin to, as it were, subvert, open, and expose it from inside" (in Jhally, 1997). Again, whether or not such an approach is successful in undercutting the influence of stereotypes is an empirical question worth investigating.

Second, I agree with scholars such as Sonia Livingstone, Justin Lewis, and Sut Jhally when they call for critical media literacy aimed at producing sophisticated public *citizens* and not just savvy private consumers of popular culture (Lewis & Jhally, 1998; Livingstone, 2005; Rockler, 2006). Such a move is necessary to encourage students to recognize the civic importance of audience activities and to encourage them to learn about other models of organizing and funding mass media (rather than just lament the evils of capitalism).

Third, media scholars are well positioned to act as public pedagogues. Whether we write or speak as concerned citizens or experts, we need to reach out to a larger audience than just our students and professional colleagues (Robbins, 1993; Schiappa, 1995). Whether we write columns for newspapers, work with groups such as "See Jane" (http://www.seejane. org) or "Dads and Daughters" (http://www.dadsanddaughters.org), appear on programs that analyze the media, such as "On the Media" (http://www.onthemedia.org) and "Mental Engineering" (http://www. mentalengineering.com), or engage in direct advocacy, the point is that we need to practice what we preach to our students in terms of being engaged citizens. Eli M. Noam (1993) notes that "while communications research has often been openly and legitimately political" in its theories and subject matter, communication scholars have "absented themselves from actual policy" (p. 199). Declaring that scholars "underestimate their own weight" (p. 200), Noam states that communication studies "must broaden beyond the bounds of pure academia. Communications scholars must both address and occasionally venture into a real world, whether in production, government, media business, or public-interest advocacy" (p. 204).

It is my hope that some readers will find these suggestions helpful. Even if every one of my suggestions turns out *not* to be persuasive to readers, I believe that it is beneficial at this historical moment to rethink the relationship between our critical aspirations and our theoretical, critical, and pedagogical practices.

Notes

Chapter 1

1. "Popular media" refers to any mass-marketed and distributed popular culture artifact, though in this book I use the phrase as shorthand to refer to "popular television and film." By "texts" I simply mean individual television shows, films, books, songs, and so on that consumers experience and that can be "read" by critics. As I acknowledge later, a good deal of theoretical literature has complicated a simple notion of a unitary text. Even the temporal and spatial demarcation of a particular film or program is a matter of social construction, let alone the "meaning" of any text. For current purposes, however, a fairly mundane sense of the word "text" will suffice.

2. Hargrave and Livingstone (2006) provide a review of recent research on how often popular media users are offended, though most of their data is limited to the United Kingdon.

3. For an overview of the relevant research, see Hargrave and Livingstone (2006, pp. 54–72) and Sparks (2006, pp. 81–95).

4. A far more nuanced examination of Black masculinity can be found in bell hooks's *We Real Cool: Black Men and Masculinity* (2003) and *The Will to Change: Men, Masculinity, and Love* (2004).

Chapter 2

1. See also note 1 in chapter 1 of this book.

2. My thanks to University of Minnesota student Sgt. Brandon Hlavka (2005) for drawing my attention to how masculinity is performed in *Jarhead*.

3. Note that the text encountered was far from randomly selected. *Cagney and Lacey* was a show with a self-conscious ideological perspective

(D'Acci, 1994) and the episode Condit (1989) studied concerned the volatile issue of abortion. How meanings are contested with such texts could be quite different than with the many programs that try to avoid being "political." Only with further audience research can we learn how typical or generalizable Condit's findings are.

4. For example, Rockler (2001a) notes that while all of her research subjects agreed that the film *Fried Green Tomatoes* did not include an overt depiction of lesbian sex, the subjects' willingness to call the relationship between the main two characters (Idgie and Ruth) a lesbian relationship depended on how they defined such relationships prior to viewing the film.

5. I am grateful for the assistance of Jennifer Stromer-Galley, Jessica Prody, and Emanuelle Wessels in reviewing the contents of these journals.

6. Examples of audience conjectures advanced without audience research are plentiful. Five examples are discussed in this chapter, but many more would be possible: (1) Abel (1999) argues that films such as *Fargo* encourage viewers to adopt a "masochistic position" in which the excitement or interest lies less in acts of violence than in their anticipation. (2) Bellon (1999) suggests that the television show *The X-Files* teaches viewers to distrust authority and to trust themselves. (3) Cooper (2001) applies Foss and Foss's idea of the feminine gaze to *Ally McBeal* to argue that the show's first season encouraged viewers to adopt a feminist perspective, and that gender-based humor functioned as "subversive narrative devices to encourage viewers' participation in ridiculing sexist behaviors and questioning traditional definitions of masculinity" (p. 425). (4) Klein's (2005) analysis of *Black Hawk Down* argues that the film conflates personal support of American soldiers with support of U.S. military policy, and that the text has the power to "encourage its audience to embrace uncritically the policies driving soldier culture" (p. 446). (5) Burns (2001) conjectures that *X Files* audiences understand that representations of aliens are meta-phors for marginalized groups, and that such representations increase audience anxiety and paranoia over immigration and multiculturalism. (6) Railton and Watson (2005) suggest that audiences see music video representations of Black women, specifically Lil' Kim and Beyonce, in stereotypically racist and sexist ways. (7) Mann (2004) claims that *Invasion of the Body Snatchers* encourages audience identification with an idealized form of suburban whiteness. (8) Rowe (2004) suggests that *American Beauty* gives pleasure to middle-class viewers even while divisive; it conjectures that those who like the film are those who find its attitude toward the protag-onist ambivalent. (9) Oake (2004) argues that through the act of spec-tatorship, cult spectators both produce and express their

difference and contends that such identities cannot be considered in isolation from certain defining media texts. (10) Hillis (2005) claims that film noir texts encourage audience members ultimately to identify with the father and state over the tragic protagonist. (11) Capino (2005) suggests that to solicit spectators' engagement and pleasure, "porn films must constantly thematize the process of the production of sexual pleasure." (12) Keller and Ward (2006) contend that minimalism guides viewers to discover the meaning of an object via examination of how it interacts with its context. (13) Beckham (2005) argues that *Touch of Evil* and *The Border* did not have commercial success because they critiqued U.S. policy and authorities, while the highly successful *Traffic*, while it challenged U.S. policy, framed Mexico as the cause of U.S. problems. (14) Davis and Womack (2001) argue that James Cameron, in his film *Titanic*, relies on the audience's "aesthetic reading strategies" in order to allow it to shed its postmodern cynicism and experience sentimentality and hope for the reconciliation of the divergent social worlds represented by his main characters. (15) Placing the film *Freaks* into its historical context, Larsen and Haller (2002) argue that the film's poor reception was due to the social shift that was occurring that caused members of society to alter their perceptions of disabled individuals from dangerous freaks to pitiful people. (16) Admittedly making claims without empirical audience research, Loy (2003) argues that the B-Westerns of the World War II era served to reinforce the lessons their young viewers were learning from society and its institutions about the importance and glory of war. (17) Nachbar (2000) places the film *Casablanca* into its historical context to argue that the film's easily identifiable story and lesson of self-sacrifice helped those living during World War II to cope with the uncertainty of their situation. (18) Lacroix (2004) claims that there is a connotative "unity of images" regarding race and gender in the "orientalized" presentation of females in recent Disney animated films. (19) Atkinson (2003) finds an implicit "resistance narrative" in the alterations of corporate billboards and advertisements that "provides empowerment" needed for community building in the anti-corporate movement and culture. (20) Li-Vollmer and LaPointe (2003) argue that recent animated films promote a "villain-as-sissy" archetype to signify the villain's deviance, and that such representations reinforce heteronormativity and promote negative associations about gay people. (21) McHugh (2002) claims that the film *Babe* invites viewers to understand the characters as a collective and discourages them from viewing one particular individual as central. (22) Gerhard (2005) argues that *Sex and the City* brings viewers to a metanarrative of Queer family structure by its depiction of close female bonds. (23) Helford (2006) posits that viewers are on the side of *The Stepford Wives'* main female protagonist, and that they also are aligned with feminism. Helford states that the film invites viewers to adopt the male gaze for the purpose of critiquing it and causing discomfort, thus raising viewer consciousness on the politics of The Gaze. (24) Richardson (2006) conjectures that audiences of *Desperate Housewives* understand the irony of the ways in which Bree Van Dee Kamp "camps up" the idea of traditional femininity. (25) Ramsey (2005) claims that *The People versus Larry Flynt,* by personalizing the pornography issue, increases the likelihood that audiences will blame *Hustler's* bad taste and misogyny on Flynt's personal foibles as opposed to a legal system that protects such words and images. (26) Tierney (2006) argues that the acquisition of martial arts skills by White protagoists in such movies as *Kill Bill* and *Bulletproof Monk* constitutes "a significant filmic form of cultural colonialism and appropriation that reinforce hegemonic ideas of racial and cultural superiority and inferiority, with consequences that reach far beyond the movie theater" (p. 622). (27) Darling-Wolf (2006) states that the Japanese fashion magazines *non-no* and *Men's non-no* provide hybrid constructions of race, gender, and culture that nonetheless constitute commodified ideals that are likely to continue to legitimate existing inequalities of class, gender, and race. (28) Pitcher (2006) conjectures that *Girls Gone Wild* videos function hegemonically to reinforce a neoliberalist mentality of personal responsibility.

7. Matthew 13:13: "That is why I speak to them in parables, because seeing they do not see, and hearing they do not hear, nor do they understand."

8. It would be hard to prove that *The Cosby Show* had any negative effect at all, given that Entman and Rojecki (2000) report that other famous Black celebrities, such as Oprah Winfrey and Michael Jordan, are cited already by those who believe that "Blacks can make it if they only try harder" (p. 29).

9. As a result of conversations with Goodnight concerning an earlier draft of this chapter, Stromer-Galley and I were convinced that he reads his own essay both as opening up interpretive possibilities (creative-mediational) and as a critical commentary on the texts' complicity with postmodern skepticism (corrective). Accordingly, both ways of reading the essay are discussed.

10. An earlier draft of this chapter was shared with Dana Cloud, Karen and Sonja Foss, Marty Medhurst, Nick Trujillo, and Tom Goodnight. While we did not reach agreement on all points, we did agree on many, and we are thankful for the spirit of collegiality and cooperation demonstrated in the fruitful discussions that led to the final version.

11. I owe this observation to David Zarefsky.

12. I regret the fact that I was introduced to the books of Janet Staiger (see 1992, 2000, 2005) too late to integrate her useful work into this project. Nonetheless, I certainly recommend her work for readers interested in a thorough historical and theoretical survey of media reception research.

Chapter 3

1. The concept of a "trained incapacity" was originally introduced by Thorstein Veblen and developed by Kenneth Burke. For a useful summary see Wais (2005).

2. See, for example, Ayres (2003), Bell, Haas, and Sells (1995), Brockus (2004), Budd and Kirsch (2005), Dorfman and Mattelart (1975), Giroux (1999), and Lacroix (2004).

3. In e-mail exchanges, I confirmed with both authors that they did, in fact, believe that these were actual "effects" of the text, at least for straight audience members, though they both made it clear that alternate readings are certainly possible.

4. The percentage of students who were willing to agree that *Will & Grace* "has encouraged me to think positively about homosexuals" is particularly noteworthy given the well-established "third-person effect"; that is, people tend to underestimate the influence of persuasive messages on themselves and overestimate the influence on others. See Diamond (1978), Davison (1983), and Bryant, Salwen, and Dupagne (2000).

5. For example: The closest relevant data challenge the reading of Jack as a weak foil, as noted earlier from Cooper (2002). Furthermore, 80% of the participants in our study did not agree with the statement that "Grace acts like a child or buffoon who is not to be taken seriously," and twice as many viewers picked her as their favorite character than picked Will, which suggests that she may not be the "parodic stereotype" that Shugart conjectures.

Chapter 4

1. For details concerning the various interpersonal scales used, see Rubin, Palmgreen, and Sypher (1994).

Chapter 5

1. Sales information concerning *Disclosure* is based on records regularly reported in *Publisher's Weekly*, the *New York Times*, and *Entertainment Weekly*.

2. A few words are appropriate about the film version of *Disclosure*. Like the novel, the film enacts impersonal narration to create sympathy for and identification with the lead male character, played by Michael Douglas. The film portrays Meredith Johnson (Demi Moore) as devoid of any redeeming qualities and parallels the book's negative stereotype of her as a female executive. The story's framing of stereotypical men's and women's roles in society is generally the same as in the book, but with enough minor differences that we cannot simply assert that the ideological functions are identical. The film repeats, but without as much detail, attacks on feminism and feminist agendas. Although we believe that the film and novel function in very similar ways, obviously such a conjecture could be usefully explored with audience research.

3. According to the EEOC (2006), in fiscal year 2005 over 85% of all sexual harassment charges were brought by women.

4. Our thanks to our colleague, Patricia Ryden, for administering the survey and running the subsequent statistical analysis.

5. A one-way ANOVA test, using the three sex-role types as the independent variable and social desirability as the depended variable, yielded $F(2, 47) = 26.3$, $p < .001$. A Tukey-B multiple comparison test indicated that all of the groups differed from one another. Specifically, the test demonstrated that cross-typed characters ($M = 4.5$) were rated significantly lower in social desirability (or "higher in social undesirability") than androgynous characters ($M = 4.0$) and sex-typed characters (mean $= 3.2$) ($p < .05$).

Chapter 6

1. The research reported in this chapter was conducted with Peter B. Gregg, with Martin Lang providing additional data.

2. See Nora Vincent's interesting and accessible book *Self-Made Man* (2006).

3. Cronbach's αs were similar to those reported by Mahalik: Disdain for Homosexuality ($\alpha_1 = .92$, $\alpha_2 = .92$), Self-Reliance ($\alpha_1 = .84$, $\alpha_2 = .86$), Violence ($\alpha_1 = .81$, $\alpha_2 = .82$), Winning ($\alpha_1 = .87$, $\alpha_2 = .87$), Emotional Control ($\alpha_1 = .91$, $\alpha_2 = .91$), Risk Taking ($\alpha_1 = .83$, $\alpha_2 = .83$), Power over

Women ($\alpha_1 = .82$, $\alpha_2 = .81$), Dominance ($\alpha_1 = .70$, $\alpha_2 = .71$), Playboy ($\alpha_1 = .85$, $\alpha_2 = .86$), Primacy of Work ($\alpha_1 = .80$, $\alpha_2 = .84$), and Pursuit of Status ($\alpha_1 = .73$, $\alpha_2 = .77$).

4. Earlier tests of the Hetnorm scale rendered αs in excess of .85. In this sample, Cronbach's αs were similar to those found earlier $\alpha_1 = .89$, $\alpha_2 = .86$).

5. Cronbach's $\alpha_1 = .75$, $\alpha_2 = .86$.

6. See Diamond (1978), Davison (1983), and Bryant, Salwen, and Dupagne (2000).

Chapter 7

1. In contrast, see Entman and Rojecki's (2000) constructive suggestions in *The Black Image in the White Mind* (pp. 216–25).

2. Like McWhorter (2003), I am guilty of oversimplifying Bogle's account to make my argument clearer. Though I must confess to a sense of frustration with how rarely Bogle ever offers unqualified praise for a film or television program or character, he is not nearly as pessimistic as McWhorter implies. His account of Bill Cosby, for example, is thorough, masterful, and overwhelmingly positive. There also is a subtle and relevant wording change that was made between the third and fourth editions of *Toms, Coons, Mulattoes, Mammies, & Bucks*. In the original 1994 preface, as I emphasize in the passage just quoted, Bogle declares that the "thesis of my book is that *all* black actors" have played stereotyped roles (p. xxiii). In the fourth edition this is changed to "*many*" black actors (Bogle, 2001b, p. xxii).

3. I knew that the term *stereotype* had been stretched too thin when I came across an article titled "Beyond stereotypes of IT [information technology] professionals: Implications for IT HR practices" (Enns, Ferratt, & Prasad, 2006). The first sentence claims that "IT professionals are complicated—managers need to go beyond stereotypes to truly understand them" (p. 105).

4. See, for example, Cacioppo and Berntson (1994), Ito, Larsen, Smith, and Cacioppo (1998), and Carretie, Mercado, Tapia, and Hinojosa (2001).

5. For example: (1) Schrag, Hudson, and Bernabo (1981) praise *Taxi*, *Barney Miller*, *Lou Grant*, and *M*A*S*H* for advancing a vision of a humane and sympathetic awareness of and concern for the group. (2) Foss and Foss (1994) credit Garrison Keillor's radio monologues on

Prairie Home Companion for offering a feminist perspective for listeners. (3) A notable exception to the pattern of textual critics finding fault with *Will & Grace* is an analysis by Karin Quimby (2005) that argues that *Will & Grace* provides "a significant critique of the marriage contract and other normative heterosexual structures" (p. 726). Quimby suggests that the show encourages a far more "queer" spectator position for viewers than usually found in mainstream mass-culture productions (p. 719). (4) Through a mix of content analysis and accounts from fan mail, Enns (2000) explores the themes of U.N.C.L.E. and the role of the female spectator, arguing that the creators of the show designed the series to provide women with a point of identification and thus promoted their position of female viewership. (5) Edwards (2004) admonishes critics who immediately dismiss the film *Barb Wire* because of its overt sexuality and star, Pamela Anderson. Instead he argues that critics must not allow this sexualization to cause them to dismiss the text outright; rather, they must look deeper and acknowledge that there is potential for the film and the strength of its main character to be inspiring and motivating to the audience. (6) In a pair of articles, Mascaro (2004, 2005) praises the television series *Homicide: Life on the Streets* for its portrayal of the complexity of Black culture and Black men and women. (7) Peek (2003) challenges the prevalent claims that Westerns have existed as celebrations of masculinity; rather, she argues that they are celebrations of competence that often involve characters negotiating between masculine and feminine traits in order to address the problems at hand. (8) Looking at movies such as *School Daze, House Party 2, Higher Learning*, and *Boyz N the Hood*, Speed (2001) argues that "Black youth films" contain important positive messages for Black youth. The most significant messages of these types of films involve the importance of education for members of the Black community and the importance of mediation in the lives of young Blacks. This message of mediation often is presented through the roles of strong Black women, thus allowing these films to challenge traditional patriarchal attitudes. (9) Though not without reservations, Reser (2005) notes that the film *The Full Monty* was able to achieve mainstream commercial success while preserving "its potential to promulgate alternative visions of how masculinity was challenged and reclaimed during the Thatcher era" (p. 235). (10) Weiss (2005) argues that the language performed by the stars of *Queer Eye for the Straight Guy* enacts "queer" ways (conflicting, fluid, and uncategorizable) of constituting its speakers' sexual identities that challenge stereotypes and deepen our understanding of identity.

6. For a useful discussion over the ends and means of media criticism involving a purely anti-capitalist position and a more accommodationist position, see the exchange between Celeste M. Condit (1994, 1996, 1997) and Dana L. Cloud (1996, 1997).

7. As Bruce Robbins puts it, "The most dangerous complacencies are often those that accompany the harshest, most monotonously pessimistic readings of present history, thereby justifying in silence the space in the ivory tower that the writer does not otherwise acknowledge, and that the writer is therefore unmotivated to step outside of" (1993, p. 223).

8. "The racial inequities that scarred the United States before the Civil Rights movement can only be rectified by instituting major structural changes in the nation's social, political, and economic life. The [Reagan/Bush-era] White House has, since 1980, withdrawn from any notion of intervention against an iniquitous system, committing itself instead to promoting a freewheeling capitalist economy. . . . The economic laws of free market capitalism keep these [racist] class barriers in place with cavalier efficiency" (Jhally & Lewis, 1992, p. 132).

9. Vavrus's reading is not purely laudatory: She argues that representations of "Mr. Mom" challenge some notions of gender but "reinscribe significant aspects of patriarchal privilege within domestic space" (2002a, p. 353). One can concede her argument for this conclusion while still insisting that a patriarchy that "normalize[s] male nurturance and domesticity" (ibid.) is better than one that does not.

References

Abel, M. (1999). *Fargo*: The violent production of the masochist contract as a cinematic concept. *Critical Studies in Mass Communication, 16*, 308–328.

Advocate.com. (2004). Poll: Is *Queer Eye for the Straight Guy* a step forward for the gay rights movement? Retrieved June 8, 2004, from http://www.advocate.com. Original page is no longer available, but a summary can be accessed at http://www.findarticles.com.

Alcoff, L. (1991–1992, Winter). The problem of speaking for others. *Cultural Critique*, 5–32.

Aleiss, A. (2005). *Making the white man's Indian: Native Americans and Hollywood movies.* Westport, CT: Praeger.

Alexander, J. C., & Giesen, B. (1987). From reduction to linkage: The long view of the micro-macro debate. In J. C. Alexander, B. Giesen, R. Munch, & N. J. Smelser (Eds.), *The micro-macro link* (pp. 1–44). Berkeley: University of California Press.

Allor, M. (1988). Relocating the site of the audience. *Critical Studies in Mass Communication, 5*, 217–233.

Allport, G. W. (1954). *The nature of prejudice.* Cambridge, MA: Perseus Books.

Altemeyer, B. (2001). Changes in attitudes toward homosexuals. *Journal of Homosexuality, 42*, 63–76.

Altman, R. (1999). *Film/Genre.* London: British Film Institute.

Amir, Y. (1976). The role of intergroup contact in change of prejudice and race relations. In P. A. Katz (Ed.), *Towards the elimination of racism* (pp. 245–280). New York: Pergamon.

Anderson, J. A. (1996). The pragmatics of audience in research and theory. In J. Hay, L. Grossberg, & E. Wartella (Eds.), *The audience and its landscape* (pp. 75–96). Boulder, CO: Westview Press.

Anderson, J. B. (2001, April 16). The black box. *The Nation, 272,* 28–32.

Ang, I. (1985). *Watching Dallas: Soap opera and the melodramatic imagination.* London: Methuen.

Armstrong, G. B., Neuendorf, K. A., & Brentar, J. E. (1992). TV entertainment, news, and racial perceptions of college students. *Journal of Communication, 42,* 153–176.

Aronson, E., Willerman, B., & Floyd, J. (1966). The effect of a pratfall on increasing personal attractiveness. *Psychonomic Science, 4,* 227–238.

Aström, L. (1993). Generationskamrater—finns de? Om gränsdragning och likriktning inom och mellan generationerna. *Nord Nytt, 49,* 17–21.

Atkinson, J. (2003). Thumbing their noses at "The Man": An analysis of resistance narratives about multinational corporations. *Popular Communication, 1,* 163–180.

Aubrey, J. S., & Harrison, K. (2004). The gender-role content of children's favorite television programs and its links to their gender-related perceptions. *Media Psychology, 6,* 111–146.

Auter, P. J., & Palmgreen, P. (2000). Development and validation of a parasocial interaction measure: The audience-persona interaction scale. *Communication Research Reports, 17,* 79–89.

Ayres, B. (Ed.). (2003). *The emperor's old groove: Decolonizing Disney's magic kingdom.* New York: Peter Lang.

Bagdikian, B. H. (2004). *The new media monopoly.* Boston: Beacon Press.

Bandura, A. (2002). Social cognitive theory of mass communication. In J. Bryant & D. Zillmann (Eds.), *Media effects: Advances in theory and research* (2nd ed.) (pp. 121–153). Mahwah, NJ: L. Erlbaum Associates.

Banet-Weiser, S. (2004). Girls rule!: Gender, feminism, and Nickelodeon. *Critical Studies in Media Communication, 21,* 119–139.

Battles, K., & Hilton-Morrow, W. (2002). Gay characters in conventional spaces: *Will & Grace* and the situation comedy genre. *Critical Studies in Media Communication, 19,* 87–105.

Beaty, Bart. (2005). *Fredric Wertham and the critique of mass culture.* Jackson: University Press of Mississippi.

Beckham II, J. (2005). Placing *Touch of Evil, The Border,* and *Traffic* in the American imagination. *Journal of Popular Film & Television, 33,* 130–141.

Bell, E. (1995). Somatexts at the Disney shop: Constructing the pentimentos of women's animated bodies. In E. Bell, L. Haas, & L. Sells

(Eds.), *From mouse to mermaid: The politics of film, gender, and culture* (pp. 107–124). Bloomington: Indiana University Press.

Bell, E., Haas, L., & Sells, L. (Eds.). (1995). *From mouse to mermaid: The politics of film, gender, and culture.* Bloomington: Indiana University Press.

Bellon, J. (1999). The strange discourse of *The X-Files*: What it is, what it does, and what is at stake. *Critical Studies in Mass Communication, 16,* 136–154.

Bem, S. L. (1974). The measurement of psychological androgyny. *Journal of Clinical and Consulting Psychology, 42,* 155–162.

Bem, S. L. (1993). *The lenses of gender: Transforming the debate on sexual inequality.* New Haven, CT: Yale University Press.

Bem, S. L. (2004). *Bem Sex Role Inventory Manual.* Redwood City, CA: Mindgarden.

Berger, C. R., & Calabrese, R. J. (1975). Some explorations in initial interaction and beyond: Toward a developmental theory of interpersonal communication. *Human Communication Research, 1,* 99–112.

Bogle, D. (1994). *Toms, coons, mulattoes, mammies, and bucks: An interpretive history of blacks in American films.* New York: Continuum.

Bogle, D. (2001a). *Primetime blues: African Americans on network television.* New York: Farrar, Straus, & Giroux.

Bogle, D. (2001b). *Toms, coons, mulattoes, mammies, and bucks: An interpretive history of blacks in American films* (4th ed.). New York: Continuum.

Booth, W. C. (1983). *The rhetoric of fiction* (2nd ed.). Chicago: University of Chicago Press.

Bordwell, D. (1989). *Making meaning: Inference and rhetoric in the interpretation of cinema.* Cambridge, MA: Harvard University Press.

Bowers, J. W. (1968). The pre-scientific function of rhetorical criticism. In T. R. Nilsen (Ed.), *Essays on rhetorical criticism* (pp. 126–145). New York: Random House.

Boyer, E. L. (1990). *Scholarship reconsidered: Priorities of the professoriate.* San Francisco: Jossey-Bass.

Brannon, R., & Juni, S. (1984). A scale for measuring attitudes toward masculinity. *JSAS Catalog of Selected Documents in Psychology, 14,* 6.

Brewer, M. B., & Brown, R. J. (1998). Intergroup relations. In D. T. Gilbert, S.T. Fiske, & G. Lindzey (Eds.), *The handbook of social psychology* (4th ed.) (pp. 554–594). Boston: McGraw-Hill.

Brock, B. L., Scott, R. L., & Chesebro, J. W. (1990). *Methods of rhetoricial criticism* (3rd ed.). Detroit: Wayne State University Press.

Brockriede, W. (1971). Toward a blending of criticism and science. In Lloyd F. Bitzer & Edwin Black (Eds.), *The prospect of rhetoric* (pp. 123–139). Englewood Cliffs, NJ: Prentice Hall.

Brockriede, W. (1974). Rhetorical criticism as argument. *Quarterly Journal of Speech, 60*, 165–174.

Brockus, S. (2004). Where magic lives: Disney's cultivation, co-creation, and control of America's cultural objects. *Popular Communication, 2*, 191–211.

Bronowski, J. (1956). *Science and human values.* New York: Harper & Row.

Brookey, R. A., & Westerfelhaus, R. (2001). Pistols and petticoats, piety and purity: *To Wong Foo*, the queering of the American monomyth, and the marginilazing discourse of deification. *Critical Studies in Mass Communication, 18*, 141–156.

Brookey, R. A., & Westerfelhaus, R. (2002). Hiding homoeroticism in plain view: The *Fight Club* DVD as Digital Closet. *Critical Studies in Mass Communication, 19*, 21–43.

Brown, D. (2003). *The Da Vinci code.* New York: Doubleday.

Bruhn, J. G., & Murray, J. L. (1985). "Playing the dozens": Its history and psychological significance. *Psychological Reports, 56*, 483–494.

Brummett, B. (1991). *Rhetorical dimensions of popular culture.* Tuscaloosa: University of Alabama Press.

Bryant, P., Salwen, M. B., & Dupagne, M. (2000). The third-person effect: A meta-analysis of the perceptual hypothesis. *Mass Communication & Society, 3*, 57–85.

Buckingham, D. (1998). Media education in the UK: Moving beyond protectionism. *Journal of Communication, 48*, 33–43.

Budd, M., & Kirsch, M. H. (2005). *Rethinking Disney: Private control, public dimensions.* Middletown, CT: Wesleyan University Press.

Buhler, S. M. (2003). Shakespeare and company: *The Lion King* and the Disneyfication of Hamlet. In B. Ayres (Ed.), *The emperor's old groove: Decolonizing Disney's magic kingdom* (pp. 117–129). New York: Peter Lang.

Bunn, A. (2002, March 19). Our siblings, our secrets. *The Advocate*, 38–39.

Bunzl, M. (2000). Inverted appellation and discursive gender insubordination. *Discourse & Society, 11*, 207–236.

Burke, K. (1945). *A grammar of motives*. New York: Prentice Hall.

Burke, K. (1966). *Language as symbolic action*. Berkeley: University of California Press.

Burns, C. L. (2001). Erasure: Alienation, paranoia, and the loss of memory in *The X Files. Camera Obscura 45, 15,* 195–226.

Cacioppo, J. T., & Berntson, G. G. (1994). Relationship between attitude and evaluative space: A critical review. *Psychological Bulletin, 115,* 401–423.

Cagle, V. M. (2002). *Current representations of LGBT people in entertainment television: The case of* Will & Grace. GLAAD Center for the Study of Media & Society. Retrieved April 1, 2002, from http://www.glaad. org/documents/csms/w&gpdf.

Campbell, J. A. (1990). Between the fragment and the icon: Prospect for a rhetorical house of the middle way. *Western Journal of Speech Communication, 54,* 346–376.

Cantril, A. H. (1982). *The invasion from Mars: A study in the psychology of panic.* Princeton, NJ: Princeton University Press. Originally published in 1940.

Capino, J. B. (2005). Homologies of space: Texts and spectatorship in all-male adult theaters. *Cinema Journal, 45,* 50–66.

Carretie L., Mercado F., Tapia M., & Hinojosa J. A. (2001). Emotion, attention, and the "negativity bias," studied through event-related potentials. *International Journal of Psychophysiology, 41,* 75–85.

Carter, B. (1992, February 4). Rather pulls CBS News back to the assassination. *New York Times,* p. C11.

Charpentier, J. D. (2006). *Teasing in adult peer relationships: Using Lazarus' model of stress and coping to understand the effects of teasing.* Unpublished doctoral dissertation, University of Minnesota.

Cloud, D. L. (1992). The limits of interpretation: Ambivalence and the stereotype in *Spenser: For Hire. Critical Studies in Mass Communication, 9,* 311–324.

Cloud, D. L. (1996). Hegemony or concordance?: The rhetoric of tokenism in Oprah Winfrey's rags-to-riches biography. *Critical Studies in Media Communication, 13,* 115–137.

Cloud, D. L. (1997). Concordance, complexity, and conservatism: Rejoinder to Condit. *Critical Studies in Media Communication, 14,* 193–197.

Clymer, A. (1992, March 27). Bill would open Kennedy death files. *New York Times,* p. A17.

Cohen, J. (2001). Defining identification: A theoretical look at the identification of audiences with media characters. *Mass Communication & Society, 4,* 245–264.

Cohen, J. (2004). Parasocial break-up from favorite television characters: The role of attachment styles and relationship intensity. *Journal of Social and Personal Relationships, 21,* 187–202.

Cohen, J. R. (1991). Intersecting and competing discourses in Harvey Fierstein's *Tidy Endings. Quarterly Journal of Speech, 77,* 196–207.

Condit, C. M. (1989). The rhetorical limits of polysemy. *Critical Studies in Mass Communication, 6,* 103–112.

Condit, C. M. (1990). Rhetorical criticism and audiences: The extremes of McGee and Leff. *Western Journal of Speech Communication, 54,* 330–345.

Condit, C. M. (1994). Hegemony in a mass-mediated society: Concordance about reproductive technologies. *Critical Studies in Media Communication, 11,* 205–230.

Condit, C. M. (1996). Hegemony, concordance, and capitalism: Reply to Cloud. *Critical Studies in Media Communication, 13,* 382–384.

Condit, C. M. (1997). Clouding the issues? The ideal and the material in human communication. *Critical Studies in Media Communication, 14,* 197–200.

Condit, C. M., Bates, R. G., Givens, S. B., Haynie, C. K., Jordan, J. W., Stables, G., & West, H. M. (2002). Recipes or blueprints for our genes? How contexts selectively activate the multiple meanings of metaphors. *Quarterly Journal of Speech, 88,* 100–120.

Connell, R. (1995). *Masculinities.* Oxford: Polity Press.

Conway, J. C., & Rubin, A. M. (1991). Psychological predictors of television viewing motivation. *Communication Research, 18,* 443–464.

Cooper, B. (1999). The relevancy and gender identity in spectators' interpretations of *Thelma & Louise. Critical Studies in Mass Communication, 16,* 20–41.

Cooper, B. (2001). Unapologetic women, "comic men" and feminine spectatorship in David E. Kelley's *Ally McBeal. Critical Studies in Media Communication, 18,* 416–435.

Cooper, B. (2002). *Boys Don't Cry* and female masculinity: Reclaiming a life and dismantling the politics of normative heterosexuality. *Critical Studies in Media Communication, 19,* 44–63.

Cooper, E. (2003). Decoding *Will & Grace*: Mass audience reception of a popular network situation comedy. *Sociological Perspectives, 46,* 513–533.

Cope, V. (1992, August 1). Senate votes for release of secret JFK files. *Congressional Quarterly Weekly Report, 50,* 2250.

Coppock, V., Haydon, D., & I. Richter. (1995). *The illusions of "post-feminism": New women, old myths.* London: Taylor & Francis.

Cornford, F. M. (1941). *The Republic of Plato.* London: Oxford University Press.

Coupland, D. (1991). *Generation X: Tales from an accelerated culture.* New York: St. Martin's Press.

Crichton, M. (1994). *Disclosure.* New York: Alfred A. Knopf.

Crichton, Michael. (1990, December). They are us: Are the sexes battling each other or some imaginary enemy? *Men's Health,* p. 92.

D'Acci, J. (1994). *Defining women: Television and the case of Cagney & Lacey.* Chapel Hill: University of North Carolina Press.

Darling-Wolf, F. (2006). The men and women of *non-no*: Gender, race, and hybridity in two Japanese magazines. *Critical Studies in Media Communication, 23,* 181–199.

D'Augelli, A. R., & Rose, M. L. (1990). Homophobia in a university community: Attitudes and experiences of heterosexual freshmen. *Journal of College Student Development, 31,* 484–491.

Davis, T., & Womack, K. (2001). Narrating the ship of dreams. *Journal of Popular Film & Television, 29,* 42–48.

Davison, P. W. (1983). The third-person effect in communication. *Public Opinion Quarterly, 47,* 1–15.

de Moraes, L. (2005, January 27). PBS's "Buster" Gets an Education. *The Washington Post,* p. C1.

Diamond, E. (1978). *Good news, bad news.* Cambridge: MIT Press.

Dion, K., Berscheid, E., & Walster, E. (1972). What is beautiful is good. *Journal of Personality and Social Psychology, 24,* 285–290.

Dorfman, A., & Mattelart, A. (1975). *How to read Donald Duck: Imperialist ideology in the Disney comic* (D. Kunzle, Trans.). New York: International General.

Dorling, D. (1997). *Mapping: Ways of representing the world.* London: Longman.

Doug135711. (2006). Comments. Posted on January 15, 2006. Retrieved May 21, 2006, from http://www.thedisneyblog.typepad.com/tdb/2006/01/interview_with_.html.

Dovidio, J. F., Gaertner, S. L., & Kawakami, K. (2003). Intergroup contact: The past, present, and the future. *Group Processes and Intergroup Relations, 6,* 5–21.

Dow, B. J. (1990). Hegemony, feminist criticism, and *The Mary Tyler Moore Show. Critical Studies in Mass Communications, 7,* 261–274.

Dow, B. J. (1996). *Prime-time feminism: Television, media culture, and the women's movement since 1970.* Philadelphia: University of Pennsylvania Press.

Dow, B. J. (2001a). Criticism and authority in the artistic mode. *Western Journal of Communication, 65,* 336–348.

Dow, B. J. (2001b). Ellen, television, and the politics of gay and lesbian visibility. *Critical Studies in Media Communication, 18,* 123–140.

Dyer, R. (1997). *White.* New York: Routledge.

Dyer, R. (2002). *The matter of images: Essays on representations* (2nd ed.). New York: Routledge.

Eagly, A. H., & Karau, S. J. (2002). Role congruity theory of prejudice toward female leaders. *Psychological Review, 109,* 573–598.

Edwards, G. C. (1996). Presidential rhetoric: What difference does it make? In M. J. Medhurst (Ed.), *Beyond the rhetorical presidency* (pp. 242–263). College Station: Texas A&M University Press.

Edwards, M. (2004). The blonde with the guns. *Journal of Popular Film & Television, 32,* 39–47.

EEOC (U.S. Equal Employment Opportunity Commission). (2006). Sexual harassment. Retrieved August 1, 2006, from http:///www.eeoc.gov/types/sexual_harassment.html.

Eisler, R. M., & Skidmore, J. R. (1987). Masculine gender role stress: Scale development and component factors in the appraisal of stressful situations. *Behavior Modification, 11,* 123–136.

Elahi, B. (2001). Pride lands: *The Lion King,* proposition 187, and white resentment. *Arizona Quarterly, 57,* 121–152.

Eleftheriotis, D. (2005). Historical metaphor and European cinema. *Screen, 46,* 315–328.

Enns, A. (2000). The fans from U.N.C.L.E. *Journal of Popular Film & Television, 28,* 124–132.

Enns, H. G., Ferratt, T. W., & Prasad, J. (2006). Beyond stereotypes of IT [information technology] professionals: Implications for IT HR practices. *Communications of the ACM, 49,* 105–109.

Entman, R. M., & Rojecki, A. (2000). *The black image in the white mind: Media and race in America.* Chicago: University of Chicago Press.

Faludi, S. (2000). *Stiffed: The betrayal of the American man.* New York: HarperPerennial.

Fecteau, T . J., Jackson, J., & Dindia, K. (1992). Gender orientation scales: An empirical assessment of content validity. In L. A. M. Perry, L. H. Turner, & H. M. Sterk (eds.), *Constructing and reconstructing gender: The links among communication, language, and gender* (pp. 17–35). Albany: State University of New York Press.

Fejes, F., & Petrich, K. (1993). Invisibility and heterosexism: Lesbians, gays, and the media. *Critical Studies in Mass Communication, 10,* 396–422.

Festinger, L. (1954). A theory of social comparison processes. *Human Relations, 7,* 117–140.

Festinger, L. (1957). *A theory of cognitive dissonance.* Evanston, IL: Row & Peterson.

Fisch, S. M. (2004). *Children's learning from educational television: Sesame Street and beyond.* Mahwah, NJ: L. Erlbaum Associates.

Fisch, S. M., & Truglio, R. T. (Eds.). (2004). *"G" is for growing: Thirty years of research on children and Sesame Street.* Mahwah, NJ: L. Erlbaum Associates.

Fischoff, S., Franco, A., Gram, E., Hernendez, A., & Parker, J. (1999). Offensive ethnic clichés in movies: Drugs, sex, and servility. Unpublished paper.

Fishbein, M., & Ajzen, I. (1975). *Belief, attitude, intention, and behavior: An introduction to theory and research.* Reading, MA: Addison-Wesley.

Fiske, J. (1986). Television: Polysemy and popularity. *Critical Studies in Mass Communication, 3,* 391–408.

Fiske, J. (1989a). Moments of television: Neither the text nor the audience. In E. Seiter, H. Borchers, G. Kreutzner, & E-W. Warth (Eds.), *Remote control: Television, audiences, and cultural power* (pp. 56–78). London: Routledge.

Fiske, J. (1989b). *Understanding popular culture.* London: Routledge.

Foss, S. K., & Foss, K. A. (1994). The construction of feminine spectatorship in Garrison Keillor's radio monologues. *Quarterly Journal of Speech, 40,* 410–426.

Franzen, J. (2001). *The corrections.* New York: Farrar, Straus & Giroux.

Frow, J. (1995). *Cultural studies and cultural value.* Oxford: Oxford University Press.

Fujioka, Y. (1999). Television portrayals and African American stereotypes: Examination of television effects when direct contact is lacking. *Journalism & Mass Communication Quarterly, 76,* 52–75.

Gadamer, H. G. (1989). *Truth and method* (2nd rev. ed.) (J. Weinsheimer & D. G. Marshall, Trans.). New York: Continuum. Originally published in 1960.

Gairola, R. (2001). *Will & Grace:* Watching with ambivalence. Retrieved April 1, 2002, from http://www.popmatters.com/tv/reviews/w/will-and-grace.html.

Gallup, G. (1995). *The Gallup poll: Public opinion 1994.* Wilmington, DE: Scholarly Resources.

Gardiner, G. S. (1972). Complexity training and prejudice reduction. *Journal of Applied Social Psychology, 2,* 326–342.

Garlick, B., Dixon, S., & Allen, P. (Eds.). (1992). *Stereotypes of women in power.* Westport, CT: Greenwood Press.

Gavin, R. (1996). *The Lion King* and *Hamlet:* A homecoming for the exiled child. *English Journal, 85,* 55–57.

Gelfand, L. (2002) Reader. saw SUV headline as a smear. *Minneapolis Star-Tribune.* Published April 14, 2002. Retrieved April 20, 2002, from http://www.startribune.com.

Gerbner, G., Gross, L., Morgan, M., Signorielli, N., & Shanahan, J. (2002). Growing up with television: Cultivation processes. In J. Bryant & D. Zillmann (Eds.), *Media effects: Advances in theory and research* (2nd ed.) (pp. 43–67). Mahwah, NJ: L. Erlbaum Associates.

Gerhard, J. (2005). Sex and the city: Carrie Bradshaw's queer postfeminism. *Feminist Media Studies, 5,* 37–50.

Getlin, J. (1994, January 19). Crichton's "Disclosure." *Los Angeles Times,* pp. E1, E6.

Giles, D. C. (2002). Parasocial interaction: A review of the literature and a model for future research. *Media Psychology, 4,* 279–305.

Giltz, M. (2003, September 2). Queer eye confidential. *The Advocate,* 40–44.

Giroux, H. A. (1999). *The mouse that roared: Disney and the end of innocence.* New York: Rowman & Littlefield.

Giuliana, B. (1993). Ramble city: Postmodernism and *Blade Runner.* In C. Sharrett (Ed.), *Crisis cinema* (pp. 236–249). Washington, DC: Maisonneuve.

Gleich, U., & Burst, M. (1996). Parasoziale Beziehungen von Fernsehzuschauern mit Personen auf dem Bildschirm. *Medienpsychologie, 8,* 182–200.

Goldberg, D. T. (1993). *Racist culture: Philosophy and the politics of meaning.* Oxford: Blackwell.

Goldner, D. (1994, January 7–9). Michael Crichton: The plot thickens. *USA Weekend,* pp. 4–6.

Goodnight, G. T. (1982). The personal, technical, and public spheres of argument: A speculative inquiry into the art of public deliberation. *Journal of the American Forensics Association, 18,* 214–227.

Goodnight, G. T. (1987). Argumentation, criticism, and rhetoric: A comparison of modern and postmodern stances in humanistic inquiry. In Joseph W. Wenzel (Ed.), *Argument and critical practices* (pp. 61–67). Annandale, VA: Speech Communication Association.

Goodnight, G. T. (1995). The firm, the park, and the university: Fear and trembling on the postmodern trail. *Quarterly Journal of Speech, 81,* 267–290.

Goodwin, C. (1994). Professional vision. *American Anthropologist, 96,* 606–633.

Gould, R. F. (1973). Homosexuality on television. *Medical Aspects of Human Sexuality, 7,* 116–127.

Gray, H. (1995). *Watching race: Television and the struggle for "Blackness."* Minneapolis: University of Minnesota Press.

Greenberg, B. (1988). Some uncommon television images and the drench hypothesis. In S. Oskamp (Ed.), *Television as a social issue: Applied social psychology* (pp. 88–102). Newbury Park, CA: Sage Publications.

Gregg, P. B. (2005). *Parasocial relationships' similarity to interpersonal relationships: Factor analyses of the dimensions of parasocial interaction.*

Unpublished doctoral dissertation, University of Minnesota, Minneapolis.

Grey, S. H. (1999). The statistical war on equality: Visions of American virtue in *The Bell Curve*. *Quarterly Journal of Speech, 85,* 303–329.

GRIID. (2003). *Tell me who I am: Race representation at the movies.* A Report by the Grand Rapid Institute for Information Democracy (GRIID). Retrieved August 1, 2006, from http://www.griid.org/pdfs/race_in _films.pdf.

Gross, A. G. (2006). *Starring the text: The place of rhetoric in science studies.* Carbondale: Southern Illinois University Press.

Gross, L. (1984). The cultivation of intolerance: TV, blacks, and gays. In G. Melischek, K. Rosengren, and J. Stappers (Eds.), *Cultural indi cators: An international symposium* (pp. 345–363). Vienna: Verlag der Osterreichischen Akademie der Wissenschaften [Austrian Academy of Sciences].

Gross, L. (1991). Out of the mainstream: Sexual minorities and the mass media. *Journal of Homosexuality, 21,* 19–46.

Gross, L. (2001). *Up from invisibility: Lesbians, gay men, and the media in America.* New York: Columbia University Press.

Grossberg, L. (1997). *Bringing it all back home: Essays on cultural studies.* Durham, NC: Duke University Press.

Hall, E. J., & Rodriguez, M. S. (2003). The myth of postfeminism. *Gender & Society, 17,* 878–902.

Hall, S. (1978). Some problems with the ideology/subject couplet. *Ideol ogy and Consciousness, 3,* 115–125.

Hall, S. (1980). Encoding/decoding. In S. Hall, D. Hobson, A. Lowe, & P. Willis (Eds.), *Culture, media, language* (pp. 128–138). London: Routledge.

Hall, S. (1981). The whites of their eyes: Racist ideologies and the media. In G. Bridges & R. Brunt (Eds.), *Silver linings: Some strategies for the eighties* (pp. 28–52). London: Lawrence & Wishart.

Hall, S. (1992). Race, culture, and communications: Looking backward and forward at cultural studies. *Rethinking Marxism, 5,* 10–18.

Hall, S. (1994). Reflections upon the encoding/decoding model: An in terview with Stuart Hall. In J. Cruz & J. Lewis (Eds.), *Viewing, reading, listening: Audiences and cultural perceptions* (pp. 253–274). Boulder, CO: Westview Press.

Hall, S. (1997). *Representation: Cultural representations and signifying practices.* Thousand Oaks, CA: Sage Publications.

Hargrave, A. M., & Livingstone, S. (2006). *Harm and offence in media content: A review of the evidence.* Bristol, UK: Intellect.

Harris, J. E. (1994, November). Stereotyping for fun and profit. *Christopher Street, 219*, 4.

Hart, K. R. (2000). Representing gay men on American television. *Journal of Men's Studies, 9*, 59–79.

Hartley, J. (2006). *"Read thy self"*: Text, audience, and method in cultural studies. In M. White & J. Schwoch (Eds.), *Questions of method in cultural studies* (pp. 71–104). Oxford: Blackwell.

Havelock, E. A. (1963). *Preface to Plato.* Cambridge, MA: Harvard University Press.

HBO. (2003). *Six Feet Under:* About the show. Retrieved April 1, 2003, from http://www.hbo.com/sixfeetunder/about/index.shtml.

Hebdige, D. (1979). *Subculture: The meaning of style.* London: Methuen.

Heer, J., & Worcester, K. (2004). *Arguing comics: Literary masters on a popular medium.* Jackson: University Press of Mississippi.

Heidegger, M. (1962). *Being and time* (J. Macquarrie & E. Robinson, Trans.). New York: Harper & Row. Originally published in 1927.

Heider, F. (1946). Attitudes and cognitive organization. *Journal of Psychology, 21*, 107–112.

Heisterkamp, B. L., & Alberts, J. K. (2000). Control and desire: Identity formation through teasing among gay men and lesbians. *Communication Studies, 51*, 388–403.

Helford, E. R. (2006). *The Stepford Wives* and the gaze: Envisioning feminism in 1975. *Feminist Media Studies, 6*, 145–156.

Heller, D. (2004). Taking the nation "from drab to fab": *Queer Eye for the Straight Guy. Feminist Media Studies, 4*, 347–350.

Herek, G. M. (1984). Beyond "homophobia": A social psychological perspective on attitudes toward lesbians and gay men. *Journal of Homosexuality, 10*, 1–21.

Herek, G. M. (1986). Can functions be measured? A new perspective on the functional approach to attitudes. *Social Psychology Quarterly, 50,* 285–303.

Herek, G. M. (1987). The instrumentality of attitudes: Toward a neo-functional theory. *Journal of Social Issues, 42,* 99–114.

Herek, G. M. (1988). Heterosexuals' attitudes toward lesbians and gay men: Correlates and gender differences. *Journal of Sex Research, 25,* 451–477.

Herek, G. M. (1994). Assessing heterosexuals' attitudes toward lesbians and gay men: A review of empirical research with the ATLG scale. In B. Greene & G. M. Herek (Eds.), *Lesbian and gay psychology: Theory, research, and clinical applications* (pp. 206–228). Thousand Oaks, CA: Sage Publications.

Herek, G. M. (2004). Beyond "homophobia": Thinking about sexual stigma and prejudice in the twenty-first century. *Sexuality Research and Social Policy, 1,* 6–24.

Herek, G. M., & Capitanio, J. P. (1996). "Some of my best friends": Intergroup contact, concealable stigma, and heterosexuals' attitudes toward gay men and lesbians. *Personality and Social Psychology Bulletin, 22,* 412–424.

Herek, G. M., & Glunt, E. K. (1993). Interpersonal contact and heterosexuals' attitudes toward gay men: Results from a national survey. *Journal of Sex Research, 30,* 239–244.

Herman, E. S. (1999). *The myth of the liberal media.* New York: Peter Lang.

Herman, J. (2006). Review of *Jake Long: American Dragon* on ParentCenter Family Entertainment Guide. Retrieved May 19, 2006, from http://www.parentcenter.babycenter.com/reviews/bigkid/gentertainment/view/4-3611.

Herrett-Skjellum, J., & Allen, M. (1996). Television programming and sex stereotyping: A meta-analysis. In B. R. Burleson (Ed.), *Communication Yearbook 19* (pp. 157–185). Thousand Oaks, CA: Sage Publications.

Hewitt, C. (1997, August 1). Opening makes "The Lion King" the mane event. *St. Paul Pioneer Press.* Retrieved August 1, 2006, from http://www.lionking.org/musical/Review-Pioneer.html.

Hewstone, M., Rubin, M., & Willis, H. (2002). Intergroup bias. *Annual Review of Psychology, 53,* 575–604.

Hilger, M. (1986). *The American Indian in film.* Metuchen, NJ: Scarecrow Press.

Hillis, K. (2005). Film noir and the American dream: The dark side of enlightenment. *Velvet Light Trap, 55,* 3–19.

Hilton-Morrow, W., & Battles, K. (2004, November). Queer Eye for the Straight Guy: *Queer in name only.* Paper presented at the National Communication Association Convention, Chicago, IL.

Hird, M., & Jackson, S. (2001). Where "angels" and "wusses' fear to tread: Sexual coercion in adolescent dating relationships. *Journal of Sociology, 37,* 27–43.

Hlavka, B. (2005). *Masculinity as performed by characters in war movies about Operation Desert Shield, Operation Desert Storm, and Operation Iraqi Freedom.* Unpublished manuscript.

Hoberman, J. (1994, June 21). The mouse roars. *Village Voice,* 45.

Hobson, D. (1989). Soap operas at work. In E. Seiter, H. Borchers, G. Kreutzner, G. & E-W. Warth (Eds.), *Remote control: Television, audiences, and cultural power* (pp. 150–167). London: Routledge.

Hobson, D. (1990). Women, audiences, and the workplace. In M. E. Brown (Ed.), *Television and women's culture: The politics of the popular* (pp. 61–74). Thousand Oaks, CA: Sage Publications.

Hoffman, R. M., & Borders, L. D. (2001). Twenty-five years after the Bem Sex-Role Inventory: A reassessment and new issues regarding classification variability. *Measurement and Evaluation in Counseling, 34,* 39–55.

Hogg, M. A., & Abrams, D. (1988). *Social identifications: A social psychology of intergroup relations and group processes.* London: Routledge.

hooks, b. (1992). Representing whiteness in the black imagination. In L. Grossberg, C. Nelson, P. A. Treichler, L. Baughman, and J. M. Wise (Eds.), *Cultural Studies* (pp. 338–346). New York: Routledge.

hooks, b. (1994). *Outlaw culture: Resisting representations.* London: Routledge.

hooks, b. (2003). *We real cool: Black men and masculinity.* London: Routledge.

hooks, b. (2004). *The will to change: Men, masculinity, and love.* New York: Atria Books.

Horton, D., & Wohl, R. R. (1956). Mass communication and parasocial interaction. *Psychiatry, 19,* 215–229.

Huesmann, L. R., Moise-Titus, J., Podolski, C. L., & Eron, L. D. (2003). Longitudinal relations between children's exposure to TV violence and their aggressive and violent behavior in young adulthood: 1977–1992. *Developmental Psychology, 39,* 201–221.

Hugick, L. (1992, March). Satisfaction with U.S. at a ten-year low. *The Gallup Poll Monthly*, pp. 47–50.

Hugick, L., & McAneny, L. (1992, September). A gloomy America sees a nation in decline, no easy solutions ahead. *The Gallup Poll Monthly*, pp. 2–9.

Ito, T. A., Larsen, J. T., Smith, N. K., & Cacioppo, J. T. (1998). Negative information weighs more heavily on the brain: The negativity bias in evaluative categorizations. *Journal of Personality and Social Psychology, 75*, 87–90.

Ivie, R. L. (1995). What's at stake for public discourse? *Quarterly Journal of Speech, 81*, 266.

Izzard, E. (2002). *Dress to kill* [DVD]. New York: Warner.

James, C. (2006, June 4). How to write about film. *New York Times Book Review*, 36–39.

Jamieson, K.H. (1995). *Beyond the double bind: Women and leadership*. New York: Oxford University Press.

Jensen, K. J., & Rosengren, K. E. (1990). Five traditions in search of the audience. *European Journal of Communication, 5*, 207–238.

Jhally, S. (1987). *The codes of advertising: Fetishism and the political economy of meaning in the consumer society*. New York: Routledge.

Jhally, S. (1997). *Stuart Hall: Representation & the media* [Transcript of VHS tape]. Northampton, MA: Media Education Foundation.

Jhally S., & Lewis, J. (1992). *Enlightened racism: The Cosby Show, audiences, and the myth of the American dream*. Boulder, CO: Westview Press.

Johansson, T. (1992). Music video, youth culture, and postmodernism. *Popular Music and Society, 16*, 9–22.

Johnson, T. C. (2006). *Relationships between sports viewing habits and attitudes about masculinity*. Unpublished master's thesis, University of Minnesota, Minneapolis.

Kanazawa, S. (2002). Bowling with our imaginary friends. *Evolution and Human Behavior, 23*, 167–171.

Kant, I. (1965). *The Critique of Pure Reason* (2nd ed.). (N. Kemp Smith, Trans.) New York: St. Martin's Press. Originally published in 1787.

Kanter, R. M. (1977). *Men and women of the corporation*. New York: Basic Books.

Keller, A., & Ward, F. (2006). Matthew Barney and the paradox of the new avant garde blockbuster. *Cinema Journal, 45*, 3–17.

Kellerman, K., & Reynolds, R. (1990). When ignorance is bliss: The role of motivation to reduce uncertainty in uncertainty reduction theory. *Human Communication Research, 17*, 5–75.

Kelly, J., & Smith, S. L. (2006). *Where the girls aren't: Gender disparity saturates G-rated films.* Retriebed December 1, 2006. Research report available online at: http://www.seejane.org.

Keyton, J. (1996). Sexual harassment: A multidisciplinary synthesis and critique. In B.R. Burleson (Ed.), *Communication Yearbook 19* (pp. 93–155). Thousand Oaks,.

Kielwasser, A. P., & Wolf, M. A. (1992). Mainstream television, adolescent homosexuality, and significant silence. *Critical Studies in Mass Communication, 9*, 350–373.

Kiesler C. A., & Goldberg, G. N. (1968). Multidimensional approach to the experimental study of interpersonal attraction: Effect of a blunder on the attractiveness of a competent other. *Psychological Reports, 22*, 693–705.

Kilpatrick, J. (1999). *Celluloid Indians: Native Americans and film.* Lincoln: University of Nebraska Press.

Kimmel, M. (1997). Masculinity as homophobia: Fear, shame, and silence in the construction of gender identity. In M. Gergen and S. Davis (Eds.), *Toward a new psychology of gender* (pp. 223–242). New York: Routledge.

King, G. (2002). *Film comedy.* London: Wallflower Press.

Kite, M. E., & Whitley, B. E. (1998). Do heterosexual women and men differ in their attitudes toward homosexuality? A conceptual and methodological analysis. In G. M. Herek (Ed.), *Stigma and sexual orientation* (pp. 39–61). Thousand Oaks, CA: Sage Publications.

Klawans, S. (2004, November 29). Dark habits. *The Nation.* Retrieved May 20, 2006, from http://www.thenation.com/doc/20041129/klawans.

Klein, S. A. (2005). Public character and the simulacrum: The construction of the soldier patriot and citizen agency in *Black Hawk Down. Critical Studies in Media Communication, 22*, 427–449.

Koenig, F., & Lessan, G. (1985). Viewers' relationship to television personalities. *Psychological Reports, 57*, 263–266.

Kolodny, A. (1985). A map for rereading: Gender and the interpretation of literary texts. In E. Showalter (Ed.), *New feminist criticism* (pp. 46–62). New York: Random House.

Krämer, P. (2000). Entering the magic kingdom: The Walt Disney Company, *The Lion King*, and the limitations of criticism. *Film Studies: An International Review, 2,* 44–50.

Krueger, R. A. (1994). *Focus groups: A practical guide for applied research* (2nd ed.). Thousand Oaks, CA: Sage Publications.

Kubey, R. (1998). Obstacles to the development of media education in the U.S. *Journal of Communication, 48,* 58–69.

Kurdek, L. A. (1988). Correlates of negative attitudes toward homosexuals in heterosexual college students. *Sex Roles, 18,* 727–738.

Lacroix, C. (2004). Images of animated others: The orientalization of Disney's cartoon heroines from *The Little Mermaid* to *The Hunchback of Notre Dame*. *Popular Communication, 2,* 213–229.

Ladd, E. C. (1993, January–February). The twentysomethings: "Generation myths" revisited. *The Public Perspective, 5,* 14–18.

Larsen, R., & Haller, B. (2002). Public reception of real disability: The case of *Freaks. Journal of Popular Film & Television, 29,* 164–172.

Lazarsfeld, P. K., Berelson, B., & Gaudet, H. (1944). *The people's choice.* New York: Duell, Sloan & Pearce.

Legman, G. (1949). *Love & death: A study in censorship.* New York: Hacker Art Books.

Leippe, M. R., & Eisenstadt, D. (1994). The generalization of dissonance reduction: Decreasing prejudice through induced compliance. *Journal of Personality and Social Psychology, 67,* 395–413.

Lewis, J. (1991). *Ideological octopus: An exploration of TV and its audience.* London: Routledge.

Lewis, J., & Jhally, S. (1998). The struggle over media literacy. *Journal of Communication, 48,* 109–120.

Liebes, T., & Katz, E. (1989). On the critical abilities of television viewers. In E. Seiter, H. Borchers, G. Kreutzner, & E-W. Warth (Eds.), *Remote control: Television, audiences, and cultural power* (pp. 204–222). London: Routledge.

Liebes, T., & Katz, E. (1990). *The export of meaning: Cross-cultural readings of* Dallas. Oxford: Oxford University Press.

Lindlof, T. (1991). The qualitative study of media audiences. *Journal of Broadcasting and Electronic Media, 35,* 23–42.

Linneman, T. J. (2001). How do you solve a problem like Will Truman? The intersection of male homosexuality and femininity on *Will & Grace.* Paper originally posted on GLAAD's Web site (http://www.glaad.org). A summary is available at: http://www.glaad.org/documents/csms/w&g.pdf.

Linneman, T. J. (2002). How do you solve a problem like Will Truman? The intersection of male homosexuality and femininity on *Will & Grace.* Full version of the GLAAD research report. Unpublished manuscript.

Linneman, T. J. (2004). The lady and the tramp: Feminizing Will and Jack on *Will & Grace. American Sexuality Magazine, 2*(7). Retrieved July 15, 2006, from http://www.nsrc.sfsu.edu/MagArticle.cfm?Article=370&PageID=0.

Linneman, T. J. (2007). How do you solve a problem like Will Truman? The feminization of gay masculinities on *Will & Grace. Men and Masculinities.* Prepublication version at jmm.sagepub.com.

Lipsitz, G. (1998). *The possessive investment of whiteness.* Philadelphia, PA: Temple University Press.

Livingstone, S. M. (1993). The rise and fall of audience research: An old story with a new ending. *Journal of Communication, 43,* 5–12.

Livingstone, S. M. (1998a). Audience research at the crossroads: The implied audience in media and cultural theory. *European Journal of Cultural Studies, 1,* 193–217.

Livingstone, S. M. (1998b). *Making sense of television: The psychology of audience interpretation* (2nd ed.). London: Routledge.

Livingstone, S. M. (2005). On the relation between audiences and publics. In S. Livingstone (Ed.), *Audiences and publics: When cultural engagement matters for the public sphere* (pp. 17–41). Bristol, UK: Intellect Books.

Li-Vollmer, M., & LaPointe, M. E. (2003). Gender transgression and villainy in animated film. *Popular Communication, 1,* 89–109.

Lopate, P. (2006). *American movie critics: From the silents until now.* New York: Library of America.

Lowery, S. A., & DeFleur, M. L. (1995). *Milestones in mass communication research: Media effects* (3rd ed.). White Plains, NY: Longman.

Loy, R. (2003). Soldiers in stetsons. *Journal of Popular Film & Television, 30*, 197–205.

Lueptow, L. B., Garovich, L., & Lueptow, M. B. (1995). The persistence of gender stereotypes in the face of changing sex roles: Evidence contrary to the sociocultural model. *Ethology & Sociobiology, 16*, 509–530.

Lury, K. (2005). The child in film and television. *Screen, 46*, 307–314.

Mahalik, J. R., Locke, B., Ludlow, L., Diemer, M., Scott, R. P. J., Gottfried, M., & Freitas, G. (2003). Development of the conformity to Masculine Norms Inventory. *Psychology of Men and Masculinity, 4*, 3–25.

Mahalik, J. R., Morray, E. B., Coonerty-Femiano, A., Ludlow, L. H., Slattery, S. M., & Smiler, A. (2005). Development of the conformity to Feminine Norms Inventory. *Sex Roles, 52*, 417–435.

Mailloux, S. (1991). Rhetorical hermeneutics revisited. *Text and Performance Quarterly, 11*, 233–248.

Mailloux, S. (1994). Rhetorically covering conflict: Gerald Graff as curricular rhetorician. In W. E. Cain (Ed.), *Teaching the conflicts* (pp. 79–94). New York: Garland.

Mann, K. (2004). You're next: Postwar hegemony besieged in *Invasion of the Body Snatchers. Cinema Journal 44*, 49–69.

Mannheim, K. (1952 [1928]). *Essays on the sociology of knowledge.* London: Routledge & Kegan Paul.

Martin-Rodriguez, M. M. (2000). Hyenas in the Pride Lands: Latinos/as and immigration in Disney's *The Lion King. Aztlán, 25*, 47–66.

Marx, D. M., & Roman, J. S. (2002). Female role models: Protecting women's math test performance. *Personality and Social Psychology Bulletin, 28*, 1183–1193.

Mascaro, T. (2004). *Homicide: Life on the Street. Journal of Popular Film & Television, 32*, 10–19.

Mascaro, T. (2005). Shades of black on *Homicide: Life on the Street:* Advances and retreats in portrayals of African American women. *Journal of Popular Film & Television, 33*, 56–67.

McChesney, R. W. (1999). *Rich media, poor democracy: Communication politics in dubious times.* Urbana: University of Illinois Press.

McCroskey, J. C. (1984). Self-report measurement. In J. A. Daly & J. C. McCroskey (Eds.), *Avoiding communication: Shyness, reticence, and communication apprehension* (pp. 81–94). Beverly Hills, CA: Sage Publications.

McCroskey, J. C., & McCain, T. A. (1974). The measurement of interpersonal attraction. *Speech Monographs, 41,* 261–266.

McCroskey, J. C., Richmond, V. P., & Daly, J. A. (1975). The development of a measure of perceived homophily in interpersonal communication. *Human Communication Research, 1,* 323–332.

McGee, M. C. (1990). Text, context, and the fragmentation of contemporary culture. *Western Journal of Speech Communication, 54,* 274–289.

McHugh, S. (2002). Bringing up babe. *Camera Obscura 49, 17,* 149–187.

McIntyre, R. B., Lord, C. G., Gresky, D. M. T., Eyck, L. L., Frey, G. D. J., & Bond, C. F. (2005). A social impact trend in the effects of role models on alleviating women's mathematics stereotype threat. *Current Research in Social Psychology, 10,* 9. Retrieved from http:// www.uiowa. edu/~grpproc/crisp/crisp.html.

McIntyre, R. B., Paulson, R. M., & Lord, C. G. (2003). Alleviating women's mathematics stereotype threat through salience of group achievements. *Journal of Experimental Social Psychology, 39,* 83–90.

McKee, A. (2000). Images of gay men in the media and the development of self-esteem. *Australian Journal of Communication, 27,* 81–98.

McKee, R. (1997). *Story: Substance, structure, style, and the principles of screenwriting.* New York: Regan Books.

McWhorter, J. (2003). *Authentically black: Essays for the black silent majority.* New York: Gotham Books.

Medhurst, M. J. (1993). The rhetorical structure of Oliver Stone's *JFK. Critical Studies in Mass Communication, 10,* 128–143.

Miller, J. B. (1986). *Toward a new psychology of women.* Boston: Beacon Press.

Miller, M. M., & Reeves, B. (1976). Linking dramatic TV content to children's occupational sex role stereotypes. *Journal of Broadcasting, 20,* 35–50.

Miller, S., & Rode, G. (1995). The movie you see, the movie you don't: How Disney do's that old time derision. In E. Bell, L. Haas, & L. Sells (Eds.), *From mouse to mermaid: The politics of film, gender, and culture* (pp. 86–103). Bloomington: Indiana University Press.

Miller, T. (1993). *The well-tempered self: Citizenship, culture, and the postmodern subject.* Baltimore, MD: Johns Hopkins University Press.

Miller, T. (1998). Commodifying the male body, problematizing "Hegemonic Masculinity." *Journal of Sport & Social Issues, 22,* 431–447.

Mitchell, D. M. (2005). Producing containment: The rhetorical construction of difference in *Will & Grace*. *Journal of Popular Culture, 38,* 1050–1068.

Mitchell, D. M. (2006). Rhetorically contained: The construction and incorporation of difference in *Will & Grace*. In P. Bizzell (Ed.), *Rhetorical agendas: Political, ethical, spiritual* (pp. 275–280). Mahwah, NJ: L. Erlbaum Associates.

Modleski, T. (1991). *Feminism without women.* London: Routledge.

Monmonier, M. (1991). *How to lie with maps.* Chicago: University of Chicago Press.

Moore, D. W. (1995a, January). Crime legislation, deficit reduction top public's "wish list." *The Gallup Poll Monthly,* pp. 2–5.

Moore, D. W. (1995b, July). Public supports new ties with Vietnam. *The Gallup Poll Monthly,* pp. 17–18.

Morgan, G. (1997). *Images of organizations.* Thousand Oaks, CA: Sage Publications.

Moritz, M. J. (1989). American television discovers gay women: The changing context of programming decisions at the networks. *Journal of Communication Inquiry, 13,* 62–78.

Morley, D. (1980). *The "nationwide" audience.* London: British Film Institute.

Morrish, L., & O'Mara, K. (2004). *Queer Eye for the Straight Guy*: Confirming and confounding masculinity. *Feminist Media Studies, 4,* 350–352.

Morrison, T. G., Parriag, A. V., & Morrison, M. A. (1999). The psychometric properties of the homonegativity scale. *Journal of Homosexuality, 37,* 111–126.

Mulvey, L. (1975). Visual pleasure and narrative cinema. *Screen, 16,* 6–18.

Nachbar, J. (2000). Doing the thinking for all of us: *Casablanca* and the home front. *Journal of Popular Film & Television, 27,* 5–15.

Nelson, J. (1985). Homosexuality in Hollywood films: A contemporary paradox. *Critical Studies in Mass Communication, 2,* 54–64.

Newberger, C. (1994, June 27). Intolerance is the real message of "The Lion King." *Boston Globe,* p. 11.

Newport, F. (1995, August). Majority still approve use of atom bombs on Japan in World War II. *The Gallup Poll Monthly,* pp. 2–5.

NOAH (National Organization for Albinism and Hypopigmentation). (2005, January 6). "'Evil Albino' missing from 2004 movies. Will 'The Da Vinci Code' revive the cliché?" Press release. Retrieved May 18, 2006, from http://www.albinism.org/pressRelease/pressRelease2005-01-06.html.

Noam, E. M. (1993). Reconnecting communications studies with communications policy. *Journal of Communication, 43,* 199–207.

Nyberg, A. K. (1998). *Seal of approval: The history of the comics code.* Jackson: University Press of Mississippi.

Oake, J. I. (2004). *Reality Bites* and Gen X as spectator. *Velvet Light Trap, 53,* 80–98.

Oakes, P. J., Haslam, S. A., & Reynolds, K. J. (1999). Social categorization and social context: Is stereotype change a matter of information or of meaning? In D. Abrams & M. A. Hogg (Eds.), *Social identity and social cognition* (pp. 55–79). Oxford: Blackwell.

O'Neil, J. M, Helms, B., Gable, R., David, L., & Wrightsman, L. (1986). Gender Role Conflict Scale: College men's fear of feminity. *Sex Roles, 14,* 335–350.

Oppliger, P. A. (2007). Effects of gender stereotyping on socialization. In R. W. Preiss, B. M. Gayle, N. Burrell, M. Allen, & J. Bryant (Eds.), *Mass media effects research: Advances through meta-analysis* (pp. 199–214). Mahwah, NJ: L. Erlbaum Associates.

Orlofsky, J. L., Cohen, R. S., & Ramsden, M. W. (1985). Relationship between sex-role attitudes and personality traits and the revised sex-role behavior scale. *Sex Roles, 12,* 377–391.

Ortiz, M., & Harwood, J. (2007). A social cognitive theory approach to the effects of mediated intergroup contact on intergroup attitudes. *Journal of Broadcasting & Electronic Media, 51,* in press.

Park, J. H., Gabbadon, N. G., & Chernin, A. R. (2006). Naturalizing racial differences through comedy: Asian, black and white views on racial stereotypes in *Rush Hour 2. Journal of Communication, 56,* 157–177.

Peek, W. (2003). The romance of competence. *Journal of Popular Film & Television, 30,* 206–219.

Perse, E. M., & Rubin, R. B. (1989). Attribution in social and parasocial relationships. *Communication Research, 16,* 59–77.

Pettigrew, T. F. (1997a). Generalized intergroup contact effects on prejudice. *Personality and Social Psychology Bulletin, 23,* 173–185.

Pettigrew, T. F. (1997b). The affective component of prejudice: Empirical support for the new view. In S. A. Tuch & J. K. Martin (Eds.), *Racial attitudes in the 1990s* (pp. 76–90). Westport, CT: Praeger.

Pettigrew, T. F. (1998). Intergroup contact theory. *Annual Review of Psychology, 49*, 65–85.

Pettigrew, T. F., & Tropp, L. R. (2000). Does intergroup contact reduce prejudice? Recent meta-analytic findings. In S. Oskamp (Ed.), *Reducing prejudice and discrimination* (pp. 93–114). Mahwah, NJ: L. Erlbaum Associates.

Pettigrew, T. F., & Tropp, L. R. (2006). A meta-analytic test of intergroup contact theory. *Journal of Personality and Social Psychology, 90*, 751–783.

Pitcher, K. C. (2006). The staging of agency in *Girls Gone Wild. Critical Studies in Media Communication, 23*, 200–218.

Postman, N. (1985). *Amusing ourselves to death: Public discourse in the age of show business.* New York: Penguin.

Potts, A. (1998). The science/fiction of sex: John Gray's *Mars and Venus in the Bedroom. Sexualities, 2*, 153–173.

Pratt, S. B. (1996). Razzing: Ritualized uses of humor as a form of identification among American Indians. In H. B. Mokros (Ed.), *Interaction & Identity* (vol. 5, pp. 237–255). New Brunswick, NJ: Transaction Publishers.

Prelli, L. J. (1989). *A rhetoric of science: Inventing scientific discourse.* Columbia: University of South Carolina Press.

Press, A. L. (1990). Class, gender, and the female viewer: Women's responses to *Dynasty.* In Mary Ellen Brown (Ed.), *Television and women's culture: The politics of the popular* (158–182). Thousand Oaks, CA: Sage Publications.

Press, A. L. (1991). *Women watching television: Gender, class, and generation in the American television experience.* Philadelphia: University of Pennsylvania Press.

Quimby, K. (2005). *Will & Grace:* Negotiating (gay) marriage on prime-time television. *Journal of Popular Culture, 38*, 713–731.

Radway, J. (1984). *Reading the romance: Women, patriarchy, and popular literature.* Chapel Hill: University of North Carolina Press.

Railton, D., & Watson, S. (2005). Naughty girls and red-blooded women: Representations of female heterosexuality in music videos. *Feminist Media Studies, 5*, 51–63.

Ramsey, E. M. (2005). Protecting patriarchy: The myths of capitalism and patriotism in *The People versus Larry Flynt*. *Feminist Media Studies, 5*, 197–214.

Ramsey, E. M., Achter, P. J., & Condit, C. M. (2001). Genetics, race, and crime: An audience study exploring *The Bell Curve* and book reviews. *Critical Stuidies in Media Communication, 18*, 1–22.

Ramsey, E. M., & Santiago, G. (2004). The conflation of male homosexuality and femininity in *Queer Eye for the Straight Guy*. *Feminist Media Studies, 4*, 353–355.

Raney, A. A. (2004). Expanding disposition theory: Reconsidering character liking, moral evaluations, and enjoyment. *Communication Theory, 14*, 348–369.

Raney, A. A., & Bryant, J. (2002). Moral judgment as a predictor of enjoyment of crime drama. *Media Psychology, 4*, 305–322.

Rarick, D. L., Duncan, M. B., Lee, D. G., & Porter, L. W. (1977). The Carter persona: An empirical analysis of the rhetorical visions of campaign '76. *Quarterly Journal of Speech, 63*, 258–273.

Reep, D. C., & Dambrot, F. H. (1989). Effects of frequent television viewing on stereotypes: "Drip, drip" or "drench"? *Journalism Quarterly, 66*, 542–550.

Reeves, B., & Nass, C. (1996). *The media equation: How people treat computers, television, and new media like real people and places*. Cambridge: Cambridge University Press.

Reser, E. M. (2005). Strategies of negotiation in mainstream media: Vernacular discourse and masculinity in *The Full Monty*. *Popular Communication, 3*, 217–237.

Richardson, N. (2006). As Kamp as Bree: The politics of camp reconsidered by *Desperate Housewives*. *Feminist Media Studies, 6*, 157–174.

Riggle, E. D. B., Ellis, A. L., & Crawford, A. M. (1996). The impact of "media content" on attitudes toward gay men. *Journal of Homosexuality, 31*, 55–69.

Robbins, B. (1993). *Secular vocations: Intellectuals, professionalism, culture*. London: Verso.

Robertson, A. (2004). Zemeckis' "Polar Express" transforms Christmas into Clausmas. Retrieved May 22, 2006, from http://www.crosswalk.com/fun/movies/1295704.html.

Rockler, N. R. (1999a). *Beyond "It's just entertainment": Therapeutic discourse and resistance to popular culture criticism in the United States.* Unpublished doctoral dissertation, University of Minnesota, Minneapolis.

Rockler, N. R. (1999b). From magic bullets to shooting blanks: Reality, criticism, and *Beverly Hills, 90210. Western Journal of Communication, 63,* 72–94.

Rockler, N. R. (2001a). A wall on the lesbian continuum: Polysemy and *Fried Green Tomatoes. Women's Studies in Communication, 24,* 90–106.

Rockler, N. R. (2001b). Messages between the lions: The dominance of the tranmission paradigm in student interpretations of *The Lion King. Journal of Communication Inquiry, 25,* 6–21.

Rockler, N. R. (2002a). Overcoming "it's just entertainment": Perspective by incongruity as strategy for media literacy. *Journal of Popular Film and Television, 30,* 16–22.

Rockler, N. R. (2002b). Race, whiteness, "lightness," and relevance: African American and European American interpretations of *Jump Start* and *The Boondocks. Critical Studies in Media Communication, 19,* 398–418.

Rockler, N. R. (2006). Just change the channel: Media violence and the lack of sociological imagination. *Popular Communication, 4,* 39–62.

Rodman, G. B. (1996). *Elvis after Elvis: The posthumous career of a living legend.* New York: Routledge.

Rorty, R. (1991). *Objectivity, relativism, and truth.* Cambridge: Cambridge University Press.

Rorty, R. (1998). *Achieving our country: Leftist thought in 20th-century America.* Cambridge, MA: Harvard University Press.

Rorty, R. (1999). *Philosophy and social hope.* New York: Penguin.

Rosteck, T. (1995). Cultural studies and rhetorical studies. *Quarterly Journal of Speech, 81,* 386–421.

Rothbart, M., & John, O. P. (1985). Social categorization and behavioral episodes: A cognitive analysis of the effects of intergroup contact. *Journal of Social Issues, 41,* 81–104.

Rowe, K. K. (2004). Too close for comfort: *American Beauty* and the incest motif. *Cinema Journal, 44,* 69–93.

Rubin, A. M., & Step, M. M. (2000). Impact of motivation, attraction, and parasocial interaction on talk radio listening. *Journal of Broadcasting & Electronic Media, 44,* 635–654.

Rubin, R. B., & McHugh, M. P. (1987). Development of parasocial inter-action relationships. *Journal of Broadcasting & Electronic Media, 31,* 279–292.

Rubin, R. B., Palmgreen, P., & Sypher, H. E. (1994). *Communication research measures: A sourcebook.* New York: Guilford Press.

Rubin, R. B., & Rubin, A. M. (2001). Attribution in social and parasocial relationships. In V. Manusov & J. H. Harvey (Eds.), *Attribution, communication behavior, and close relationships* (pp. 320–337). Cambridge: Cambridge University Press.

Russo, V. (1987). *The celluloid closet: Homosexuality in the movies* (rev. ed.). New York: Harper & Row.

Sawyer, T. (2003). Review of *Queer Eye for the Straight Guy.* Retrieved July 9, 2004, from http://www.popmatters.com/tv/reviews/q/queer-eye-for-the-straight-guy.shtml.

Schiappa, E. (1995). Intellectuals and the place of cultural critique. In J. F. Reynolds (Ed.), *Rhetoric, cultural studies, and literacy* (pp. 21–27). Hillsdale, NJ: L. Erlbaum Associates.

Schiappa E. (2002). Sophisticated modernism and the continuing im-portance of argument evaluation. In G. T. Goodnight (Ed.), *Arguing communication and culture* (pp. 51–58). Washington, DC: National Communication Association.

Schiappa, E. (2003). *Defining reality: Definitions and the politics of meaning.* Carbondale: Southern Illinois University Press.

Schiappa, E., Allen, M., & Gregg, P. B. (2007). Parasocial relation-ships and television: A meta-analysis of the effects. In R. W. Preiss, B. M. Gayle, N. Burrell, M. Allen, & J. Bryant (Eds.), *Mass media effects research: Advances through meta-analysis* (pp. 301–314). Mahwah, NJ: L. Erlbaum Associates.

Schiappa, E., Gregg, P. B., & Hewes, D. E. (2005). The parasocial contact hypothesis. *Communication Monographs, 72,* 95–118.

Schiappa, E., Gregg, P. B., & Hewes, D. E. (2006). Can one TV show make a difference?: *Will & Grace* and the parasocial contact hypoth-esis. *Journal of Homosexuality, 51,* 15–37.

Schiappa, E., Gregg, P. B., & Lang, M. (2004). *Influencing student atti-tudes about men and masculinity in a film class.* Paper presented at the annual meeting of the National Communication Association, Chicago, IL.

Schrag, R. L., Hudson, R. A., & Bernabo, L. M. (1981). Television's new humane collectivity. *Western Journal of Speech Communication, 45*, 1–12.

Schramm, H., Hartmann, T., & Klimmt, C. (2002). Desiderata und Perspektiven der Forschung über parasoziale Interaktionen und Beziehungen zu Medienfiguren. *Publizistik, 47*, 436–459.

Seiter, E., Borchers, H., Kreutzner, G., & Warth, E-W. (1989). *Remote control: Television, audiences, and cultural power.* London: Routledge.

Sender, K. (1999). Selling sexual subjectivities: Audiences respond to gay window advertising. *Critical Studies in Mass Communication, 16*, 172–196.

Sender, K. (2006). Queens for a day: *Queer Eye for the Straight Guy* and the neoliberal project. *Critical Studies in Media Communication, 23*, 131–151.

Shadish, W. R., Cook, T. D., & Campbell, D. T. (2001). *Experimental and quasi-experimental designs for generalized causal inference.* Boston: Houghton Mifflin.

Shaheen, J. G. (2001). *Reel bad Arabs: How Hollywood vilifies a people.* Northhampton, MA: Olive Branch Press.

Shanahan, J., & Morgan, M. (1999). *Television and its viewers: Cultivation theory and research.* London: Cambridge University Press.

Shenon, P. (1988, November 18). Who killed John Kennedy? *New York Times*, p. D21.

Sheppard, B. H., Hartwick, J., & Warshaw, P. R. (1988). The theory of reasoned action: A meta-analysis of past research with recommendations for modifications and future research. *Journal of Consumer Research, 15*, 325–343.

Shugart, H. A. (2003). Reinventing privilege: The new (gay) man in contemporary popular media. *Critical Studies in Media Communication, 20*, 67–91.

Simms, S. A. (1981). Gay images on television. In J. W. Chesebro (Ed.), *Gayspeak: Gay male & lesbian communication* (pp. 153–161). New York: Pilgrim.

Simon, A. (1998). The relationship between stereotypes of and attitudes toward lesbians and gays. In G. M. Herek (Ed.), *Stigma and sexual orientation* (pp. 62–81). Thousand Oaks, CA: Sage Publications.

Slagle, R. A. (1995). In defense of *Queer Nation*: From identity politics to a politics of difference. *Western Journal of Communication, 59*, 85–102.

Sloan, T. O. (1971). Report of the committee on the advancement and refinement of rhetorical criticism. In L. F. Bitzer & E. Black (Eds.), *The prospect of rhetoric* (pp. 220–227). Englewood Cliffs, NJ: Prentice Hall.

Smeltzer, L. R., & Watson, K. W. (1986). Gender differences in verbal communication during negotiations. *Communication Research Reports, 3,* 74–79.

Solomon, R. L. (1949). An extension of control group design. *Psychological Bulletin, 46,* 137–150.

Span, P. (1994, January 20). Tyrannosaurus sex. *The Washington Post,* pp. C1–C2.

Sparks, G. G. (2006). *Media effects research: A basic overview* (2nd ed.). Belmont, CA: Thomson/Wadsworth.

Speed, L. (2001). Moving on up: Education in black American youth films. *Journal of Popular Film & Television, 29,* 82–91.

Spence, J. T., Helmreich, R. L., & Stapp, J. (1975). Ratings of self and peers on sex role attributes and their relation to self-esteem and conceptions of masculinity and femininity. *Journal of Personality and Social Psychology, 32,* 29–39.

Staiger, J. (1992). *Interpreting films: Studies in the historical reception of American cinema.* Princeton, NJ: Princeton University Press.

Staiger, J. (2000). *Perverse spectators: The practices of film reception.* New York: New York University Press.

Staiger, J. (2005). *Media reception studies.* New York: New York University Press.

Stenberg, D. (1996). The circle of life and the chain of being: Shakespearean motifs in *The Lion King. Shakespeare Bulletin, 14*(2), 36–37.

Stephan, W. G. & Stephan, C. W. (1984). The role of ignorance in intergroup relations. In N. Miller & M. B. Brewer (Eds.), *Groups in contact: The psychology of desegregation* (pp. 229–256). Orlando, FL: Academic Press.

Sun, C. F., & Scharrer, E. (2004). Staying true to Disney: College students' resistance to criticism of *The Little Mermaid. Communication Review, 7,* 35–55.

Swofford, A. (2003). *Jarhead: A marine's chronicle of the Gulf War and other battles.* New York: Scribners.

Tan, A., Fujioka, Y., & Lucht, N. (1997). Native American stereotypes, TV portrayals, and personal contact. *Journalism and Mass Communication Quarterly, 74,* 265–284.

Taylor, S. E. (1981). A categorization approach to stereotyping. In D. L. Hamilton (Ed.), *Cognitive processes in stereotyping and intergroup behavior* (pp. 83–114). Hillsdale, NJ: L. Erlbaum Associates.

Tierney, S. M. (2006). Themes of whiteness in *Bulletproof Monk, Kill Bill,* and *The Last Samurai. Journal of Communication, 56,* 607–624.

Trujillo, N. (1991). Hegemonic masculinity on the mound: Media representations of Nolan Ryan and American sports culture. *Critical Studies in Mass Communication, 8,* 290–308.

Trujillo, N. (1994). *The meaning of Nolan Ryan.* College Station: Texas A & M University Press.

Tucker, K. (2001, March 2). Color bind: Donald Bogle takes an incisive look at small-screen depictions of African Americans in *Primetime Blues. Entertainment Weekly, 585,* 62–65.

Turner, P. K., & Ryden, P. (2000). How George Bush silenced Anita Hill: A Derridian view of the third persona in public argument. *Argumentation & Advocacy, 37,* 86–97.

van Zoonen, L. (1994). *Feminist media studies.* Thousand Oaks, CA: Sage Publications.

Vares, T. (2002). Framing "killer women" films: Audience use of genre. *Feminist Media Studies, 2,* 213–229.

Vavrus, M. D. (2002a). Domesticating patriarchy: Hegemonic masculinity and television's "Mr. Mom." *Critical Studies in Media Communication, 19,* 352–375.

Vavrus, M. D. (2002b). *Postfeminist news: Political women in media culture.* Albany: State University of New York Press.

Verrinder, M. (2005). Quirky *Sideways* sends pinot noir sales soaring. Reuters News Service, retrieved February 4, 2005, from http://www.news.yahoo.com.

Vidmar, N., & Rokeach, M. (1974). Archie Bunker's bigotry: A study in selective perception and exposure. *Journal of Communication, 24,* 36–47.

Vincent, N. (2006). *Self-made man: One woman's journey into manhood and back.* New York: Viking Press.

Wais, E. ((2005). "Trained Incapacity". Thorstein Veblen and Kenneth Burke. *KB Journal*. Available online at http://kbjournal.org/node/103, accessed July 1, 2006.

Walkerdine, V. (1986). Video replay: Families, films, and fantasy. In V. Burgin, J. Donald, & C. Kaplan (Eds.), *Formations of fantasy* (pp. 167–199). London: Methuen.

Wall, J. M. (1993). Of lawyers and dinosaurs. *Christian Century, 110*, 731–732.

Walters, S. D. (2001). *All the rage: The story of gay visibility in America.* Chicago: University of Chicago Press.

Wander, P. (1984). The third persona: An ideological turn in rhetorical theory. *Communication Studies 35*, 197–216.

Ward, A. R. (1996). *The Lion King's* mythic narrative: Disney as moral educator. *Journal of Popular Film and Television, 23*, 171–178.

Weber, E. S. (2002). *Mars, Venus, and nostalgia: How therapeutic rhetoric romanticizes cave and kitchen.* Unpublished doctoral dissertation, University of Minnesota, Minneapolis.

Webster, J. G., & Phalen, P. F. (1997). *The mass audience: Rediscovering the dominant model.* Mahwah, NJ: L. Erlbaum Associates.

Weiss, D. (2005). Constructing the queer "I": Performativity, citationality, and desire in *Queer Eye for the Straight Guy. Popular Communication, 3,* 73–95.

Wertham, F. (1954). *Seduction of the innocent.* New York: Rinehart & Company.

Wessels, E. M. (2006). *A textual and audience analysis of the "Zombie Survival" film genre.* Unpublished master's thesis, University of Minnesota, Minneapolis.

West, C. (1993). *Race matters.* Boston: Beacon Press.

Westerfelhaus, R., & Lacroix, C. (2006). Seeing "straight" through *Queer Eye:* Exposing the strategic rhetoric of heteronormativity in a mediated ritual of gay rebellion. *Critical Studies in Media Communication, 23,* 426–444.

Wilchins, R. (2002, March 19). Homophobia's gender roots. *The Advocate,* p. 72.

Will, G. F. (1994, January 20). Reverse harassment. *The Washington Post,* p. A23.

Williams, R. M. (1964). *Strangers next door.* Englewood Cliffs, NJ: Prentice Hall.

Winant, H. (1998). Racial dualism at century's end. In W. Lubiano (Ed.), *The house that race built* (pp. 87–115). New York: Vintage Books.

Winship, J. (1987). *Inside women's magazines.* London: Pandora Press.

Wood, D. (1992). *The power of maps.* New York: Guilford Press.

Wood, J. V. (1989). Theory and research concerning social comparisons of personal attributes. *Psychological Bulletin, 106,* 231–248.

Yang, A. (1997). Trends: Attitudes toward homosexuality. *Public Opinion Quarterly, 61,* 477–507.

Zephoria. (2006). Gender representation on King Kong. Posted at http://www.zephoria.org (a blog by Danah Boyd) on January 11, 2006. Retrieved May 19, 2006, from http://www.zephoria.org/thoughts/archives/2006/01/11/gender_represen.html.

INDEX